New Concepts in Latino American Cultures
A Series Edited by Licia Fiol-Matta & José Quiroga

Ciphers of History: Latin American Readings for a Cultural Age
by Enrico Mario Santí

Cosmopolitanisms and Latin America: Against the Destiny of Place
by Jacqueline Loss

Remembering Maternal Bodies: Melancholy in Latina and Latin American Women's Writing
by Benigno Trigo

The Ethics of Latin American Literary Criticism: Reading Otherwise
edited by Erin Graff Zivin

Modernity and the Nation in Mexican Representations of Masculinity: From Sensuality to Bloodshed
by Héctor Domínguez-Ruvalcaba

White Negritude: Race, Writing, and Brazilian Cultural Identity
by Alexandra Isfahani-Hammond

Essays in Cuban Intellectual History
by Rafael Rojas

Mestiz@ Scripts, Digital Migrations, and the Territories of Writing
by Damián Baca

Confronting History and Modernity in Mexican Narrative
by Elisabeth Guerrero

Cuban Women Writers: Imagining a Matria
by Madeline Cámara Betancourt

Other Worlds: New Argentine Film
by Gonzalo Aguilar

Cuba in the Special Period: Culture and Ideology in the 1990s
edited by Ariana Hernandez-Reguant

Carnal Inscriptions: Spanish American Narratives of Corporeal Difference and Disability
by Susan Antebi

Telling Ruins in Latin America
edited by Michael J. Lazzara and Vicky Unruh

Hispanic Caribbean Literature of Migration: Narratives of Displacement
edited by Vanessa Pérez Rosario

New Directions in Latino American Cultures
Also Edited by Licia Fiol-Matta & José Quiroga

New York Ricans from the Hip Hop Zone
by Raquel Z. Rivera

The Famous 41: Sexuality and Social Control in Mexico, 1901
edited by Robert McKee Irwin, Edward J. McCaughan, and Michele Rocío Nasser

Velvet Barrios: Popular Culture & Chicana/o Sexualities
edited by Alicia Gaspar de Alba, with a foreword by Tomás Ybarra Frausto

Tongue Ties: Logo-Eroticism in Anglo-Hispanic Literature
by Gustavo Pérez-Firmat

Bilingual Games: Some Literary Investigations
edited by Doris Sommer

Jose Martí: An Introduction
by Oscar Montero

New Tendencies in Mexican Art: The 1990s
by Rubén Gallo

The Masters and the Slaves: Plantation Relations and Mestizaje in American Imaginaries
edited by Alexandra Isfahani-Hammond

The Letter of Violence: Essays on Narrative, Ethics, and Politics
by Idelber Avelar

An Intellectual History of the Caribbean
by Silvio Torres-Saillant

None of the Above: Puerto Ricans in the Global Era
edited by Frances Negrón-Muntaner

Queer Latino Testimonio, Keith Haring, and Juanito Xtravaganza: Hard Tails
by Arnaldo Cruz-Malavé

The Portable Island: Cubans at Home in the World
edited by Ruth Behar and Lucía M. Suárez

Violence without Guilt: Ethical Narratives from the Global South
by Hermann Herlinghaus

Redrawing the Nation: National Identity in Latin/o American Comics
by Héctor Fernández L'Hoeste and Juan Poblete

Cuba in the Special Period

Culture and Ideology in the 1990s

Edited by

Ariana Hernandez-Reguant

CUBA IN THE SPECIAL PERIOD
Copyright © Ariana Hernandez-Reguant, 2009.

All rights reserved.

First published in hardcover in 2009 by
PALGRAVE MACMILLAN®
in the United States—a division of St. Martin's Press LLC,
175 Fifth Avenue, New York, NY 10010.

Where this book is distributed in the UK, Europe and the rest of the world,
this is by Palgrave Macmillan, a division of Macmillan Publishers Limited,
registered in England, company number 785998, of Houndmills, Basingstoke,
Hampshire RG21 6XS.

Palgrave Macmillan is the global academic imprint of the above companies
and has companies and representatives throughout the world.

Palgrave® and Macmillan® are registered trademarks in the United States,
the United Kingdom, Europe and other countries.

ISBN: 978–0–230–10479–2

Library of Congress Cataloging-in-Publication Data

Hernandez-Reguant, Ariana.
    Cuba in the Special Period : culture and ideology in the 1990s / Ariana
  Hernandez-Reguant.
       p. cm.—(New concepts in Latino American cultures)
    Includes bibliographical references and index.
    ISBN 0–230–60654–7
      1. Cuba—Civilization—1959– 2. Politics and culture—Cuba. 3. Cuba—
  History—1990– I. Title.

F1788.H42 2008
306.097291′09045—dc22   2008021629

A catalogue record of the book is available from the British Library.

Design by Newgen Imaging Systems (P) Ltd., Chennai, India.

First PALGRAVE MACMILLAN paperback edition: August 2010

10 9 8 7 6 5 4 3 2 1

Printed in the United States of America.

Transferred to Digital Printing in 2010.

Contents

Preface and Acknowledgments — vii

About the Contributors — ix

1 Writing the Special Period: An Introduction — 1
   Ariana Hernandez-Reguant

I Foreign Commerce

2 Truths and Fictions: The Economics of Writing, 1994–1999 — 21
   Esther Whitfield

3 Filmmaking with Foreigners — 37
   Cristina Venegas

4 Spiritual Capital: Foreign Patronage and the
   Trafficking of *Santería* — 51
   Kevin M. Delgado

2 Plural Nation

5 Multicubanidad — 69
   Ariana Hernandez-Reguant

6 Preemptive Nostalgia and *La Batalla* for Cuban
   Identity: Option Zero Theater — 89
   Laurie Frederik

7 Wandering in Russian — 105
   Jacqueline Loss

8 The "Letter of the Year" and the Prophetics of Revolution — 123
   Kenneth Routon

3 Transnational Publics

9 El Rap Cubano: Can't Stop, Won't Stop the Movement! 143
   Roberto Zurbano Translated by Kate Levitt

10 Audiovisual Remittances and Transnational Subjectivities 159
   Lisa Maya Knauer

11 Ending the Century with *Memories...*: Paper Money,
   Videos, and an *X-Acto* Knife for Cuban Art 179
   Antonio Eligio Fernández, "Tonel" Translated by Kate Levitt

Bibliography 197

Index 221

Preface and Acknowledgments

The idea for this volume emerged in conversation with Esther Whitfield, six years ago when we were both recent Ph.D. graduates. However, it was only after I joined the University of California, San Diego, in 2004, that I was able to secure funds to launch this project. On December 9–11, 2005, some of the best scholars writing about arts and culture during Cuba's Special Period gathered at a conference entitled *The Special Period: Cuban Culture in the 1990s*, which took place at UCSD. Dennise Blum, Kevin Delgado, Ana Dopico, Steve Fagin, Laurie Frederik Meer, Betti Sue Hertz, Dick Hebdige, Berta Jottar, Lisa Maya Knauer, Jacqueline Loss, Lillian Manzor, Ernesto Menéndez, Ivor Miller, Jennifer Paz, Marc Perry, Antonio Eligio Fernández "Tonel," Cristina Venegas, Esther Whitfield and myself, Ariana Hernandez-Reguant, presented their work and participated in debates, along with other attendees, which fueled and sharpened our collective understanding of the Special Period. Those sessions form the basis for this volume.

In addition to all the conference participants, special thanks are due to Luis Garzón Masabó, author of the conference poster reproduced in this book cover. Thanks also to all the individuals who in one way or another have contributed to the success of this endeavor; among them: Alfredo Alonso, Emilio Bejel, Jorge Ferrer, Betty Gago, Anitra Grisales, Sarah Mahler, Lourdes Martinez-Echazábal, José Quiroga, Jean Muteba Rahier, Doris Sommer, and Ignacio Vera. Finally, thanks are due to the institutions that supported both that conference and this book. These are: The University of California Humanities Research Institute (UCHRI), the University of California-San Diego Center for the Humanities, the University of California-San Diego Institute for International, Comparative and Area Studies (IICAS), the University of California-San Diego Department of Communication, and La Jolla's Haudenschild Garage.

About the Contributors

Editor

Ariana Hernandez-Reguant is a cultural anthropologist and assistant professor in the Department of Communication at the University of California in San Diego. Her book *Radio Taino. Socialism and the Market in Post-Soviet Cuba* is forthcoming from Duke University Press. Her recent articles in various edited volumes and in the journals *Public Culture* and the *Journal of Latin American Anthropology* focus on Cuban cultural production in the 1990s.

Contributors

Kevin M. Delgado is an assistant professor of Music and Coordinator of World Music and Ethnomusicology at San Diego State University, and a graduate of UCLA's Ph.D. program in Ethnomusicology. In addition to being a bassist and a percussionist, his academic research focuses on the music, performance, and cultural representation of the Afro-Cuban Santería religion. His articles have appeared in *Black Music Research Journal*, *Selected Reports in Ethnomusicology*, and *A Contracorriente*.

Antonio Eligio Fernández (Tonel) is an artist, art critic, curator, and adjunct professor of studio art at the Art History, Visual Arts and Theory Department of the University of British Columbia, in Vancouver, Canada. His art works have been collected by Havana's National Museum of Fine Arts; Ludwig Forum, Aachen, Germany; Van Reekum Museum, Apeldoorn, The Netherlands; Daros Collection, Zurich, Switzerland; Arizona State University Museum; and the Jack S. Blanton Museum of Art of the University of Texas at Austin, USA. Tonel is also the author of numerous articles on contemporary Cuban art published in art journals, exhibition catalogues, and edited books.

Laurie Frederik is a cultural anthropologist and an assistant professor of performance studies at the University of Maryland. Her long-term ethnographic research in Cuba has focused on professional theater artists living and working in the rural regions of Cienfuegos and Guantánamo provinces.

She has published in the *Journal of Latin American Anthropology*, *The Drama Review* (*TDR*), *Gestos*, and the Cuban journal *Conjunto*, and is preparing a book manuscript entitled "Pure Cuba: Performance, Playmaking, and Politics in the Rural Zones of Silence."

Lisa Maya Knauer is an assistant professor of anthropology at the University of Massachusetts-Dartmouth. Her research on Afro-Cuban music, religion, and media in both New York and Cuba has been published as journal articles and book chapters. She is coeditor of *Memory and the Impact of Political Transformation in Public Space* (2004) and *Memory, Race and the Nation in Public Space* (2008), both from Duke University Press.

Jacqueline Loss is an associate professor of Latin American Literary and Cultural Studies at the University of Connecticut. Her book, *Cosmopolitanisms and Latin America: Against the Destiny of Place*, was published by Palgrave in 2005, and her *New Short Fiction from Cuba*—coedited with Esther Whitfield—was published by Northwestern University Press in 2007. She is currently working on a manuscript tentatively entitled, "Dreaming in Russian," and on an edited volume, "Caviar with Rum: Cuba-USSR and the Post-Soviet Experience."

Kenneth Routon is a sociocultural anthropologist. He carried out 18 months of ethnographic fieldwork between 2003 and 2005 on ritual constructions of power and history in Havana, Cuba. His work has appeared in the *Journal of Latin American Anthropology*, *Identities: Global Studies in Culture and Power*, and *Anthropology News*.

Cristina Venegas is an assistant professor in Film and Media Studies at the University of California Santa Barbara. She specializes in contemporary Latin American and U.S. Latino media and visual culture. Her book *Digital Dilemma*, about Cuban digital media since the 1990s, is forthcoming from Rutgers University Press. She has curated numerous film programs on Latin American and Indigenous film in the United States and Canada, and is cofounder and artistic director of the Latino CineMedia Film Festival in Santa Barbara.

Esther Whitfield is an assistant professor of Comparative Literature at Brown University and author of *Cuban Currency: The Dollar and Special Period Fiction* (University of Minnesota Press, 2008). She is editor of a critical edition of Antonio Jose Ponte's *Un arte de hacer ruinas* (Mexico: FCE, 2005) and coeditor, with Jacqueline Loss, of *New Short Fiction from Cuba* (Northwestern University Press, 2007). Her articles on contemporary Cuban and Latin American literature have appeared in books and journals in the United States, Spain, and Cuba.

Roberto Zurbano is a poet, essayist, and cultural critic. He is the vice president of the Association of the Union of Cuban Writers and Artists (UNEAC), director of the Fondo Editorial of the Casa de las Americas in Havana, and editor in chief of *Movimiento*, a magazine devoted to Cuban rap music.

1

Writing the Special Period: An Introduction

Ariana Hernandez-Reguant

It is always a challenge to bracket a time period and categorize it as a historical epoch. The Special Period, not unlike the Cold War, the twentieth century, or the 1960s, is not only a historical convention, or an analytical construct, but also a defining category of experience. For most people, the invocation of these chronological referents is metonymic of a broad range of events, aesthetics, experiences, emotions, acts, and attitudes. Alain Badiou (2007) in *The Century* attempts precisely to identify the unifying tropes that define the twentieth century, the period's imagination—its epochal dreamworlds, to use Susan Buck-Morss's (2000) felicitous expression. There is, no doubt, something powerful about conventional time frames, like a century. Such a time frame, within a specific geographical space, is often identified with a collective type of consciousness—in Badiou's case, the European West. Badiou's project is to pin down "how the century thought itself," that is, the epochal consciousness that key Western intellectuals expressed in their works during that time; how they imagined, or rather abstracted, the time in which they were living as a centurial period and how they represented it. Just as importantly, how they confronted it. In a nutshell, Badiou examined what type of "epochal thinking" developed in trying to make sense of the century's major events and processes; what ideas about humanity, what visions of the future, what fears and obsessions were internalized and expressed in salient artistic and intellectual documents.

For those who lived through it, Cuba's Special Period—roughly, the decade of the 1990s, immediately following the country's loss of Soviet trade and support—was without a doubt one of those defining periods. Across the board, its invocation brings up memories of deprivation and hopelessness; of hunger and heat; of wheeling and dealing, of dreams of a life elsewhere. Raising pigs in bathtubs, making omelets without eggs and pizzas with melted condoms, getting married for the state-allocated free case of beer, and other epic tales of survival, seldom void of black humor, form the lore of the time. As the state was forced to withdraw from everyday economic activity, leaving the population to fend for itself, many began to wheel and deal, unleashing a thriving black market of goods and services. The fierce competition for extremely scarce resources further cleaved a society already divided by suspicion and distrust, but also created a strong cohort-type consciousness based on the common experience of those years. A sort of anachronistic self-awareness—as socialist survivors in a sea of global capitalism—together with the national gloom over Soviet abandonment, further colored the experience as a radical break from the past. In the Special Period, there was a "before," which was stable, perhaps purer in its altruism and high ideals, a "now," which was confusing and unsettling, and a future that was, for many, another country. The experience was intense, yet the period was construed as a time of waiting; as an irresolute transition.

The models of transformation invoked by academics of various ideological affiliations appeared remote from the vantage point of those trapped in the Special Period's quotidian struggle. The analysis of these collective imaginaries would be limited if it only focused on the highest philosophical and poetic works of the type preferred by Badiou. Writing eight decades earlier about Weimar Germany, Siegfried Kracauer offered an alternative to the types of analyses to which Badiou's owed its genesis: "The position that an epoch occupies in the historical process can be determined more strikingly from an analysis of its inconspicuous surface-level expressions than from that epoch's judgments about itself" (Kracauer 1995 [1927]: 75).

Kracauer was searching for spacial patterns, forms of mass entertainment and collective beliefs that produced the person of the times and which reflected new understandings and experiences of time, work, community, and leisure. No doubt, Special Period Cuba saw an explosion of forms of popular culture that questioned the canonic divide between "high" and "low," sharply upheld by socialist cultural policies. It was the most popular of expressions that immediately reflected on the intensity of everyday life, while art, literature, theater, and music sought to approximate those and bridge the divide to reach the embittered population. This book lies between the two poles represented by Badiou and Kracauer respectively, in order to undertake a reflection on the Special Period as an instance of "late socialism."

This book focuses on the ways in which artists, intellectuals, and various expressive communities operated within a temporal framework that was critiqued and selectively represented, yet was accepted as a fact of life. This temporal framework was the years known as the Special Period—a time that, as Badiou pointed out for his twentieth-century European intellectuals, people had to confront in their creative works as much as in their lives. But, like Kracauer, the authors in this volume, for the most part, are not as concerned with specific intellectual figures as with particular groups of cultural producers, such as filmmakers, writers, religious practitioners, visual artists, performers, musicians, and dancers, whether professional or amateur. As the spaces for public expression increased, partly due to the state's weakening and partly due to new commercial opportunity, so did reflective and critical visions of the social experience. As the essays in this collection show, multiple positions and consciousness of self and others based on race, generation, and sexuality, as well as diverse visions of citizenship, labor, property, community, altruism, and profit, marked a departure from an earlier social pressure to express a uniformity of experience. Can we speak, then, of a Special Period culture?

The Set Up

In early April 1991, in commemoration of the Union of Communist Youth's anniversary, Fidel Castro and Roberto Robaina, then head of the organization, addressed a crowd of 400,000 in Havana's Revolution Square. The international weekly edition of the Communist Party daily, *Granma*, transcribed Castro's speech in its entirety and also included a short summary of Robaina's—both of which incited Cuban youth to remain loyal to the nation and the Revolution through the difficult times ahead. "Cuban youth will not sell out our nation, not for lentils nor spangles!" extolled Robaina. The paper also included a short commentary on the event's distinct atmosphere. "Two new things happened," observed the journalist (Cabrera 1991: 4). The first was "the proliferation of bicycles," which during the rally apparently inundated the surrounding streets. The second was "the rebirth" of a Che Guevara motto: "Ever onward to victory" (In Spanish: *Hasta la Victoria Siempre*), which Robaina reintroduced.

While the extraordinary profusion of the two-wheel vehicles noted by the paper—about a quarter million in Havana alone—signaled dramatic shortages of fuel and spare parts, the recuperation of an early revolutionary slogan was an indication of the government's determination to survive. By that point in early 1991, the Special Period was a fait accompli, and a change of direction in economic policy appeared as the only possible way to confront the crisis provoked by the disappearance of the Soviet bloc. Reforms had the goal of both inserting the Cuban economy into international markets and stimulating domestic production so that the population's basic needs could be met; but, they were to do so without disrupting the social structure or, much less, the government and the political system. That is, Cuba could enter "the era of the bicycle," but material deprivation should not make people forget the nation's historical commitment to socialism and revolution (Castro 1990e). Cuba's National Assembly proclaimed that the island would sink to the bottom of the ocean before it would renounce socialism and revolution (Cabrera 1990), and Fidel Castro added "socialism or death" (*socialismo o muerte*) to his usual "fatherland or death" (*Patria o muerte*) motto with which he typically closed his speeches.[1] But as state socialism faded from the Western world, the meaning of such proclamations was more symbolic than literal. Furthermore, as the Cuban state fell into bankruptcy and was forced to retreat from everyday economic activity, so did socialism. The state became the nucleus of both socialism and revolution, leaving, for a short period of time, broad spaces for autonomous social action.

Modeled after a hypothetical "Special Period in Times of War"—designed decades earlier for the eventuality of a U.S. invasion attempt—the "Special Period in Times of Peace" entailed severe measures to confront a siege-type of situation, and therefore extreme scarcity. As soon as the Soviet Union exhibited symptoms of structural crisis at the end of the 1980s, the Cuban government began hinting at its eventuality. Still, the successive demise of all Eastern European socialist regimes after 1989 was invariably underplayed. Only following months of mixed statements—like, "if there is a Special Period, we will be able to resist it," and "we are not in a special period but we are almost in a special period" (Castro 1990a)—did the Cuban government acknowledge the irreversibility of the Soviet process.[2] Finally, on December 30, 1990, the front page of the international edition of the Communist Party paper *Granma*, under a "Happy 1991!" wishes for the New Year, featured a headline reading "Cuba has entered the Special Period; the situation is not yet very acute" (Lee and Oramas 1990). Invoking an earlier utopian moment, Fidel Castro announced that the little that people had would be shared equitably. Belt-tightening measures were put in place to confront the loss of Soviet bloc subsidies and trade, which up until then amounted to 84 percent of all trade (Jatar-Hausmann 1999).

Fuel and food shortages led first to an exhortation of thrift, which included door-to-door inspections of household appliances in order to issue individually tailored saving measures. Then, a strict rationing of energy and most other necessities was imposed, and food rations—in place since 1962—were severely curtailed. For example, bread allocations were decreased to 80 grams per person per day, gas sales to individuals were suspended altogether, and the utilities' supply was limited, in many cases, to a few hours a day.[3] To address the emergence of malnutrition-related illnesses, the media sought to reeducate the population's eating habits, promoting such recipes as sweet potato leaf salad, mashed banana peel, and fried grapefruit peel.[4] A return to an ox-based agriculture, the promotion of bicycling as a means of transportation, the reduction of the workday as well as of media broadcasts and organized entertainment—from movie theaters to carnival parades—further recalled the war economy that had originally been planned for a Special Period. As a remedy, foreign investment and international tourism were identified as promising strategies. Old hotels were remodeled and new ones were built; small airports situated near beach areas were revamped to deal with seasonal flight traffic from countries such as Germany and Canada.[5] The government had no choice but to generate hard currency and rejoin the international trade networks that it had shunned for three decades. To that end, the country's socialist constitution was reformed to permit new forms of private and corporate property, regulate foreign investment, turn state companies into for-profit enterprises, and decriminalize the circulation of the U.S. dollar.[6]

The summer of 1994 marked an all-time low in revolutionary history with the hijacking of a tugboat by would-be migrants and its sinking by government vessels in Havana bay (killing 35 people), riots in the old downtown, and a mass exodus, known as the balsero crisis, which took tens of thousands of destitute Cubans to the United States. Those who stayed behind consumed their time and energy in an obsessive search for food. Stories of people raising pigs in their bathtubs and traveling to rural areas to barter everything imaginable for food were overwhelmingly common. Electricity blackouts of many hours a day and the constant and unpredictable interruption in the supply of all other utilities made quotidian tasks such as cooking and cleaning an ordeal. In Havana the pitch-black, traffic-free nights became havens for petty crime. The widespread expressions of discontent forced the government to speed up reform and permit spaces for both debate and independent economic activity.

By 1996, the market reforms began to yield results. Soon, many imported and domestically produced necessities were made available outside the rationing system at much higher prices, whether on the black market, in new private farmers and crafts markets, or at new state hard-currency stores. The possibility of better times ahead raised popular expectations, particularly as the incipient domestic market seemed to provide some avenues for advancement, but also generated feelings of uncertainty and anxiety. The growing influx of remittances as well as the income generated by foreign visitors, who often preferred to rent private rooms and eat at private restaurants, stimulated an informal economy that rapidly improved the living standards of strategically situated professionals. In addition, artists and artisans, among others, were allowed to perform freelance work as self-employed workers setting their own fees.[7] Others were able to start their own family business or work in the tourist industry and for foreign-owned companies. Access to foreign currency became the defining element of increasing social stratification. Some people got richer, mostly those in key positions at state-owned enterprises or plugged into transnational economic networks, while many others got poorer, particularly blacks and the elderly (de la Fuente 2001). At the same time, cheerful radio sounds, commercial billboards, new expensive nightclubs and hard currency stores, crowded street markets, books, crafts, and pirated CDs, tourists and traffic, along with the conspicuous jetsetting lives of the rich and famous—musicians, actors, television personalities, foreign residents, and their Cuban spouses—concocted an image of Havana as an emergent cosmopolis. However, the double currency—the *peso* and *dollar*—corresponded to a double life to which only some could aspire. Those who could crisscross the two with ease—namely, Havana's new showbiz elite—became youth's new role models.

Soon, few bicyclists dared to navigate the heavy traffic of the once-empty Havana thoroughfares, and an atmosphere of cautious optimism spread through those sectors who most benefited from the changes: remittance recipients, independent entrepreneurs, employees in hard-currency sectors, and managers of state enterprises. But as economic policies yielded positive results, the government rolled them back. Heavy taxation squeezed the rising independent sector, while state managers and bureaucrats in favorable positions were selectively supervised and in some cases fired in an effort to root out corruption. Effectively, the government returned to its role as the gatekeeper of both wealth and discourse and reversed its earlier attitude of *laisser-penser* to eliminate public challenges to its ambitioned hegemony. The regime had survived the worst and could therefore return to its old ways. But could it? Even as the government regained control of the economy and reasserted its political control, the arrival of foreign stakeholders—companies, entrepreneurs, tourists—had extended the horizons of possibility for many people. Specifically, and as the texts in this collection evidence, modes of expression, ethical views, and practical approaches to work, property, profit, and community were dramatically altered for many artists, media producers, cultural entrepreneurs and, even, religious practitioners.

For the revolutionary government, intellectuals and artists were influential social actors to be sought as allies. Now the task was harder, as new incoming stakeholders offered them fresh avenues for promotion and publicity, and the expansion of audiences beyond the island and the introduction of new aesthetic agendas created an impression of plurality and openness. Furthermore, the increasing opportunities for international travel, mail service, telephone communication, and, email access allowed many to maintain active contact with émigré and foreign relatives, friends, and colleagues. International academic exchanges, mostly with Mexico, Spain, and the United States, significantly intensified after 1991, allowing intellectuals, academics, and artists to travel abroad, and growing numbers of foreign students to enroll in courses and conduct research on the island—among them, many of the contributors to this volume (Stanton 2006; Sublette 2004; Vincent 1993e). Both Cuban and foreign scholars and artists increasingly learned about their respective intellectual universes, and began to refer to each other's work and engage in dialogue. Cuban intellectuals—like visual artists before then—had to negotiate diverse intellectual circles while acquiescing to revolutionary ideology and hierarchy, for it was precisely their official status within the island that endowed them with a cultural capital desirable abroad.

As economic indicators improved, the government redoubled its control of oppositional discourses. Beginning in July 1994, extensive police raids in homes and roofs tore out the homemade TV parabolic antennas that had sprung up throughout Havana (Alvarez García and González Núñez 2001). Subsequently, a number of institutional closures and new legislation sought to curtail the emerging public sphere. In 1995, the independent Pablo Milanés Foundation, established two years earlier with great fanfare and an endowment of $160,000 U.S. dollars donated by the internationally acclaimed singer Pablo Milanés, was suddenly shut down (Vicent 1993c, 1995). Shortly after, the Centro de Estudios de América, a high-profile think tank dedicated to assessing, predicting, and advising on the social, political, and economic prospects of Cuba within a broader global context, suffered a similar fate when its research staff was disbanded and relocated. As icing on the cake, new legislation (Law 80 of 1996 for the Reaffirmation of Cuban Dignity and Sovereignty, and Law 88 of 1999 for the Protection of National Independence and the Economy of Cuba) further restricted free speech.[8] Crackdowns on dissident groups and propaganda campaigns such as the Battle of Ideas, along with the Elián González international child-custody dispute, closed the decade of the 1990s and the last hopes for a political opening.

In the end, as many have indicated, there was no structural transformation of the socialist economy. Economic reforms were designed to overcome the dire situation of the early 1990s without relinquishing political power. That is, they sought to alleviate material scarcity and popular pressure for change, but only for as long as they would not subvert revolutionary governance. Exactly how far changes in economic policy could go before revolutionary hegemony would be called into question was the quandary of the decade, both for the Cuban government and for international observers. For a few years, a strategy of trial and error, rather than a master plan, seemed to guide the government's actions, as it sought to balance the need for economic remedy with the determination to avoid social change and political opposition; juggling the expressive opening brought by the introduction of new market-driven stakeholders with the need to avoid political challenges; alternating the carrot of economic opening with the stick of political repression. As Jorge Domínguez (2004: 23) has noted, the policies merely intended to "buy political time." In sum, economic policy was subordinated to the political survival of both the revolutionary government and the socialist state.

A Period's Telos

From the onset, the Special Period was defined by the Cuban government in economic terms. The break in the flow of supplies from the Soviet bloc countries had material implications whose correction was said to entail economic, not political, reform. This was a point reiterated numerous times. In a Gramscian fashion, market reform was considered a necessary evil to ensure the Revolution's survival.[9] Discursively, the Cuban government separated politics from economics, and based its legitimacy on a glorious history of independence struggles, above and beyond the contingencies of the day. Socialism ceased to be a holistic project and instead became increasingly identified with little more than basic social rights, such as education and health, which were to be guaranteed and managed by the state. Yet the question remained whether the redefinition of socialism in strictly political terms would allow the Cuban government to avoid the pitfalls that led to Gorbachev's demise.

Particularly in Havana, where most foreign companies and visitors gravitated, the new opportunities for business and enterprise created an impression of systemic change. The double economy—driven by the U.S. dollar and the Cuban peso, respectively—corresponded to a two-tiered quotidian experience. Society was re-stratifying according to people's regular access to hard currency, and a discourse of possessive individualism seemed to take hold. While some mourned the socialist values of altruism and solidarity, wheeling, dealing, and gleaning became the order of the day. Everything seemed to acquire a cash value; everything was for sale or lease, and not only material objects, but also time, labor, and affect. It appeared as if Cuban society on the whole was embarking on an unstoppable journey of capitalist transformation that encompassed all spheres of daily life, down to the most intimate. Both in scholarly circles and on Havana's streets, talk of transition became commonplace. As the former Soviet bloc disbanded and its countries joined international markets and adopted liberal forms of democratic governance with more or less success, all eyes were on Cuba. Cuba was to provide a test case for theories formulated on the basis of the Soviet and Eastern European transitions from socialism to capitalist democracy, and predicated on a notion of state socialism as a totalitarian system of government that engulfed all social life. Accordingly, any challenge or reform to any element of the system had the potential to destabilize the whole structure. Would Cuba's reforms jeopardize revolutionary governance?

Political theories of regime change formulated on the basis of the Soviet and Eastern European socialist transitions to democracy established the inevitability of political change as both a precondition and a consequence of market reform. The prevailing idea was that market reform required changes to socialist governance that would end the state's monopoly over economic activity. Market policies, in addition, entailed the empowerment of non-state economic actors, resulting in the rise of autonomous social sectors which, eventually, would exert political pressure for further change. In Gorbachev's case, that led to a split within the leadership and a takeover of reformist factions (complicated by the centrifugal tendencies in the Soviet Republics). At the same time, as the state loosened its grip over social life, popular discontent was increasingly expressed in the open leading to disruptive civil unrest and, eventually, to a political crisis and the centralized government's fall. For the former Eastern European socialist governments, the weakening of the Soviet regime crippled their main source of both support and legitimacy, and without the active backing of their citizens, their rule soon came to an end as well. As numerous scholars have pointed out, people's passive acquiescence to these regimes led to a quick transition and the welcoming of new democratic pro-market regimes.[10]

In Cuba, as the 1990s progressed and market practices and capitalist attitudes took hold throughout society, the expectation, both among the public and scholars, was that political change would be the ultimate outcome. This belief guided both the Cuban government's fear of full-fledged market reforms, and rationale for U.S. policy toward the island. The hypothesis was that if reforms were far-reaching enough as to satisfy people's needs and wants, the formation of civil society would be unavoidable and history would unfold as in Eastern Europe. And if they were not, civil unrest would disrupt the government's unity, and repression would only lead to popular resistance and regime delegitimation. While Cubanologists abroad waited for the "transition" to unfold, the Cuban think tanks were busy studying the evolution of the Eastern European, Vietnamese, and Chinese economies. They examined all possible options for Cuba, including that of a market-type of socialist democracy, and some argued for the need to implement political reform in order to successfully reform and thus sustain a socialist society.[11] Without going as far as China, neither on reform nor on repression, the Cuban government was open to exploring whether a mixed economy and a socialist government were compatible and viable. It appeared that the key element to watch out for was civil society.

The empowerment of non-state stakeholders and the development of an independent public sphere had been the weak link in the processes that turned change into demise in the former Soviet bloc. In Cuba, throughout the 1990s, numerous debates and scholarly publications assessed the shape and limits of an autonomous civil society within both socialism and capitalism (Chanan 2001; Dilla and Oxhorn 2002). While it was obvious that the visibility of dissident groups, particularly when financed by foreign powers, constituted a threat to revolutionary hegemony, the lessons from Eastern Europe had shown that it was the organization of autonomous economic actors that posed the most danger. Not only could they potentially convert their economic capital into political clout, but most importantly in the Cuban context, they could withdraw from the displays of revolutionary allegiance that were essential to political citizenship. Hence, the rising self-employed sector and other professionals such as commercially successful artists were not allowed to associate and organize (Dilla and Oxhorn 2002; Hernandez-Reguant 2004a). For instance, musicians and composers were not permitted to form an association to manage their international royalties, despite a World Trade Organization mandate to that end. They were also heavily taxed.

By the end of the 1990s, the Cuban government had regained control of both the economy and the public sphere. As the child Elián returned to Cuba, so did the ideological order. It became clear that no political change would take place as a result of economic reform, and that, moreover, the so-called reform had consisted of only fleeting policies implemented for the sake of political survival. Talk of transition subsided, and an elitist view of Cuban politics regained its centrality in political analysis. Political observers recuperated the view that regime change would probably occur only as a result of a consensus break among the political elite—something that, in Cuba, would presumably happen only after Fidel Castro's death (Pérez-Stable 2006). In the meantime, Cuban music, literature, film, and art had made noise throughout the world, to a great extent as a result of the opportunities brought by commercial stake holders. At the same time, a new migrant cohort had extended through Europe and the Americas, forcing political, religious, and media discourses to accommodate an increasingly deterritorialized notion of Cuban culture. In the island, being Cuban no longer meant, necessarily, being revolutionary—in the sense of being committed to a nationalist political project. It meant, more than ever, being cosmopolitan. In addition, in the absence of other forms of material capital, creativity, broadly conceived, was both a way to transcend economic and political geographies and a means to social and financial ascension. This made Cuba's Special Period attractive not only to cultural entrepreneurs, but also to cultural scholars who, thanks to the opening academic exchanges, were able to conduct research, and often reside, on the island during the decade.

The Special Period and the Culture of Late Socialism

Teleologies of transition loomed in the background for cultural scholars, but in a different way. Their work was influenced by the booming body of globalization theory, which sustained a narrative of unstoppable social progress toward neoliberal capitalism, and directly attributed cultural change to the increasing permeability of national borders and the flexibility of communication and transportation systems (Appadurai 1990; García Canclini 1989; Harvey 1989). Their approach, however, was cautious, following post-socialist debates concerning the need to question teleological discourses of forward development by considering a longer historical trajectory, one that might show both the continuity and change of values and practices between a pre-socialist period and the post-socialist moment (Humphrey 1995; Lampland 1995). However, the assumption that an opening to international markets and the transnational circulation of goods, people, and popular culture fostered social and cultural change was not in dispute. The question, for cultural theorists, was not *if* but *how*, and their method was to engage with very specific and quotidian practices. The picture that they presented in their microstudies on the relation between market reforms, cultural production, aesthetics, and ideology was less teleological than expected; it was filled with halted trajectories and hesitations, breaks and continuities—neither treating socialism as an eternal present nor as a mere hiatus in capitalism's *longue durée*.

Fredric Jameson's 1984 piece concerning the relation between "late capitalism" and "post-modernity"—which emphasized cognitive mappings as a sort of collective imaginaries that linked epochal-defining material conditions and cultural forms—was a major influence. The text provided a referential point from which to think about the cultural predicament of a period that ran parallel to "late capitalism" and that could be referred to as "late socialism." In these "late" times, East and West experienced cultural and economic globalization, as well as the cracking of long-standing ideological hegemonies. On both sides of the Iron Curtain, the grand narratives of modern times became artifacts to be critically scrutinized. In the late Communist world, as the Party began to lose its centrality as the ideological guide of society, an emergent public sphere allowed for other voices to come to the fore (Erjavec 2003; Yurchak 2006). In the thoroughly regulated cultural arena, the sharp distinction between the official and the unofficial, between the state-controlled public and the dissident, began to wane and alternative expressions (e.g., youth popular culture) challenged the elitism of the art and culture apparatus.

Cuban late socialism, it appeared, differed from the Eastern European in significant ways. In Eastern Europe, as Alexei Yurchak (2006) and Alexei Monroe (2005) have shown with their studies of youth culture in 1980s USSR and Slovenia, respectively, the cracking of the regimes—resulting partly from economic reform—was evidenced through very specific forms of popular critique, like the ironic use of communist symbols and referents, the invocation of totalitarian images, and the recuperation of elements from folklore and traditional culture. Something similar took place in Cuban art and theater just before the height of the Special Period (Manzor-Coats and Martiatu Terry 1995; Mosquera 2003). Yet in the 1990s, most artists chose not to directly collide with revolutionary ideology, strategically insisting instead on the separation of art from politics.[12] It was popular culture, rather, that provided a space for cultural critique.

The introduction of commercial and foreign stakeholders in the 1990s expanded the arenas for public expression. *Timba* music, for instance, became a powerful space for critique both of revolutionary ideology and of the dollarization process that precisely turned this musical genre into a youth phenomenon (Hernandez-Reguant 2006b).[13] Furthermore, the introduction of commercial interests destabilized the cultural hierarchies of socialism. Commercial forms, such as *timba* music, so-called Special Period writers such as Pedro Juan Gutiérrez (see chapter 2, this volume), comedic film languages that undid 40 years of experimentation (see chapter 3, this volume), and other previously considered "lesser" genres moved to center stage due to their popular appeal—something unthinkable in previous times, when the role of culture and the media was to lead over the masses and not the other way around. The boundaries between professional and amateur artists, "high" culture and low-brow popular culture, neatly and administratively defined under socialism, begun to blur. A source of challenge came precisely from youth groups at the fringes, like rockers and rappers, who forced the state cultural apparatus to loosen up its monopoly over cultural production and permit the expression of alternative formulations. These groups often voiced social discontent in the name of various youth, black, and neighborhood groups, and their process of incorporation into the state administrative infrastructure was often rocky. Mainstream Cuban artists catering to broader publics often developed a sort of "double consciousness," as they presented their works according to what they thought foreigners might value. They began looking at the surrounding reality with a distancing gaze, as if trying to imagine what foreigners sought. In particular, the juxtaposition of socialist practices and capitalist landscapes was a fruitful inspiration for humorous commentaries. Yet in the end, the price for their public projection was to refrain from frontal opposition to the regime.

Commercial culture was everywhere. Determining whether significant social change occurred and to what extent required further investigation, but the alteration of the urban landscape was swift and obvious. The socialist differentiation between ideology and commodity as mutually exclusive frameworks for understanding society had broken down. For instance, advertising billboards stood side-by-side with placards featuring revolutionary slogans, and dingy *bodegas* or distribution centers for rationed products contrasted with the new hard-currency supermarkets flashing brand-name items. The value of goods and services was the first element to fall into confusion, and fluctuating prices often defied all logic. Cuba became a hyperrealist collage, and postmodern aesthetics found their foremost expression in the many objects recycled for uses totally different from that for which they had been intended—what theater theorists referred to as an "aesthetics of difficulty," and art critics termed as an "architecture of necessity."[14] Indeed, there was neither a sudden nor complete transformation of the symbolic order. The socialist order continued, but it was now fading within a collage of assorted referents that eventually would force the revolutionary government into an ideological offensive.

During these years, in addition to the discussions taking place among social scientists about the shape and form that a civil society would take in a mixed economy, art and literary critics reflected on the relevance of postmodernist visions for the Cuban predicament. Ironically, as Mateo Palmer (2007) notes in a collection on postmodernism published in Cuba, while in Europe and North America postmodernism spoke to a postindustrial society, in Cuba it was precisely to its absence. It was the material involution of the Special Period that sparked concerns about the relationship among artists, media, and audiences, and the possibility of queer, black, feminist, and diasporic vantage points. Ironically, improvements in telephone service, increasing access to electronic mail, and an ease in foreign travel requirements for academics and professional artists contributed to a consciousness of anachronicity, of lagging behind. While Cuban artists and academics grappled with these issues, foreign scholars—who unlike their Cuban peers, were free to disengage from the surrounding circumstances—struggled to understand and write about an experience that they could never fully own.

Cultural Engagements

During the 1990s, all sorts of entrepreneurs—music producers, literary editors, art dealers, journalists and academics—flocked to Cuba to be the first to publicize its cultural treasures. As a result, Special Period Cuba acquired a distinct aesthetic quality, devoid of the moral judgments that invariably surrounded any reference to the Cuban Revolution. Thus images of ruin and decay and the music sounds of yesteryear were presented as signifiers of authenticity and resilience rather than as of socialism's failure. One only has to recall the successful *Buena Vista Social Club* recording series and film, numerous photography coffee-table books, and a wealth of articles in magazines such as *National Geographic* and *Cigar Aficionado*—all of which showed old traditions, houses, cars, and people in ruins, yet surviving thanks precisely to capitalism's absence (Dopico 2004; Hernandez-Reguant 2000; Quiroga 2007). If anything, socialism appeared as capitalism's past; or, as a famous Polish joke had it, as a detour between capitalism and capitalism. But, increasingly, the members of a growing expatriate community in Havana—academics, filmmakers, musicians, correspondents, and artists—sought to generate firsthand representations and accounts that would counterbalance these orientalist representations of Cuban life and dispel images of socialism as a monochromatic society.[15]

This collection of essays gathers North and South American, Cuban and European cultural anthropologists, ethnomusicologists, and literary, film, and art scholars who examine cultural production as a site for individual agency and social action. Influenced by Stuart Hall (1977) and Pierre Bourdieu's (1993) models of cultural and media production, these contributors seek to dispel simplistic notions of socialist governance to show cultural production as occurring within a field of action marked by conflicts and negotiations among interest groups. Hence, the contributors to this volume investigate the emergence of semiautonomous spheres of cultural practice during the Special Period and track the agency of various social actors faced both with the constraints of the socialist bureaucracy and the possibilities opened by both new commercial stakeholders and foreign constituencies.

Thus the essays zero in on various interpretive communities formed around cultural expression, including film, theater, literature, music, and religion, and focus on the discursive adjustments and representative strategies developed by the government, intellectuals, and artists to cope with the crisis of the Special Period.

The book is divided into three sections. While all the articles frame cultural production within networks that transcend the island nation, the logic of the division corresponds to a focus, respectively, on the commodification of the cultural industries and religious expression, on the reactive attempts to present national culture as rooted in Cuban history, and on the development of new cultural forms out of a transnational dialogue with communities in and out of the island. Hence the first part deals with the direct engagement of Cuban cultural producers, trained under socialism, with commercial practices and monetary profits; the second part is concerned with the government's and intellectuals' reactive discourses formulated against the alleged commodification of Cuban culture to stress Cuba's historical specificities; and the third section focuses on artistic practices that, though identified as specifically Cuban, engage with new technologies and address both the impending crisis and a transnational public.

In the first part, the chapters by Esther Whitfield, Cristina Venegas, and Kevin Delgado examine the production of literature and film and the celebration of religious ritual within a context dominated by monetary transactions. In their essays, they all pay attention both to the practices of cultural producers within the new imperatives and to the types of narrative forms that result from the need to attract foreign capital. While, according to Venegas and to Delgado, filmmakers and religious leaders seemed to deal with the predicament rather pragmatically, adjusting their formulas to both maintain their professionalism and appeal to foreign publics, Whitfield shows the anxieties and ambivalences expressed in the writings of key authors during these years. Writing during the Special Period entailed, more than ever, a double duty on the part of the writer: it involved expressing one's own self vis-à-vis the overwhelming surrounding hardships as well as infusing the experience with universal appeal. Many authors' preoccupation with producing true literature rather than mere popular entertainment was, in the end, an anxiety about the crisis of socialism, its moral categories, and its social and cultural stratification: The boundaries between "high" and "low" culture no longer marked social status and respectability. How could then Cuban culture be defined in such a moment of social and moral change?

The chapters in the second section of the book address this question by analyzing the discursive reactions on the part of both cultural producers and the state apparatus to confront what was often perceived as a flood of foreign cultural influences. That is, on the face of the need for economic restructuring, discourses about the threat of cultural imperialism and loss of national identity gained ground. The essays here examine a variety of intellectual discourses undertaken to both reflect on and confront the feared erosion of nationalist hegemony. My chapter traces the shift, within government and intellectual discourse, from a revolutionary nationalism based on political community to a national ideology of belonging based on local culture and history. Similarly, Laurie Frederik examines the trope of the "noble *campesino*" and the revaluation of rural authenticity and purity put forth by grassroots theater groups in the provincial areas in order to counteract a view of the paradigmatic Cuban citizen as urban, cosmopolitan, and corrupted by modern life. Jacqueline Loss, in turn, highlights an active referent often overlooked, and that is the Russian/Soviet influence in Cuban culture. Only very slowly, after the disappearance of the Soviet bloc and coinciding with the coming of age of a generation of Cuban-Soviet offspring, were there timid attempts to recuperate a certain pride in the Soviet past. This was not nostalgia for a purer form of a socialism now in process of extinction, but rather an attempt to reclaim the educational and professional experiences of many Cubans in the Soviet bloc as well as an iconic and cultural landscape that was formative and unique for the so-called Children of the Revolution. Last in this section, Kenneth Routon outlines the conflicts and debates that rid the traditional formulation of annual predictions on the part of Afro-Cuban religious leaders. As the Cuban government struggled to maintain its legitimacy during the Special Period, the support of religious communities could no longer be overlooked. Strategic agreements between rival Afro-Cuban religious organizations and the Cuban government led to the visibility of a religion that had been marginalized for decades as incompatible with socialist society and morality. Once again, nationalist discourses sought the inclusion of and support from a myriad of communities that, as the socialist state retreated from the social arena, had come to the fore.

The last section of the book is devoted to the development of cultural forms and narratives within transnational contexts and new communication technologies. Roberto Zurbano's chapter on the emergence of rap music in East Havana shows the influence that North American rap and its associated racial experience had among Cuban youth; yet it also shows that young rappers owned it by both indigenizing lyrics and rhythms and agreeing to inscribe themselves within a cultural bureaucracy that previously excluded them. Lisa Maya Knauer, in turn, writes about the circulation of rumba music and dance between New York and Havana thanks to the popularization of digital cameras and the increasing facility of travel between the two cities. She shows the mutual influence that *rumberos* in New York and Havana hold on each other to both maintain standards of tradition and innovation within mutually accepted parameters. To end, Antonio Eligio Fernández, Tonel, examines the development of postmodern painting and video-art among Cuban artists, some of whom reside outside the island. He traces their influence from an iconographic tradition linked to Cuban colonial and postcolonial history, yet their work developed thanks to both the introduction of new audiovisual technologies in Cuba in the 1990s and an awareness of the contemporary concerns of international art.

For these scholars, both foreign and Cuban, whose outlook was framed by the concerns of postcolonial and postmodern paradigms as well as by models of cultural circulation that emphasized Black Atlantic circuits and multiple directionalities, questions of transition were not central. Instead, their concern was change; a type of change that could be non-dialectical and non-teleological, and that could only be apprehended through examining the contingencies of the every day, without forgetting broader contexts of circulation. Hence, the expression of social identities and the specific forms that creativity took during the Special Period were placed within fields of action that went beyond the island. This book therefore argues that the Special Period, despite its intense demand for a commitment to the here and the now, required the engagement with trends beyond the island. As a result, subjectivities and identities—often identified with a multicultural sort of postindustrial capitalism—found expression and visibility during this period, even as the state apparatus sought to maintain the nation united in a common culture. Hence cultural expressions, while inextricable from the experiences of daily life at that time, were often framed within transnational scales of reference. In so doing they showed a consciousness of connectedness that transcended the island territory, and valued elements such as race, religion, and generation, which had been traditionally underplayed within a revolutionary framework.

All the texts in this book reveal the intense dialogue between their authors and those communities they write about. All but two contributors born and raised in the island, Tonel and Zurbano, could be considered neither tourists nor natives—as anthropologist and filmmaker Ruth Behar (2002) put it in reference to herself. Rather, they are intimate onlookers, participant observers whose lives were intertwined with their subjects in economies of favors and affects that generated mutual expectations and often provoked a sort of double consciousness in the Cubans they engaged with, who at times saw themselves through the foreigners' lens and acted accordingly. The unequal relation between foreign scholars and their Cuban interlocutors was a direct and unavoidable consequence of life in Special Period Cuba, when hierarchy was defined by access not only to foreign currency but, most dramatically, to a foreign passport. Fueled by the influential concerns of the booming postcolonial theory, the manifest inequality between foreign residents and Cuban citizens raised questions as to the hierarchical distance between these scholars and their otherwise peers. In a gregarious society in which interactions were always ambiguous—ideologically, materially, sexually—and where intimacy and distrust coexisted, the position of the foreign person vis-à-vis his or her interlocutors was always questionable, as the contributions in this book implicitly and explicitly address.

* * *

After Fidel Castro's illness in 2006 and his resignation in February 2008, popular expectations of transition picked up steam, leading to congratulatory statements by exiled intellectuals such as "Cuba has rejoined the present" (de la Nuez 2008). Soon, however, it became apparent that Raúl Castro's government was one of continuity. There was no official end to the Special Period.[16] Without the Soviet Union, the Cuban Revolution survived by turning itself into a new temporal category: the Special Period. Cuba became, for Cubans and foreigners alike, an island outside history, lingering in a sort of timeless eternal—to use Edward Said's famous expression. This book focuses on the decade of the 1990s, when the Special Period meant stagnation (political) but it also meant change. During that time, the uncertainty of Cuba's position in the world brought a widespread ideological pessimism, while market reform generated expectations of change. The result was a popular search for meaning as well as for means of expression. This book brings to the fore the new aesthetic forms, expressive cultures, ethical practices, visions of the future, and considerations of community that forever changed the landscape of what was known as the Cuban Revolution.

Notes

* I am indebted to Jorge Ferrer, Anitra Grisales, Berta Jottar, Lourdes Martinez-Echazábal, Lucía Suárez, and Ignacio Vera for their critical commentaries and helpful input, which have greatly improved this introduction.

1. Fidel Castro (1989) began adding "socialism or death" (socialismo o muerte) as a second line to his usual motto of "fatherland or death" (Patria o muerte) in December 1989.
2. See also Castro (1990b and 1990c). On September 28, 1990, in a speech to the Committees of Defense of the Revolution, he announced the inevitability of the Special Period: "Without a doubt we are entering the Special Period. It is almost unavoidable that we will have to experience that special period in a time of peace" (Castro 1990d).
3. According to Mauricio Vicent (1993d), black-outs lasted longer in the provinces than in Havana: between 16 and 20 hours a day.
4. A neuritis epidemic was widely reported in the international press. See Vicent (1993b). Concerning food recipes on radio and television, see Vicent (1993a).
5. See *Granma International* in 1990 and 1991. Every issue included news on the latest measures. See also then numerous articles by Mauricio Vicent in *EL PAIS* during these years.
6. See Jatar-Hausmann (1999).

7. This had been the case, briefly, during the early 1980s (see Jatar-Hausmann 1999).
8. These laws followed, respectively, Cuba's shooting of two U.S.-based rescue planes that allegedly entered its air space (in March, 1996), and the Varela Project, in 1998: an aborted citizens' initiative to reform the Constitution and launch democratic reforms. See Alvarez García and González Núñez (2001).
9. Chanan (2001) noted the revaluation of Gramscian Marxism in the 1990s, precisely because of Gramsci's pragmatic approach to market relations as a means to maintain socialist governance.
10. See, e.g., Bauman (1994), Kumar (1992), Przeworski (1993), Verdery (1991b), and Yurchak (2006).
11. See, e.g., Carranza Valdés, Gutiérrez Urdaneta, and Monreal González (1995).
12. See Manzor-Coats and Martiatu Terry (1995) for an account of the theater scene in these years.
13. Steve Fagin's experimental film *Tropicola* (1997), shot mostly in Havana in the early 1990s, created an improvisatory space in which actors powerfully and critically commented on the commodification of social relations occurring in Cuba at the time.
14. The Teatro del Obstáculo (or Theater of Obstacles) used "aesthetics of difficulty" as their motto, according to Manzor-Coats and Martiatu Terry (1995). See also Oroza, Maja Asaa et al. (n.d.).
15. Among these, there were film students such as the Spaniard Benito Zambrano, who went on to direct the film *Habana Blues* (2002) about foreign music producers seeking to commercialize Cuban music abroad, and journalists such as longtime *EL PAIS* correspondent Mauricio Vicent, who since 1991 published hundreds of chronicles of the Special Period's daily life.
16. Through the 2000s, Fidel Castro (2001, 2005) has continued to refer to the Special Period as ongoing. I owe this point to Ignacio Vera.

I

Foreign Commerce

2

Truths and Fictions: The Economics of Writing, 1994–1999

Esther Whitfield

"¿Pathos o Marketing?" screamed the heading in *El Caimán Barbudo*, the cultural journal of Cuba's young communists' union (UJC) in 1998, echoing a tension between literature and the unfortunate necessity of selling it that has tormented writers since at least the Romantic period.[1] But Rafael de Aguila, the article's author, set his question specifically in the rapidly globalizing literary sphere of Cuba's "Special Period in Times of Peace," going on to ask why a Cuban writer should feel obliged to engage in "un séptico flirteo para agradar a una casa editora extranjera" [a septic flirtation to please a foreign publishing house, 3]. As if this were not direct enough a question, he invoked as the epitome of market-driven fiction a bizarre but highly saleable amalgam of "Special Period" types: "un cuento sobre una frikie jinetera drogadicta de padres balseros y hermano con sadismo anal" [a story about a freaky drug-addicted hustler whose parents left on a raft and whose brother is an anal sadist, 3]. De Aguila pitted literature against the market in especially vivid terms, but his concern was shared by milder-toned contemporaries and it fueled serious debate about the survival of aesthetic principles against the threats of a foreign publishing industry perceived as lowbrow. Alongside de Aguila and others, the writer Abilio Estévez and even the Madrid-based Jesús Díaz, then editor of the influential journal *Encuentro de la Cultura Cubana*, effectively joined forces to defend what they each called "true literature."[2] The uncompromising nature of this term is striking, and it begs questions: Why uphold a "true" literature, opposed to an implicitly false one, in a field long cluttered with works of varying ambition? Why did "true" and "false" surface at this moment, and what did they mean in the context of the now-established Special Period? Cuban writers' aesthetic integrity, cast as aesthetic freedom, had faced challenges before—but from very different foes. Most notably, Castro's 1961 "Address to the Intellectuals" chastised writers for retreating to art when revolution itself was more urgent; and, although it did not encroach upon artistic form, it was famously ambiguous on the question of permissible content (Castro Ruz 1977). But what de Aguila perceived in 1998 as a new attack on content was qualitatively different from the 1960s version. Market values threatened to usurp revolutionary values as the antagonists of aesthetic integrity, and they caused an unmistakable sense of panic.

De Aguila's alarmist article coincides with the rise of what would be known as *el nuevo boom cubano*—the "new Cuban boom" that, ignited by booming foreign tourism to Cuba and buoyed by the success of Cuban exports in music and the visual arts, marked the entry of Cuban-authored works into European and American bookstores in unprecedented numbers. The term *nuevo boom*, introduced in Spain and Mexico in 1997 and soon adopted elsewhere, including in the international edition of Cuba's *Granma*, invokes the Boom with a capital B that in the 1960s brought the novels of Gabriel García Márquez, Mario Vargas Llosa, Julio Cortázar and Carlos Fuentes, and others to an international readership.[3] Naming the 1990s Cuban phenomenon thus was no doubt an attempt on the part of publishers, booksellers, and industry journalists to recreate the commercial success of the earlier Boom; and, despite the term's skeptical reception on the part of some critics—Estévez (1999), for example, preferred to think of Cuba as being "de moda," in fashion—there is no doubt that, on the one hand, the late 1990s saw a surge in publications of both new and reprinted books by Cuban authors; and, on the other, that this phenomenon shares certain traits with the earlier Boom. The 1990s saw Spain's elaborate system of literary prizes push many Cuban authors to prominence, and a sharp increase in the number of Cuban-authored books, principally novels and short stories, published outside Cuba. Between 1994 and 2002 Cuban writers were conspicuous on the lists of major international publishing houses in Spain, France, Germany, the United Kingdom, and the United States; not to mention the smaller presses—notably the Spanish houses Colibrí, Lengua de Trapo and Siruela and the Puerto Rican Ediciones Plaza Mayor—with special interests in Cuba (Strausfeld 2000).

The Boom of the 1960s, too, was propelled by a rapidly expanding market for Latin American fiction beyond the places in which it was written; a market incited, as Angel Rama (1981) commented, by widespread fascination at the triumph of the Cuban Revolution. And yet it is this factor in the success of the first Boom—its coincidence with the rise of the young Fidel Castro—that most distinguishes it from the "new Cuban boom" of the 1990s; for while the 1960s Boom coincides with the Revolution's ascension, Cuba's "new boom" was bolstered by representations of socialism's demise. One of the first Cuban-authored novels to be widely translated in the 1990s was Zoé

Valdés's *La nada cotidiana* (1995) written in Havana during the harshest years of the Special Period, and smuggled to Europe just before Valdés herself went into exile in Paris. *La nada cotidiana*, like Valdés's award-winning *Te di la vida entera* (*I Gave You All I Had*, 1999) that followed a year later, is woven from a signature blend of physical squalor, political excess, and sexual proclivity that sets an ironic standard for Special Period fiction, grounding an aesthetic that has its basis in material lack. Decay, despair, and making ends meet—the particularly creative practice of *inventar*, finding sustenance where there is none—became the stuff of fiction, setting off serious warning signs for the guardians of Cuban literature. It is in fact in a direct attack on Zoé Valdés's novels that the Cuban author Jesús Díaz, a fellow exile in Europe, invoked the notion of a "true literature." Valdés's success, claimed Díaz (1998), was due to her having met European demands for a sexualized, politically charged, and decadent Cuba. He charged her work with being "una forma de turismo literario, en el momento en que Cuba se convierte en un paraíso del sexo barato" [a form of literary tourism, in a moment when Cuba is becoming a paradise for cheap sex, 103]; while, in contrast, "la literatura, la verdadera, es el lugar imposible donde tratan de expresarse la tragedia y la comedia, el abismo y la ambigüedad entre los que se mueve este siglo; toda la complejidad del destino humano" [literature, true literature, is the impossible place where both tragedy and comedy try to find expression, the abyss and the ambiguity between which this century moves; all the complexity of human fate, 103].

Díaz's condemnation of Zoé Valdés voices the fears of writers and critics working within Cuban institutions during the late 1990s: fears about the relationship between fiction and tourism, between demand and supply and, most fundamentally, between "good" and "bad" or "true" and "false" literature. For while Valdés might have been an early pioneer of the "new Cuban boom," she did not fuel it single-handedly; and nor did her status as a vociferously anti-Castro exile distinguish her thematic repertoire as categorically as some might have hoped from that of writers within Cuba. In fact, the *nuevo boom cubano* took an extraordinary combination of circumstances wherein, on the one hand, the implosion of the domestic publishing industry, accelerated by new copyright legislation in 1994, would open the field for non-Cuban publishers; and, on the other, foreign tourists' and readers' ever-increasing interest in Cuba would spur demands for stock representations of life on the island. It is against these two coordinates—the overnight disintegration of domestic institutional support, and the potentially lucrative attention of nonnational publishers—that the literary terrain of the 1990s was mapped, as writers cautiously negotiated between the old and the new, the Cuban *peso* and the newly depenalized U.S. dollar, the domestic and the foreign. What follows is an attempt to chart the negotiations both contextually and textually. Writers within Cuba, I propose, engaged a scenario of institutional and legislative change both economically and artistically, making their fiction a venue for both exploring and complicating the changing market demands to which literature, like much of society, was suddenly subjected.

Although de Aguila (1998) laments the marketability of his hypothetical "Freakie," figures from a repertoire that to outside readers is more recognizably Cuban were more easily accommodated into fiction of the post-dollarized period than the drug binges and references to Anglo-American rock that had made an earlier generation of *novísimo* writers countercultural.[4] These recognizably Cuban motifs—chief among them the U.S. dollar that was legalized for a ten-year period between 1994 and 2004 after decades of sustaining the black market; and the foreign tourist, whose often illicit relationships with individual Cubans came to mark the Special Period landscape indelibly—function in late 1990s fiction as part of a complex exploration of the writer's place in Special Period society, rather than as a simple response to demand. By tracing their deployment in the work of Ronaldo Menéndez, Marilyn Bobes, Karla Suárez, Souleen dell'Amico, and Pedro Juan Gutiérrez, we can discern a body of Cuban fiction that takes the Special Period seriously, incorporating and reweighting its stock motifs as a challenge to this period's new markets for fiction. This writing is representative of Cuban literary production of the 1990s in a bounded but important way: although its narrow thematic repertoire does not do justice to the vast and varied output of Cuban writers during this period, it nevertheless mines a socioeconomic context that forms an implicit subtext to much writing of the period. It performs, in fact, as a specifically Cuban manifestation of what Graham Huggan (2001) has called "the cultural field of the postcolonial exotic." This is a field in which the practice of exoticizing can be understood both conventionally, "as an aestheticizing process through which the cultural other is translated, relayed back through the familiar" (ix); and at the same time, because of the particularities of the postcolonial context, as a practice that is "repoliticized, redeployed both to unsettle metropolitan expectations of cultural difference and to effect a grounded critique of differential relations of power" (x). Stock images of the tropics, colored by signs of a dwindling socialist power, operate as a Cuban version of the "postcolonial exotic," appearing as both familiar to, and dangerously critical of, the non-Cuban consumers amongst whom they circulate.

The fall of the Berlin Wall reverberated in Cuban literary production, as in all areas of the country's cultural and economic life. As Pamela Smorkaloff (1997) has explored, the 1980s represented a "golden age" in Cuban publishing, with record numbers of books produced across a range of fields. Yet at the beginning of the 1990s a reduction in material imports and the exit of many technical personnel brought the national publishing industry to a near standstill as annual publications of 500 titles and 37.6 million books in 1990 slipped to 223 titles in 1993 and 3.6 million books by 1994, with priority given to educational rather than literary texts (Campa 2002). Fiction was hit particularly hard by this situation and, in 1994, the Cuban Writers' Union

(UNEAC) published a compilation of the year's fiction with a prefatory apology, symptomatic of the hardships the industry and its authors were facing.

"La crisis de papel en Cuba," it stated soberly, "ha reducido a límites antes insospechados lo que, hasta hace poco, era su importante industria editorial... Por consiguiente, la literatura de ficción ha sido confinada por las circunstancias a las contadas revistas literarias que continúan apareciendo y, sobre todo, a lo que, poco a poco, ha ido configurando un vasto movimiento nacional de publicación de folletería y *plaquettes* que se sustenta aprovechando recortes y deshechos de algunas impresoras."

[The paper crisis in Cuba has reduced to previously unsuspected limits what was, until recently, its important publishing industry. ... As a consequence, fiction has been confined by the circumstances to the few literary journals that still circulate and, especially, to the vast national movement in publishing leaflets and makeshift books that is sustained by taking advantage of off-cuts and waste from certain presses.] (UNEAC 1994: 9)

Writers in the early 1990s had few opportunities to publish their work in Cuba.

It is at this time that Cuban institutions embarked upon joint ventures with foreign publishers, wherein the Cubans tended to perform editorial work while their partners provided material and printing facilities: this was the case, for example, with the Pinos Nuevos collection, a collaboration between Cuban and Argentine that aimed to generate 100 new titles a year (Lightfoot 1998). Although closely overseen by the collaborating home institution these joint ventures marked one of Cuban fiction's first post-Soviet forays into foreign publishing markets; a trend that was to grow fiercely, and with increasing detachment from the Cuban institutions themselves, as the 1990s progressed. And although generally welcomed as an economically viable means to disseminate Cuban fiction, the anthologies issuing from such joint ventures also raised concerns about demand and supply, and about the packaging of literature as authentically Cuban—concerns, that is, that anticipate de Águila's 1998 lament for the fate of "true" literature. In 1995 the writer Ronaldo Menéndez Plasencia complained that foreign-financed anthologies misrepresented Cuban literature, or at least steered it toward a representation that both privileged Cuban exceptionalism and met certain cultural expectations. Such anthologies, argued Menéndez, "pretenden dar al lector foráneo una información exhaustiva y un paquete de venta" [purport to give the foreign reader exhaustive information and a sales package, 1, 54]; a complaint that heralds subsequent debates over foreign interests in Cuban literature.

In August of that same year, 1995, Menéndez completed his short story "Money"; a subtle and important exploration of Cuban writers' changing relationship to commercial publishing and of the fears that such change aroused. Although not published until 1997, "Money" is set in the economic and political watershed of 1994. This was the first year in which Cubans were permitted to possess and spend U.S. dollars, rather than merely the Cuban *peso*; a shift with lasting consequences for literature as for other areas of Cuban life. The dollar's depenalization was announced on July 26, 1993 in recognition on the government's part that "[it] was confronting a multidimensional economic crisis to which the old remedies of intensifying controls and regulations or mounting state-led campaigns and programs seemed irrelevant" (Ritter and Rowe 2003: 430). Although the dollar had sustained Cuba's black market since the onset of the Special Period, the penal codes of 1979 and 1987 had prohibited its possession by Cubans and its sudden elevation to omnipotence was dazzling. After 1993 the dollar could legally extend its reach beyond state-level transactions and into the pockets and lives of private citizens. It could be used by individuals in the government-run outlets that operated alongside, and as an indispensable bolster to, the far more scantily stocked stores that charged in Cuban *pesos* and dispensed according to the ration-book. As is implied by the official name for these dollar stores, *centros de recaudación de divisas* [centers for the recovery of hard currency], all money spent there was recuperated by the state. This justified the dollar's legalization, allowing the government to benefit from the hard currency that would otherwise circulate only in the informal economy.

The effects of the dollar's depenalization were many and far-reaching. Replacing Cuba's currency with the dollar involved ideological cartwheels, for the dollar is the standard-bearer of the United States—what Jean-Joseph Goux (1999: 116) has called "a potent political symbol" of U.S. might. Moreover, until the U.S. dollar's circulation was discontinued in November 2004 its concurrency with the Cuban *peso* set a pattern of social inequalities—between those who had dollars and those who did not—that the revolutionary project had claimed to eliminate. Among dollarization's most significant consequences for literary production was a November 1993 law decree allowing writers to negotiate contracts with foreign publishers independently of state organizations. Such contracts could then be drawn in hard currency, affording writers access to new sources of income, but also, as de Aguila warns, presenting new costs.[5] It is these costs, in their social and literary dimensions, that Menéndez's "Money" engages from its conspicuously Anglicized title onward; as such, it stands as a key text in Cuban fiction's confrontation with the economic climate of the mid-1990s.

"Money" narrates the unresolved loss of thirty dollar bills, the balance for a young couple's escape to México. The title is portentous: "Money" is located inside a book (Menéndez's) in a tale of concealing money inside a book, such that a book becomes a cover for dollars and money and writing become dangerously near to one another. Set in July 1994, the story closely follows Cuba's legalization of the dollar as domestic tender alongside the rapidly devaluing Cuban *peso*, an economic shift that would facilitate the subsequent "booms" in tourism and publishing. "Money" is both a symptom and an articulation of deep mistrust toward the dollar. The protagonist's search for his lost 30 dollars leads him to a duplicity that seems to mirror that of the dual currency: there is but a small conceptual shift, he discovers, between *doble moneda* (the dual currency) and *doble moral* (double standards) and, indeed, between truth and falsehood. He commits his first act of falsehood against his wife: inspired by the thirty dollars that he still has in his pocket at the time, he initiates a love affair with another woman. Later he deceives his lover too, stealing from her bedside thirty dollars that, despite his best efforts, he cannot convince himself are his. One consequence of this dollar-inspired duplicity is a profound and irrecoverable disruption of domestic relations, as the husband is wrought with guilt at his betrayal and forced to accept that there can be no *"happy end"* to such double-dealing (Menéndez Plasencia 1997: 76). This ultimately unhappy ending, provoked by the dollars whose color haunts the husband in the very moment of transgression, lends itself to broader allegories about the disruption the foreign dollar might bring to the domestic scene; one that is further complicated by the presence of literature in the story.

It is not merely the household, or the monogamous relationship, that splinters under the strain of the thirty lost dollars. In a potent figuration of the authorial anxieties of years to come, money is imagined between the pages of a book, thus securing its proximity to writing and to literary production. Before it was lost, the money had been kept for security inside a book whose title is relayed in code. Its author is named as Reinaldo Arenas, but it is only by reading between the lines that we can assume it to be *Antes que anochezca* (*Before Night Falls*): "tras nombrar el libro ambos se derrumban como si acabaran de comprobar el resultado positivo de un análisis sobre el SIDA" [after naming the book they both collapse as though they had just been given the results to a positive AIDS tests]; "se resignan antes que anochezca definitivamente y puedan dormir" [they resign themselves before night falls completely, so that they can sleep]. When the couple recovers this book, the money is not there, yet the expectation that it might be, or indeed that it should be, leads to a series of associations that chart a speculative course for literature in an increasingly dollar-driven market. First, the husband imagines selling the book, assuring his wife that, in a local market where Arenas's work is taboo, "es un *best seller* por el que me darán los treinta dólares" [it's a bestseller for which they'll give me thirty dollars]. The potential profits of this *bestseller* soon multiply, however, as the book is provisionally launched outside the domestic space. It is as he is about to throw the book into the Caribbean that has so recently been the refuge of over 30,000 rafters that *Antes que anochezca* appears to the husband not as a thirty-dollar *bestseller* but as an untold amount of money. "Saca el libro de Reinaldo Arenas y lo manosea como quien manosea un fajo de billetes" [he takes out the Reinaldo Arenas book and flicks through it as one flicks through a wad of banknotes] (Menéndez Plasencia 1997: 75). Cementing the link between paper and monetary value that new economic critics have explored, this image displays both prescience and preoccupation regarding what Cuban writing, in particular self-revelatory writing like that of Arenas's autobiography, would be worth beyond national territory. When "Money" was written, there was of course no way to know how successful an international *bestseller* Julian Schnabel would make of *Antes que anochezca* in his film *Before Night Falls*, magnanimously retrieving Arenas for a world to which, as Jacqueline Loss (2003) has argued, he was supposed to be unknown. Nor could the extent of commercial interest in Cuban literature at the close of the decade be foreseen from Menéndez's vantage point in 1995; and yet there is in this story the seed of a relationship that would become more important as the decade wore on. In making a book a cover for money, and in visualizing its pages as a wad of bills in the moment the book moves from domestic circulation into a broader international space, "Money" anticipates the movement of Cuban fiction beyond national borders and into lucrative foreign contracts; an anticipation that becomes a challenge through the story's thinly veiled insistence that doubleness offers no *happy end*. It is perilous, the ending implies, to look for money in books that are to be launched abroad; and the story implicitly serves as a warning against venturing away from home ground, beyond the cocoon of domestic harmony.

While "Money" takes the U.S. dollar as its figure for exploring Cuba's changing literary terrain, and for posing the explicit question of how remuneration in foreign currency might damage domestic fiction, other stories shape the same exploration through a particular economic relationship that emerged in the 1990s: *jineterismo*. Paraphrased by Coco Fusco (1998) as "hustling for dollars" and often translated too rigidly as "prostitution," *jineterismo* became an increasingly visible side-effect of Cuba's large-scale embrace of tourism following its loss of Soviet support. The year 1994 saw the creation of Cuba's Ministry of Tourism, under whose direction Cuba's physical landscape and social hierarchies were dramatically altered. Tourism to Cuba had not had a heyday since the 1950s, when it was often portrayed as a playground for visitors from the United States. (Schwartz 1997); and after the imposition of the U.S. trade embargo, high-spending, hard-playing vacationers were replaced by "a small number of more frugal and less demanding visitors from the former Eastern Bloc" (Martin de Holan and Phillips 1997: 783). In the decades leading up to the Special Period, Cuba's foreign tourist industry was severely limited by the country's underdeveloped accommodation and transportation infrastructure. From 1994 on, however, tourism from Europe, Canada, and Latin America increased rapidly, surpassing one million visitors a year by the end of the decade and far outstripping revenues from sugar, until then Cuba's principal export (CEPAL 2000).

As I have noted earlier, the increase in tourism to Cuba coincided with, or spurred, foreign readers' interest in Cuban literature; and, indeed, the structure of what we might call the "tourist encounter" saw itself replicated in many of the interactions surrounding the dissemination of literature. Dean MacCannell (1999) reads the tourist as a figure whose quest to experience modernity leads him or her to celebrate differentiation and, crucially, to engage in a "dialectic of authenticity" wherein the assurance that what is being witnessed is "the real thing" is enough to validate the experience. When this dialectic plays out along national or cultural lines, as it has increasingly with the growth and globalization of the tourist industry, these differentiations, and their basis in an assumed authenticity, take on greater dimensions. John Frow (1991: 150) elicits a paradox wherein the quest for authenticity, although always mediated and doomed to disappointment, facilitates the commodification not only of material services but of immaterial relationships. "The product sold to the tourist industry," writes Frow, "in its most general form is a commodified relation to the Other." This relationship provides a structural model for the tourist encounter that is replicated in the imagined encounter between Cuban fiction and its readers outside the country. Foreign readers in the 1990s, whether or not they had visited Cuba, came to share tourists' interests in what the country had to reveal of its purportedly authentic culture; as did the literary agents and publishers who flocked to Havana's annual book fair in search of new material to take home. Reciprocally, Cuban authors who published abroad were increasingly invited to travel to launch their books—including to the United States, whose Clinton-era policy permitted cultural exchange. As Milene Fernández Pintado (1999) recounts wistfully in her short story "El día que no fui a Nueva York," the authors thus became tourists themselves.

Intercultural encounters that privileged difference were replayed in many areas of Cuban society, particularly in cultural exports such as music and film, but the encounter repeatedly depicted in fictional portrayals of the 1990s is both the most intensely physical and the most heavily publicized. It is the encounter between a Cuban woman and a foreign man, approximated to the discourse of prostitution through the figure of the *jinetera*. Much showcased in non-Cuban magazines in the 1990s—including a 1990 issue of *Playboy* and a 1999 photo-shoot in *National Geographic*—*jineterismo* became the face of the Cuban government's failure to curb the widespread prostitution that it had supposedly eradicated in the early 1960s. In more nuanced readings, *jineterismo* also functioned as an umbrella concept for all sorts of dealings between Cubans and foreigners. These range from the mutual exchange of "cultural" information—the mutual satisfaction of curiosity for places never seen, or what the writer Antonio José Ponte (2001) has called the exchange of history (Cuba's story) for geography—that is, the promise of a ticket to somewhere else, or the trading of food, clothes, entrance to nightclubs, or money for sexual companionship. Coco Fusco (1994: 151), in one of the earliest of several studies of the topic, is careful to describe *jineteras* as "women who exchange a range of favors, including sexual ones, for money from foreigners"; and Nadine Fernández (1999: 85) has observed that "though often overlooked in the literature on tourism in Cuba, *jineterismo* is actually used to describe a broad range of activities related to tourist hustling (including selling black market cigars, rum, coral jewelry etc.), providing private taxi services or access to 'authentic' *Santería* rituals, or simply serving as informal tourists guides in return for a free meal or some token gifts from the tourist."

Jineterismo as a theme appears frequently in Cuban fiction of the 1990s; to the extent that we might think of the sexual relationship between a Cuban and a foreigner as a metaphor for other relationships, and other anxieties, shaped by the Special Period. Chief among the relationships invoked by this metaphor, I would like to suggest, is that between Cuban writers and the new hard currency markets into which their work might now, in the new dynamics of the Special Period, be enticed. Long accustomed to working within the parameters of the domestic institutions that oversaw the limited and barely remunerated distribution of their work within Cuba, the appearance of new suitors offering writers international exposure and material comforts, in the form of hard currency publishing contracts, forced writers to consider in radically new ways where and how they might strike the best deal. That *jineterismo* should present itself as a metaphor for these new possibilities for engagement is poignant but, given the context, unsurprising. Early examples of fictionalized *jinterismo*, both of which are included in the National Artists' and Writers' Union's 1994 *Anuario*, are Miguel Barnet's "Miosvatis" and Miguel Mejides's "Trópico." The first tells of a Cuban traveler who returns home from Europe bearing gifts from a Swiss man to his elusive Cuban fiancée; in the second, the tourist is a German woman whose preconceived ideas of the delights of the tropics—including their potential for quick romance—are disappointed, as she becomes the deluded victim of those whom she had sought to exploit. Anna Lida Vega Serova's later "Erre con erre" ("R and "R") (1998) explores a relationship between two women, a Cuban and a Cuban-American, the first taking advantage of her Cuban-American lover only to leave her for a man as soon as their life in the United States begins. More often, however, the encounter explored in fiction replicates the paradigm of a young Cuban *jinetera* and her older foreign lover; and it is in examining some of these manifestations of the *jineterismo* theme that we might begin to read fictional restagings of the tourist encounter as a reflection upon the shifting demands that Cuban writers faced during the Special Period.

Karla Suárez's "Aniversario" (1999) is structured as one side of a conversation between a young journalism student and her friend. The latter is on the other end of the line while the former, speaking from a five-star hotel room in which she has spent the night with her French lover, gives a blow-by-blow account of the luxuries she is enjoying, and of her privileged access to a world of English television and vodka martinis of which her friend, as she is constantly reminded, is "pretty ignorant" (36). The oasis in which the woman who insists that she is not a *jinetera* finds herself is contrasted directly to the city outside: it has hot running water while outside there is none, and its occupants smoke Camel cigarettes rather than "those nasty Populares" (Suárez 1999: 33). The comforts of the hotel room appear to be unlimited and the friend on the other end of the line is given little opportunity to speak. And yet the response to her implied interjections suggest that all is not well, and that she thinks the student's relocation to the foreign side of the fence—literally, to the foreign journalists' section of a commemorative parade—has made her a bad reader of Cuba. The student's comments that "no-one was thinking about all the scarcities or about not having beer; everyone was cheering and feeling good" (34), "this country is gorgeous, really...like a foreign film" (36) cause friction between her and her friend, and suggest that her embrace of foreign luxuries has severed her cognitive ties to her homeland.

Souleen dell'Amico Ciruta's "Contradicciones" (1999) shares both the structure and the implicit concerns of Suárez's story. This time, a Cuban woman addresses her friend from France, where she has gone to live with her old and jealously protective husband. This young woman's distance from Cuba, and her sense of being out of place in her new surroundings, is more discomfiting than in Suárez's story: she knows her Cubanness to be an attraction of only superficial interest, and she is soon taken to task for both her ignorance of French behavioral codes and her presumed tendencies toward infidelity. In France she suffers from her husband's cruelty and her own ensuing loneliness; the freedom she had sought by leaving Cuba is overtly denied her, as her husband keeps her under lock and key. Her experience soon translates into both a deep regret at having left Cuba, and a sustained attack on the French. While still in Cuba she and her friend "nos sentábamos a la captura de un pasaje para salirnos del desarrollo, porque Europa les iba mejor a nuestras carreras de modelo" [would sit in wait for a ticket out of the underdeveloped world, because Europe would be better for our careers as models], but little did they know that the French "más que gente parecen estatuas escapadas de algún museo de cera" [rather than humans, they seem statues escaped from a wax museum] (dell Amico Ciruta 1999: 63). The pain of separation from Cuba is more than she can bear, and her ultimate realization gives her story a clear and simple moral message: "¡Qué tonta fui al pensar que tenía la vida resuelta, que había encontrado estabilidad y que con el dinero terminarían mis angustias! [How stupid I was to think that I had my life sorted out, that I had found stability and that money would put an end to my anguish!]. Her desire to leave Cuba, and her belief that a moneyed life outside the national sphere would solve her problems, has embroiled her in the "contradictions" of the story's title, of which the closing episode—the revelation that the stranger whose gaze has her mesmerized is in fact a blind man—is just one. Written from within Cuba, "Contradicciones," like Suárez's "Aniversario," presents the *jinetera*'s decision to leave the country for financial reasons as a lapse in judgment and, essentially, a moral weakness.

The scenario common to both Suárez's and Dell'Amico's stories—a young woman who believes that her life will improve if she enters into an economically comfortable relationship with a foreign man, but ultimately realizes the error of her ways—is anticipated by an earlier rendering of this theme; one that brings the intercultural relationship of *jineterismo* closer to the dynamics of writing and publishing in Cuba's Special Period. Marilyn Bobes's story "Pregúntaselo a Dios" ["Ask the Good Lord"], included in the 1996 anthology *Estatuas de sal: Cuentistas cubanas contemporáneas de hoy* (partially translated in the English anthology *¡Cubana!*), has the same cast of characters—a Cuban woman, Iluminada Peña, the French husband whom she met one night on Havana's Malecón, and the female friend in Cuba who serves as her confidante. Like the woman in Dell'Amico's story, Iluminada has left Cuba for France and is sorely disappointed with her new life; she, too, draws comparisons between France and Cuba—particularly between French and Cuban men—that are distinctly favorable to the latter and reflect an established pride in national ideals of manhood. Although her French husband displays an endearing *tendresse*, for example, his skills as a lover are far inferior to those of her former Cuban boyfriend. Indeed, by the end of the story and after a brief vacation in Cuba, Iluminada is deeply conflicted at having ever renounced her homeland; and her name— meaning "enlightened"—becomes supremely ironic.

Bobes's story alternates between a third-person account of Iluminada and her husband Jacques's first encounter, and Iluminada's letters to her friend Yanai—who still lives in Cuba. It is through this adoption of the epistolary form that "Pregúntaselo a Dios" ("Ask the Good Lord") becomes a metaphor for writing. The inclusion of Iluminada's letters in the story allows for a reiteration of the theme of writing; a foregrounding of its place in the context of flirtations and economically driven relationships between Cubans and foreigners. Iluminada Peña is the writer in this story and she—like Suárez's character, who is a student journalist—facilitates a reading of her role as that of the Cuban writer more broadly. Iluminada is wracked with doubt at having given a foreigner rights to her—rights that are explicitly proprietory in the case of Dell'Amico's protagonist, whose husband keeps her under lock and key. Her experience as a wife stands as a warning to others who might sell their rights to personal or intellectual property too naïvely. In making the *jinetera* a writer of letters, if not of fiction, Bobes implicitly raises the question that Menéndez's "Money" formulates through the figure of the dollar: what might be the fate of the Cuban writer, or of Cuban literature more broadly, if it enters into economic exchange with foreign entities that the Special Period offered all too readily? If the stories of Menéndez, Bobes, Dell'Amico, and Suárez have a common message, it is that while the foreign offers material rewards, it also requires a sacrifice—of home, and of all that has until now been welcoming and familiar. The stories' deep suspicion toward the viability of relationships that cross national borders betrays a tacit anxiety toward what Cuba's contact with the capitalist world would mean more broadly; and, in particular, what it would mean for fiction. "Good" and "bad," or "true" and "false," literature are not named as such; but the stories are inscribed with a moral code that leaves little doubt as to where these values lie. The domestic sphere is privileged to the extent that to break out of it and enter the international marketplace, even if doing so might ultimately be the only viable option, is construed as entering a dangerous, morally corrupting world. The appeals to literary value—to a separation of the good from the bad—that de Aguila, Estévez, and Díaz voice in 1998 are echoed here, and explored through metaphoric renderings of stock Special Period figures.

A consideration of Special Period fiction's proximity to moral corruption, whether this be conceived in social or explicitly literary terms, would not be complete without taking into account the work of Pedro Juan Gutiérrez, one of Cuba's most commercially successful literary exports in recent years. Moral corruption as well as physical decay and psychological ruin are the material of the five novels of Gutiérrez's "Ciclo Centro Habana," launched in 1998 with the much-translated *Trilogía sucia de la Habana*. The novels are populated by desperate characters whose lives unfold in squalor and in the absence of any stimulation beyond sex; their erotic encounters are, consequently, recorded in graphic detail. These novels might seem ideal targets for Jesus Díaz's charge against Zoé Valdés, that of "commercializing the Cuban tragedy"; and their long-suffering and highly sexed characters could be understudies for de Aguila's "freakie jinetera drogadicta." And yet I would like to propose, in closing, that Gutiérrez's work in fact poses a challenge to both foreign consumers of Special Period Cuba *and* defenders of an idealized notion of "true" Cuban literature; a challenge that depends on an ironic overdetermination of the Special Period's roster of stereotypes, among them the *jinetera* that I have read in others' work as a metaphor for anxiety about the new markets in which fiction was to circulate.

The "Ciclo Centro Habana" was published in circumstances rather different than the stories discussed so far. Although the third novel in the series, *Animal Tropical*, was produced in a Cuban edition subsequent to its publication in Spain, Gutiérrez is primarily what the Cuban critic Desiderio Navarro (2001) has called a "tamizdat" writer: one who is resident in Cuba but whose work is published elsewhere, and is available to readers and critics in Cuba only through unofficial channels. Gutiérrez has no strong institutional affiliation within Cuba and neither his fictional work nor the authorial persona he projects in interviews subscribe to the anguished protectionism toward Cuban letters that we hear in articles such as de Aguila's. Notions of "true" and "false" literature barely enter Gutiérrez's articulations of his vocation as a writer, and one might be forgiven for thinking that the "Ciclo Centro Habana" either lies wholly outside the debate, or is situated firmly in the terrain of the "false." In fact, however, Gutiérrez's novels advance a different notion of truth, wherein the defense of "true literature" is drawn into the social sphere to become a defense of neo-realist (or dirty realist) authenticity.[6] Updating the *testimonio* genre that the Cuban Revolution espoused in the 1970s as a way to voice the collective experience of disempowerment, Gutiérrez pens scenarios of hopeless poverty, set in the collapsing yet much-photographed *barrio* of Centro Habana.

While Gutiérrez's stories are peopled with stock figures from the Special Period landscape—destitute yet oversexed *jineteras*, frustrated yet eternally machista young pimps, black marketeers, corrupt policemen, desperate economic migrants from the countryside—the novels' challenge to new markets for Cuban fiction lies in the extent to which these characters are overdetermined as attractions, or as sources and subjects of erotic pleasure. For behind each desperate Cuban character, the story implies, there lurks a voyeur: someone who consumes and vicariously enjoys scenes of depravity. This enjoyment maps closely onto the interests of the tourists depicted in the novel (a Mexican who comes to meditate but ends up with a *jinetera* girlfriend, for example) and, implicitly, onto the pleasures and illusions of intimacy that foreign readers might find in this novel.[7] By thus invoking the relationships that sustain both tourism to Cuba and the foreign consumption of Cuban fiction, *Trilogía* mounts an attack on the ethics of voyeurism; a critique, that is, of the interests that provoke people to watch and enjoy the brutal lives of others, choosing to either engage or ignore the absolute hopelessness that underpins them. As the narrator himself watches a European tourist enjoy himself with two *jineteras* on a rooftop of a neighboring building as dilapidated as his own he comments, ironically foregrounding the cultural ignorance and economic disparity that facilitate such exploitation, "Ah, el trópico espléndido, húmedo y lujurioso. El trópico al alcance de todos los bolsillos" [Oh the magnificent tropics, humid and sensuous, within reach of any budget, 123].

Gutiérrez's novels, then, occupy the apparently paradoxical but ultimately shrewd position of being commercially successful and at the same time critiquing the interests upon which such success is built. That is, they both undermine and benefit from the very demands for recognizably "Special Period" images that Jesús Díaz and Rafael de Aguila identify as grave threats to the sanctity, or at least to the "truth," of Cuban literature. While, contextually, the "Ciclo Centro Habana" may indeed have "commercialized the Cuban tragedy," textually it rehearses a deeply rooted weariness toward the depletion of human values that has ensued from their replacement with values of a different, overwhelmingly financial, kind. The *jinetera* in one of the final chapters of *Trilogía*, for example, no longer knows passion unless it is underwritten by money; "está traumatizada con los dólares" [She's hypnotized by Yankees and dollars, 351].

In its head-on engagement with what de Aguila (1998) calls directly, and certainly with paranoia—"las demandas del mercado" [the demands of the market]—the "Ciclo Centro Habana" stands as an alternative to others' more painstaking and allusive meditations on the Special Period's reshaping of the relationship between Cuban writing and foreign money and on the "falsehood" of diverging from the nonmonetary values of national literature. Nevertheless, Menéndez, Bobes, Dell'Amico, and Suárez navigate the same, rapidly shifting terrain. As the domestic institutions that had long shepherded Cuban fiction ceded ground to a vast panorama of transnational publishing interests, these five writers' response—and their innovation—was to take the new terrain and its stock emblems as their building blocks. Writing in the period of most rapid change that is also that of greatest uncertainty, between 1994, when the dollar begins to circulate domestically and 1999, when both tourism to Cuba and the literary *boom* reached new heights, they craft a fiction that explores, exposes, and implicitly challenges Cuba's emerging literary-economic order. Their allegiance to the notion of "true" Cuban literature, invoked by critics as the *nuevo boom* took hold, may be deeply ambivalent: the stories of Menéndez, Bobes, Dell'Amico, and Súarez are structured along moral parameters that retain faith in a domestic ideal, while Gutiérrez's truth is of a different order. It is in this very ambivalence, however, that they serve as a barometer of the literary and commercial climate in which they were produced. For, with the open circulation of the U.S. dollar and the visible presence of tourists in Cuba, the "truth" and "falsehood" of literature—like other previously incontestable distinctions between good and bad—were open to question.

Notes

1. Martha Woodmansee and Mark Osteen (1999), in their introduction to *The New Economic Criticism*, trace how elite writers in the Romantic period opposed a market-economics way of determining the value of their work, defending instead a specifically *literary* form of value distinct from market price or readers' popularity.
2. In "Médiations sur la littérature cubaine d'aujourd'hui," Estévez (1999: 221) states "C'est bien connu: les frontiers entre la vraie et la fausse littérature, entre le roman, la nouvelle et le simple témoignage, dans un présent chaotique comme tous les présents, ne sont pas toujours délimitées avec precision" [It is a well-known fact: the borders between true and false literature, between the novel and news and simple testimony, in a present as chaotic as all presents are, cannot always be precisely discerned]. In an interview with François Maspero for *Le Monde* that I quote subsequently, Díaz (2002) expounds on the idea of "la literatura verdadera."

3. To give just a few examples of the widespread use of the term *el boom cubano* in publishing-related articles and in the press: Rubén Cortés, in a 1998 article in Mexico's *La Crónica de Hoy* newspaper, writes that "luego de cuatro décadas publicando dentro y casi exclusivamente para la isla, los escritores cubanos asaltan las librerías de España y América Latina para destapar un Boom de la literatura cubana" [after four decades publishing within and almost exclusively for the island, Cuban writers are storming Spanish and Latin American bookstores to unleash a Boom in Cuban literature]. In Spain's *El País*, Amelia Castilla and Mauricio Vicent (1997) referred to "La explosión literaria de La Habana" [Havana's literary explosion], and some time later, the monthly book review *Leer* published an article entitled "El nuevo *boom* de la narrativa cubana en España" [The New Cuban Narrative *Boom* in Spain], tracing the increasing popularity and visibility of Cuban literature in Spain (Cremades and Esteban 2000). In Cuba, the Communist Party international weekly has also referred to it (Perdomo 1999).
4. The *novísimos*, championed by the late Salvador Redonet (1993), were writers born after 1959 whose work, in comparison with the more rigidly monitored literary output of earlier generations, he touted as iconoclastic. Iván Rubio-Cuevas (2000) explores their representations of the "margins," and José B. Alvarez (2002) reads their works as a continuation of the "contestatory" practice of Cuban short-story writing.
5. Law-Decree No.145 of 17 November 1993, on the conditions of labor for creators of literary works, acknowledges the status as worker of creators whose artistic work is not linked to an institution, and at the same time establishes a Ministry of Culture registry for such works. Law-Decrees No. 105 (5 August 1998) and No. 144 (19 November 1993) had established these same rights for visual artists and musicians, respectively. As stated on a Cuban government's website on cultural legislation, these law-decrees recognized the possibility of artistic work performed independently from a state institution. They also provide for the creation of a registry where these independent artists will affiliate (http://www.cubagob.cu/des_soc/cultura/legis.html).
6. Anke Birkenmaier's (2004) "El realismo sucio en América Latina: Reflexiones a partir de Pedro Juan Gutiérrez" considers Gutiérrez's "dirty realism" in a Latin American context.
7. I further explore Gutiérrez's constructions and uses of a Special Period authenticity in "Dirty Autobiography: The Body Politic of *Trilogía sucia de la Habana*" (Whitfield 2002).

3

Filmmaking with Foreigners

Cristina Venegas

For, you see, so many out-of-the-way things had happened lately, that Alice had begun to think that very few things indeed were really impossible.

—Lewis Carroll, Alice in Wonderland

The profound crisis of the Special Period transformed the nature of filmmaking in Cuba. Cuban cinema could no longer be contained within the boundaries of the island nation nor sustained by the industrial model established in 1959. From 1991 onward, Cuban industrial cinema produced through the State's Instituto Cubano de Arte e Industria Cinematográfica (ICAIC) regularly ventured into the international film market. The extreme scarcity of the period led to an increase in foreign coproductions, the emergence of an independent cinema reliant on digital technology, and an increase in production of both documentary and fiction films *about* Cuban culture from a vantage point located *outside* Cuba. An investigation of the resulting films and the conditions that surrounded their production reveals that the emotional geography of Cuba was moving beyond social revolution and toward the individual self. In addition, foreign coproductions, new digital technologies, and the production of foreign films in Cuba, led to new representations of the island and new cinematic genres for both Cuban and foreign consumption.

Locating the discussion of audiovisual culture in Cuba during the Special Period necessarily implies an emphasis on the economic issues and their impact on the state's influence over cultural production. The bankruptcy of the Cuban socialist state, and therefore of the ICAIC, directly affected state producers by removing their central plank of support while still promoting socialism as a political vision. Films began to reflect the emptiness of this vision as filmmakers had to deal with economic and political pressure. Nonetheless, extreme shortage of materials, ranging from gasoline and electricity to food and film stock, equipment failure, the closing of processing labs and exhibition venues, and the falling of international purchases led to the production of fewer films and documentaries. Film completion dates became a mirage as costs skyrocketed, and trained film personnel (art directors, actors, writers, etc.) hit long periods of unemployment, and many left the country.

The crisis affected all levels of the industrial filmmaking infrastructure. Between 1991 and 2001, only 31 feature films were made through the ICAIC (none in 1996), as compared with 10 a year before then. The production of newsreels, which had long documented Cuba's revolutionary history, simply ceased. Documentaries were mostly made by the International School of Film and Television (EICTV). The National Cinematheque, part of the ICAIC, saw its operating budget reduced, and an administrative reorganization led to an institutional battle for the control of both the international commercialization of archival materials and video concessions of ICAIC productions—both of which could generate hard currency revenues. In addition, increasing transportation costs along with the fees demanded by many historical sites resulted in the regular use of a few routine locations. Just as an example, veteran director Julio García Espinosa filmed *Reina y Rey* (Queen and King, 1994) across the street in his neighbor's house.

Until the late 1980s, state support had insulated Cuban filmmakers from the onslaught of market-driven industrial concerns, at least at the level of both production and local distribution, making them, according to filmmaker Gerardo Chijona, "the spoiled children of Latin American cinema."[1] Indeed, the revolutionary government had guaranteed financial backing for its cinema while allowing for a certain degree of autonomy. It had appointed filmmakers rather than bureaucrats to high-ranking ICAIC positions, who then were able to negotiate the terms of production, distribution, and exhibition, both domestically and internationally. In addition, the production arm of the ICAIC had been organized into three autonomous working groups each one led by a prominent filmmaker. The general social climate and the structure of apprenticeship in the ICAIC fostered creative renewal through an intimate artistic culture, mentorship, and professional partnerships. Projects were essentially work-shopped in each of the three groups, before being readied for production. In general, the then extant institutional culture facilitated creative risk taking by filmmakers, precluding the strict exigencies of financial procurement for their projects, while promoting a plurality of aesthetics without subverting revolutionary values. This important safety net allowed the ICAIC to also assist in the completion of films made in other countries. Just as importantly, it succeeded in introducing Cuban audiences to world cinema through numerous international programs, amateur film clubs, and, since 1979, the Havana Latin American Film Festival, and the Latin American Film Market (MECLA)—all but the festival were slashed by the 1990s.

At the beginning of the Special Period, as the state had to release some of its control and support, the film industry ventured into a wider filmmaking world in search of new opportunity. Yet, the revolutionary government attempted to maintain its ideological grip. The controversy over the film *Alicia en el pueblo de Maravillas* (Alicia in the Town of Maravillas, Díaz Torres 1990) effectively inaugurated the new era.

"Who Is Responsible for the Mistakes?" (Diego in "Fresa y Chocolate")

As a fully Cuban-financed project, *Alicia* shook the entire institution of the ICAIC and its culture as no foreign coproduction could have. Written in the late 1980s and released in 1991, the film reflected concerns that the economic crisis was to obscure—namely the anxiety about socialism's withering and the ensuing ideological vacuum. The film was inspired by the experimental Cuban comedy group *Nos y Otros*, whose sensibility was in turn influenced by a grotesque and absurdist humor in the tradition of Monty Python. Its title plays on "Alice in Wonderland," and its story transposes the Lewis Carroll tale to the fictitious Cuban town of *Maravillas*, inhabited by very special people (*los tronados*) who have been "demoted" from their jobs. The storyline conveys a search for new meanings within an exhausted paradigm, a search hopeful in its position but wickedly piercing in its analysis of everyday life. But by the time of its release, *Alicia*'s mocking tone was hopelessly out of sync with the nervous revolution's emerging demands for renewed adherence to its socialist project.

In hindsight, *Alicia* seems more forgiving than films made later in the decade. Nevertheless, the film unleashed a wave of negative reaction from the state-controlled national press and critics who preferred to attack the film rather than engage with its complex narrative structure and tone.[2] Yet *Alicia* provided a justification for a government's proposal to dissolve the film institute and merge it with the traditionally less autonomous Institute of Radio and Television (ICRT). The critical overkill forced ICAIC's director, the aforementioned Julio García Espinosa, to resign. Lobbying by filmmakers to stop the proposed merger led to the recalling of the diplomatically astute Alfredo Guevara for a second tenure as director to salvage the so-called disaster. Guevara (2003: 478) then publicly presented the film and defended its director at that year's Havana Film Festival with these words: "*Alicia* has often been situated as a potentially problematic or controversial film, and thus revolutionaries have to make decisions, and the first is to fight, no matter what the circumstances; in this case to prevent those who are mistaken, even though well-intentioned, from using the film against the Revolution." He had managed to turn the tables by invoking the Film Institute's long-established revolutionary values against "mediocre" and "opportunistic" criticism. At the same time, however, he withdrew the film from theaters, just four days after its premiere. This strategy allowed the government to retract from its merger proposal, but also set in motion fundamental changes within the ICAIC.

The contest over the content of Cuban consciousness was also at the core of other films from this period. Fernando Perez's *Madagascar* (1994) and Enrique Álvarez's *Miradas* (The Gaze, 2001) both deal with the insularity and cyclical nature of the individual self amidst disillusionment, tedium, and fatigue. In *Madagascar*, the characterization of Laurita's aimlessness and malleable consciousness set beside her mother's weariness and resignation recognizes the relatively greater weight of future uncertainty for the younger generation. Laurita believes she will find meaning by going to the African nation that names the film, ignoring Cuba's travel impediments. In her metaphorical journey, constant relocation within the city signifies not political exile and the rejection of Cuba, but rather an inward exploration of the self, now liberated from univocal identification with the revolutionary process. Likewise, Álvarez in *Miradas* extricates his characters' emotional burdens from broader processes. He takes a new path by interpreting enigmatic arrivals and returns, paradoxical perspectives, and deceptive knowledge as arising mainly from personal history. While produced at different stages of the Special Period and sharply differing in their aesthetic, *Madagascar* and *Miradas* are indicative of the emotional tenor of the moment. Incisive in their search for new meanings, Special Period narratives brought the possibility of a separation of State and self.

"Thirty Years of Revolution and Struggle so that the Spaniards Can Come Back Again!" (Maité)

Under financial constraints and the direction of non-filmmakers, ICAIC dissolved the three working groups established by García Espinosa in the 1980s, thus losing a democratic structure that had fostered egalitarian access, creative flexibility, and open artistic dialogue.[3] Different values and practices, adjusted to hard commercial realities, took their place. Reduced state subsidies and bureaucratic centralization forced the new ICAIC leadership to pursue options for international coproductions, most notably with the expanding Spanish film industry as well as with emerging European initiatives.[4]

International coproductions appeared key to the industry's survival, despite fears of a loss of independence, and effectively expanded the market for Cuban film. The majority of them were made with Spain, after a 1988 bilateral agreement to that effect—followed by Germany, France, Denmark, and various Latin American countries. These coproductions were flexible and negotiated arrangements. A "standard" coproduction consisted of a partnership between a Cuban filmmaker with a script to be shot in Cuba and a largely Cuban cast including, perhaps, a few members from the coproducing countries. In contrast, in a "service" coproduction a foreign partner paid the ICAIC to organize the shooting of a foreign film, including the identification of locations, the hiring of actors, the provision of stock footage, and/or the conduction of related research.

As a result, state approval for film projects—once in itself assurance of financial backing—became a lengthier process involving the ICAIC's search for coproduction capital. New partnerships resulted in new professional practices. Filmmakers with no experience in the funding process outside the state subsidy system had to adapt, learning to navigate international partnership and financing systems. Working mainly with European partners, Cuban filmmakers found themselves at a disadvantage as they earned fixed salaries paid through the ICAIC, while their foreign counterparts were free to negotiate higher salaries, profit points, and the like. As analyzed by Hernandez-Reguant (2004a: 2–3) the tensions that ensued in the clash between "old socialist ethics and capitalist practices" set the stage for "a decisive shift in signifying practices of authorship." Copyright protections now extended to individual filmmakers: even though they continued to be salaried employees, many of them were able to cash in royalty payments, particularly as they joined the Spanish authors' society—which opened an office in Havana in 1997—or were able to obtain Spanish citizenship, thus evading both Cuba's travel restrictions and the strictures of the U.S. embargo. One result of these developments was a new, elite film community whose professional survival depended not so much on state support but on foreign partnerships and professional relationships.

This increasingly international and complex structure of the Cuban film sphere of the 1990s was a major factor in shaping new views of Cuba. Just as the events of the Special Period contributed to a visual representation of the individual self as apart from the state, the nation began to be constructed as independent from the revolutionary state. The traditionally usual suspects such as guerilla fighters, the worker, the educator, and the rebels moved offstage as films delved into a greater, more nuanced range of characters and scenarios. The most notable of all was the Oscar-nominated *Fresa y Chocolate* (Strawberry and Chocolate, 1993), codirected by the late Tomás Gutierrez Alea and Juan Carlos Tabío. A social comedy and exile narrative, the film featured black market dealings, and gay sexuality when homosexuality was still a taboo—therefore turning the Cuban gaze in new directions.

The numerous coproductions spurred by the Special Period often dealt with social concerns and economic problems taking place in Cuba, but those were treated in a way that could be understood by foreign viewers. The most commercially successful narrative vehicle employed in them to bridge cultural differences while exploring the existential and absurd drama of Cuban daily life was comedy—used in about half of those films coproduced by foreign parties. In this fashion, Cuban cinema joined an increasing international trend in a global market where laughter would make money.

Nothing Seemed True

In a rundown bus station, somewhere in the middle of Cuba, the bored demeanor of its small staff belies the precarious condition of public transportation on the island at the end of the Special Period. Stranded passengers proceed to fix up the depot, turning it into a comfortable shelter. So goes the plot of Juan Carlos Tabío's *Lista de espera* (The Waiting List, 2000) in reference to the etiquette of waiting in line to board a bus. The first line of dialogue begins the comedic exchange: "Who is last in line?" The answer comes: "It depends. Are you going to Havana or Santiago de Cuba?" (cities located in opposite ends of the island and therefore requiring of different buses). A chaotic dialogue ensues, until a blind passenger attempts to use his disability—unsuccessfully—to jump ahead in the line. Any Cuban would relate to what happens next: all wait in vain for hours for a bus that never comes. An announcement is made that no bus will come and they should all go home. In an unexpected turn of events, a handful of passengers resolve to stay and repair both the station and a broken bus. They then work communally in order to build an ideal environment where children can play, romance is rekindled, and strangers become friends through the bond of a common project. The stationary travelers represent people typical of Cuba's Special Period: a young woman engaged to a Spanish businessman, a young Cuban engineer unable to find work returning to his hometown in the countryside, a con-artist, a staunch Party member, a pragmatic citizen, a middle-aged herbalist woman, and two men who would not admit to their latent homosexuality. The bus station *cum* utopia displaces the dream society onto a functioning and manageable site. But as the travelers wake to the simple fact that no bus will ever arrive, they slowly decide to return to their normal lives. They realize, however, that they have experienced a common dream; one that may spill over into their waking lives. The viewer is left to question how ideals affect culture and everyday life.

The answers lie in the manner real Cuban people made sense of day-to-day existence under difficult and unstable conditions. As the guiding ideological, social, and political structures, that is, *patria, socialismo, pueblo*, and *partido* faltered, individuals had to contend with the increasing complexity of a society losing fundamental ideological grounding. What did the ubiquity of Communist Party slogans mean when the infrastructure had almost completely collapsed? Under what terms were the new sacrifices to be endured? What meaning could work bring? How does one sustain love and romance in the absence of collective dreams? This unraveling but fertile emotional and social landscape formed the setting for the comedies of the 1990s. Although intensely national in their semantic references, these films nevertheless appealed to international audiences.

Longtime documentary filmmaker Gerardo Chijona also turned to comedy as a means of addressing pressing concerns. Developed at the Sundance Institute's Film Lab, *Adorables mentiras* (Adorable Lies, 1991) allowed Chijona to establish close collaborative relationships with various North American scriptwriters. Subsequently, both his 1999 *Un paraíso bajo las estrellas* (Paradise Under the Stars) and his 2004 *Perfecto amor equivocado* (Love by Mistake) have found their largest audiences in Havana, while also achieving significant international success. The latter was conceived as a contemporary tragi-comedy of manners about Julio, a novelist who has not been able to write a second novel since the success of his first, and whose complicated personal life includes a wife, daughter, and a lover. Unable to find a publisher for his second novel, struggling to keep up the façade of a family life, and in desperate need of money to repair the family's crumbling Cuban house, Julio turns to writing politically charged, incendiary lyrics for both salsa and hip-hop music. He ends up winning a Grammy award with a popular music group, Hard Sex, a result that leads to a contract with a Spanish publisher for his second novel. The fact that Julio's earnings from publishing in Europe can maintain his life in Cuba illustrates the principal point that the world of the characters responsible for Julio's success is completely defined by foreign economies.

The theme in which personal relations and transactional parallels appeared to be intertwined is recurrent in Spanish-Cuban coproductions. These often reflect on emerging social relations defined by transnational economies, politics, and travel. Preferred themes included romance, sexuality, and exchange between Cubans and foreigners, as well as the vicissitudes of life as an émigré outside the island. The theme of binational romantic affairs as vehicles for less gritty premises was central for *Flores de otro mundo* (Flowers from Another World, by Bollaín 1999), *Cuarteto de la Habana* (Havana Quartet, by Colomo 1999), and *Maité* (Olasagasti 1994), all directed by Spanish filmmakers. The latter took up the topic of a Cuban-Spanish trade transaction as the pretense for an "impossible" love story between Daisy, a black, single mother and high-level representative for a Cuban export company, and Juan Luis, a white, middle-aged Spanish importer. Although they have a questionable business deal in the works (eels to Cuba, cigars to Spain), the ensuing romance provides the real conflict for Daisy, even as she appears opportunistic in dating Juan Luis—as might any other Cuban seeking an exit visa through a relationship with a foreigner. Similarly, a coproduction with Germany and Spain, *Hacerce el sueco* (Playing Swede, 2001) explored the contradictions between the new economy and socialist morality. In this film, Daniel Díaz Torres, director of the controversial *Alicia en el pueblo de Maravillas*, found a more welcoming audience with the tale of a German tourist who passes himself off as a university professor doing research in Cuba. He is in reality a jewel thief on the lam, hoping to hide in Cuba from the authorities. He seals his fate, however, when he rents a room in the home of a retired Cuban policeman, which leads to a number of conflicts generated among Cubans by the need to earn hard currency while upholding a socialist morality.[5]

Whether through documentary, romance, comedy, or absurdity, 1990s Cuban cinema found new forms in its association with foreign partners. In 1991, the *Alicia* controversy signaled a shift in the way artists and filmmakers expressed social complexities, first in regard to the Rectification process of the 1980s, and later to the difficulties of the Special Period. According to Díaz Torres, in the 1990s, in addition to the economic crisis, filmmakers had to contend with the widespread "double morality, boredom, a troubling level of conformity, lack of individual participation [in society], bureaucratization, and neglect."[6] As products of the age, its instability, and changing parameters, it can be no surprise that the films of the 1990s reflect on the meaning of Cuban identity, its social complexities, the socialist project, the revolutionary self, and the madness of the Special Period itself.

Digital Cinema

Under the extreme economic circumstances of the 1990s, digital technology promised low-cost access to production equipment. The Havana International Film Festival in 1997 and 1998 explored this potential through special seminars that examined costs, and viability. The seminars formed part of a broader official discourse about digital media, which began in the mid-1990s with the Internet's advent. Debates expressed caution about the deep reach of media globalization, raising fears of cultural colonization and domination. These concerns aside, video technology—both digital and analog—did indeed provide access to many Cuban filmmakers, and facilitated the forging of new visual perspectives outside the province of the ICAIC.

The seeds of Cuban digital production were sown by the nongovernmental group *Movimiento Nacional de Video de Cuba* (National Video Movement of Cuba), founded in 1989. The National Video Movement developed into an important venue for amateur directors, artists, writers, especially those outside the center of production in Havana. The group provided training, seminars, and information to videomakers throughout Cuba. At the height of the Special Period, underwater videographers could be seen carrying their cameras on bicycles, building special water-proof boxes for their equipment, and producing videos at any cost. Gloria Rolando, notorious in the United States due to her preference for themes related to the African diaspora, was able to create the production group *Imágenes del Caribe* (Images of the

Caribbean) under the auspices of the National Video Movement. Many of its members also worked in television and publicity, either for the tourism sector or for organizations such as the ICAIC and other entities producing commercials, music videos, graphic art, and animation.

Later, a *Muestra de Cine Joven* (Festival of Young Cinema), established through the ICAIC in 2001, provided a platform for emerging talent, including many women.[7] At the same time, a *Semana de Crítica Cinematográfica* (Film Criticism Week) was set up in Camaguey province by noted film critic Juan Antonio García Borrero, acting on his long-held concern with decentralizing film culture in Cuba. Both the *Muestra de Cine Joven* and the *Semana de Critica* represent attempts to renew Cuba's cinema discourse. There, every year, aspiring filmmakers screen their shorts—documentary and fictional, experimental and conventional, and video art—to a select jury of critics, filmmakers, and artists. Working independently, and using any means possible, but principally digital technologies, filmmakers who came of age during the 1980s and 1990s are thus reshaping the parameters of industrial cinema in Cuba. The embrace of digital production is key to the movement, but its members are also savvy about the economics of the industry, and aware of international marketing.

Filmmakers such as Juan Carlos Cremata, Humberto Padrón, and Pavel Giroud who have gained notoriety through the annual Muestra have gone on to produce independent features later distributed and exhibited through the ICAIC. In particular, Cremata's first two features, *Nada +* (Nothing More, 2001), and *Viva Cuba* (2005), garnered awards and were sold to a variety of international markets at different film festivals, making Cremata one of the most successful of the new generation of directors. Similarly, Humberto Padrón acquired notoriety partly thanks to the new technology. He directed *Frutas en el café* (2005), with renowned actor Jorge Perugorría as a producer. The film features a commercially oriented storyline that relies on some of the new habitual characters of the economy of the Special Period: foreigners, *jineteras*, black market thieves, criminals, and the good cop (played by Perugorria himself). His previous film, also shot in digital video, *Video de familia* (2001), was structured as a video letter from a young émigré in Miami to his family in Havana. As the parents learn that their son is gay, a comedic situation takes the opportunity to explore this social taboo.

Another filmmaker, Ismael Perdomo, formerly an assistant director to celebrated documentarian Santiago Alvarez and author of music videos made his debut feature using the new technologies available. *Mata, que Dios perdona* (Kill, God Forgives, 2005) has an experimental narrative structure which creates a view of the past that eschews familiar articulation. Like other young filmmakers, his formation was rather eclectic. As he publicly proclaimed, "Here, we no longer have transcendent dreams, but rather the harsh certainty of a transient presence...[my] intellectual references, 'spiritual teachers,' professional formation [are] more due to a VHS player or television where I've seen millions of images a day, than to a Bergman or Rossellini film seen in a theater."[8] Cheaper digital production and changing political parameters facilitated risqué themes and experimental narratives that nonetheless might be commercially viable for foreign audiences.

In addition to facilitating young and independent filmmakers' work, digital production became a vehicle for established ones to either experiment with a new language or merely survive in an economically difficult environment. Of note is the unconventional video feature *El plano* (1993) directed by Julio García Espinosa. Produced in conjunction with the EICTV, the film investigates the evolution of film language, its relationship to narrative conventions and technology. In a more practical vein, the technology made it possible that older and established filmmakers, affiliated with the ICAIC, and who were not able to work for lack of funding, could return to the screens. That was the case of the late legendary director Humberto Solás, who had gone for a decade without directing. Digital video afforded the opportunity of making his internationally acclaimed *Miel para Oshún* (Honey for Oshun, 2001), and later *Barrio Cuba* (2005)—a Spanish-Cuban coproduction. Solás was a staunch advocate of the digital medium not only for providing lower costs but also for departing from an elitist model of filmmaking.

Filmmakers from an older generation, as well as those in a younger age group, both independents and ICAIC-affiliates, now embrace alternative production strategies, striving for recognition as part of a broader audiovisual field. The different digital production groups are in no way mutually exclusive. They also point to a maturing film industry where survival depends on coproductions and the irreverence and independence of a generation educated within the social context of the Special Period.

Cuba through the Foreign Looking Glass

The increase in production of both documentaries and fictional films about Cuba from a vantage point outside Cuba contributed to the internationalization of a Special Period aesthetics. Furthermore, cinema became a way to circumvent the informational blockade that structured the island's social and political imaginary. Ana María Dopico (2002: 452) has pointed to the international economy of images of Cuba that developed post 1995 as stirring "political interests and market appetites." So, too, the audiovisual representation of Cuba created outside the nation fed a growing appetite in global markets for all things Cuban. Many forms of Cuban culture from music, dance, and politics, to identity and personal histories were explored through film. Narratives of "discovery" and return worked on themes of nostalgia and exoticism, taking the path of global popularity laid down by Cuban music. The proliferation of international film festivals and their growing attention to Latin America further made room in their programs for the abundance of films about Cuba.

The immense success of Wim Wender's *Buena Vista Social Club* (1999), which purported to rediscover the old and traditional *son* musicians of Cuba, engendered cultural debates within Cuba about the role of foreigners in conveying Cuban culture to the rest of the world. Some Cuban critics argued over the accuracy of these foreign representations, while others read international media attention as an opportunity to export Cuban culture.[9] According to Hernandez-Reguant (2000), the film itself boosted the mystique of Cuba, generating international demand for the elements of fake nostalgia so prevalent in the *mise-en-scène*—a "liberal" nostalgia that assigned Cuba a pure and stagnant historical character, sustained by socialism, and vulnerable to being "spoiled" by the unstoppable force of capital. Along the same lines, *Lágrimas Negras* (Black Tears, Herman Dolz 1997), produced two years prior to *Buena Vista* in the Netherlands, also followed a set of old Cuban musicians from Santiago de Cuba to the European stage. Rather than aestheticizing the island's urban decay, the film evokes the musicians' thoughtful attachment to Cuba and the revolutionary project.

Musicians were not all that was "discovered" by these films. Narratives of return were prevalent in a genre of autobiographical documentaries where emotions carried the story into unexpected, sometimes hidden, territory, as in the film *90 Miles* (Zaldívar 2001). Members of the one-and-a-half generation, who had either left Cuba in earlier decades or were born outside the island, returned in the 1990s to find family, acceptance, and roots—as in *Cuba mía* (Mitrani 2002), *Havana Nagila* (Paull 1995), or *Adió Kerida* (Behar 2002).[10] In other cases, expatriate and foreign filmmakers chose fiction to denounce the repressive Cuban state through passionate counter-politics centered on intolerance and emigration. This is the case in *Azúcar amarga* (Bitter Sugar, Ichaso 2001), *Before Night Falls* (Schnabel 2000), *For Love or Country: The Arturo Sandoval Story* (directed by Joseph Sargeant in 2000 and featuring Cuban-American stars Andy Garcia and Gloria Estefan), and *A Family in Crisis: The Elian Gonzalez Story* (Leitch 2000).[11] Finally, the use of documentary and experimental techniques elicits the experience of the Special Period among Cubans and relays it for a foreign audience (e.g., Steve Fagin's 1997 *Tropicola*, Luis Felipe Bernaza and Margaret Gilpin's 1997 *Mariposas en el andamio*, Uli Gaulke's 2000 *Havanna mi amor*, Rolando Díaz's 1998 *Si me comprendieras*, and Carlos Marcovich's 1997 *Who the Hell Is Juliette*).

Ultimately, globally circulated audiovisual products from and about the Special Period have enlarged, diversified, and propagated the images of Cuba that linger in the international imagination. A small, sometimes irritating, sometimes glamorous, widely forbidden, always exotic, always socialist speck of an island now looms as a much larger, louder, more colorful and textured, all-encompassing enigma on the world stage.

"And Then the Cinema Will Have Moved on from the Age of Barbarism" (Humberto Solás, Poor Cinema Manifesto, 2004)

A review of Cuban cinema in relation to the Special Period calls for mention of the *Festival Internacional de Cine Pobre* (Festival of Poor Cinema). Initiated in 2003, and headed by Humberto Solás (*Lucia, Cecilia*), *Cine Pobre* enjoys the support of the ICAIC. The festival takes place annually in Gibara in the province of Holguín in the eastern part of the island, the exact place where Columbus first disembarked in Cuba. *Cine Pobre*'s manifesto demands the availability of digital technology and defends its use as a way to promote democratic and alternative media practices. The manifesto envisions a cinema created within dominant economic and cultural societies or in peripheral sites of production, whether as part of official programs of production or through independent or alternative methods. Significantly, the regional location of the festival challenges the centralization of cinema culture in Cuba, if not specifically its funding infrastructure. In addition, its regional focus attempts to create an alternative space for audiovisual practices that would "refer to a cinema, not defined by scarcity of ideas but rather by economic restrictions" (Solás n.d.). This inclusion of alternative sites of production echoes the ideas and intentions of Imperfect Cinema, Third Cinema, Cinema of Hunger, and other manifestations of the New Latin American Cinema Movement, all influential in anti- and postcolonial discourses about culture and cinema since 1969.[12]

Ironically, several of Humberto Solás's own films had been among the most expensive Cuban films ever produced. At ten million dollars, his 1992 adaptation of Alejo Carpentier's *El siglo de las luces* was screened at that year's Havana International Film Festival. The film was the highest budgeted coproduction (with France and Russia) in Cuban history, and its cinematic luxury was in stark contrast with the festival's austerity—in the midst of the worst economic crisis in memory, the festival had few invited guests and could not afford official parties or sidebar events. Solás's elegant and expensive historical dramas had established his worldwide reputation, but only years later low budget digital technology would rescue him, and the impoverished industry, from the threat of oblivion. He became a staunch supporter of the *Cine Pobre* festival, which in turn endorsed a new attitude toward film production inspired by conditions of the Special Period. At the same time, its thematic nod to the past incorporated the present in order to foster a critical and creative engagement with the new conditions of globalization.

A discussion of the Special Period through the specificity of Cuban cinema highlights the new relations of film production, both locally and internationally. It also relates these to the tensions and fears represented in the filmic texts produced in and outside the island. However, any analysis would be incomplete if it considered a single media object from Cuba such as its cinema, rather than a complex landscape of media interactions. Only a broader perspective can derive a more accurate reading of Cuban cultural shifts and tensions. Consideration of the ICAIC reveals responses to political attacks, concerns about globalization, and the limits as well as benefits of centralized planning. How do these events relate to a broader media sphere?

In the new millennium, all Cuban mass media continues to be in the hands of the state. Through the ample use of websites, television shows—such as *Mesa Redonda*—the press, billboards, and so on, the state continues to deploy ubiquitous political messages, thus conveying the existence of a unified ideological discourse. Specifically, ideological campaigns such as *La Batalla de Ideas* (The Battle for Ideas) have dominated the media since 1997. The preservation of a socialist polity has taken many rhetorical forms yet citizens can no longer reconcile their daily experiences with the discourses provided by the official media. The disjuncture, understood in psychological, social, and political terms between the state's plea for citizens to make additional sacrifices to save Cuban socialism and fend off marauding capitalists, and the contradictions brought about by social decline, harsh difficulties, and weak infrastructure, creates a paradoxical situation where socialism is challenged by the very means employed to save it.

The intense politicization of culture has also produced its alternative. Despite harsh crackdowns on nonconformist social and artistic expression there continues to be a push—often underground—for an expanded public sphere. Underground networks around the use of information technologies as well as the use of homemade parabolic antennas have changed, to some extent, cinematic experiences and Cuban publics. A number of small independent production outfits have capitalized on cheaper audiovisual digital technology to produce commercials, wedding and personal videos. As a final broad stroke in a very rough projection of a larger media map, a booming underground media market exists, supplying hardware and IP numbers. Underground video clubs began operating at the neighborhood level, stocking international films, television programs, and national titles. They have filled the void left by neighborhood film clubs that closed as the stock of films dried up owing to budgetary restrictions, and by theaters in deplorable condition due to poor maintenance. As illegal businesses, the clubs have also been under heavy attack by the police. But the world of media duplication is sophisticated and resourceful, creating strong, if not vast, demand, albeit illicit. Although DVD players were prohibited by law until March 2008, pirated DVDs, VCDs, MP3, and music CDs abound. The Cuban media-scape is shifting out of necessity, driven by entrepreneurship and politics, and creating the larger context in which Cuban cinema and its own complexities must articulate its survival beyond the Special Period.

In sum, despite centralized control of the media, the 1990s brought about crucial developments that helped to alter the context for the cinema. Nonetheless, these developments, along with official controls on citizens' access to information technology and radio and television programming that viewers and listeners categorize as heavily ideological, and a decrease in leisure options brought about by the economic crisis, all contribute to a continued embrace of film on the part of Cuban audiences. Cuban cinema may battle with decreased output and worsening exhibition conditions, but it still creates places where ordinary people might recognize themselves.

Notes

1. Interview with Gerado Chijona, July 21, 2005. Habana, Cuba.
2. See clippings file for *Alicia en el pueblo de Maravillas* at the Cinemateca de Cuba, ICAIC, Havana.
3. Guevara stepped down in 2000 to head the Havana International Film Festival and was replaced by Omar González Jimenez the first non-filmmaker to ever head the institution. Guevara's departure marked the bureaucratic separation of the Film Festival from the ICAIC.
4. Funds such as IBERMEDIA became available for the production of "Iberoamerican" films (see www.programaibermedia.es). Additionally, media institutions such as Canal Plus and Televisión Española, and initiatives funded through film festivals such as the Huber Bals Fund of the Rotterdam International Film Festival, *Cine en Construcción* from the Festival Internacional de Cine de Donostia—San Sebastián, and the *Cinémas d'Amérique Latine* in Toulouse since 2002, presented funding opportunities throughout Europe.
5. Other films took up the topic of migration, real or potential. Among these: *Cosas que dejé en la Habana* (Things I Left in Havana, 1997) by Manuel Gutiérrez Aragón, *El juego de Cuba* (The Game of Cuba, 2001) by Manuel Martín Cuenca, *Balseros* (Carlos Bosch 2003), *Agua con sal* (Water with Salt, 2005) by Pedro Pérez Rosado, *Habana Blues* (Benito Zambrano 2005), and *Malas temporadas* (Bad Times, Manuel Martín Cuenca, 2005).
6. Interview with author, July 28, 2005. Havana, Cuba.
7. The official website for the *Muestra de Cine Joven* has an alphabetical listing of the young people who have presented their work in the past five years. The listing shows that there are many women who are part of this generation of filmmakers. See www.cubacine.cu/muestrajoven/ (accessed May 10, 2006).
8. *Festival Internacional de Cine Pobre* (2004).
9. See full discussion in *Temas* (2000).
10. On *Adió Kerida*, see Hernandez-Reguant (2004a).
11. On *Before Night Falls*, see Loss (2003).
12. See García Espinosa (1997).

4

Spiritual Capital: Foreign Patronage and the Trafficking of *Santería*

Kevin M. Delgado

In 2003, I returned to the coastal Cuban city of Matanzas to study the music of an Afro-Cuban religion commonly known as *Santería* (also known as *Regla de Ocha*, *Ifá*, or *Regla Lucumí*.)[1] My research focused on the only ritual house in the city that performed sacred Iyesá music, a type of music preserved by the Cuban descendants of the West African Ìjèsà people. For over 150 years, the family of this house has honored their patron deities annually with sacred songs and rhythms played on a unique set of drums. In my spare time, I also studied the *batá*: the sacred, double-headed drums considered the most powerful in the *Santería* religion. Both the Iyesá and certain *batá* drums are considered *fundamento*. That is, they are consecrated drums containing living, spiritually charged objects of the drum deity Añá.

One day, after a *batá* lesson, I took my two teachers to lunch. After several minutes, one of them, a young drummer that lived near the Iyesá house, grew serious. "Tell me, Kevin," he said, while avoiding my eyes, "they say you are going to buy the *fundamento* of the Iyesá drums and take it with you back to the United States. Is it true?" I was incredulous. Hurt by the accusation that I would unscrupulously buy a unique, living deity object from within a set of drums over 150 years old, I demanded to know who was saying such things. "People in the street" he replied, avoiding my glare. I assured him I was not negotiating a secret deal to whisk away the only Iyesá drum deity in the city, and expressed my disappointment that he would even consider the possibility that such *chisme* (gossip) could be true.

Defensively, my teacher explained that he was simply repeating what he had heard in order to clear it up. Satisfied with my response, he changed the subject, but I remained distracted. Did neighbors on the block of the Iyesá house view me as some type of cultural poacher? As my anger subsided, however, I realized that such conjecture made perfect sense on their part. The "people in the street" were speculating as to why individuals such as myself—a foreigner with money and the ability to travel internationally—would bother to come to Matanzas in the first place and then, rather than going to the beach or nightclubs in the nearby resort town of Varadero like normal tourists, would spend our days trudging around some of the poorest neighborhoods in the city, repeatedly visiting people (some elderly and poor) involved in what many Cubans view as a "primitive" religion. In short, through their experience of seeing foreigners interact with *Santería* religious practitioners, they were applying a common formula to my comings and goings: foreigner + local religion = transaction; it was simply the nature of that transaction they were trying to ascertain. They assumed some type of commodity was being exchanged. And they were indeed correct.[2]

This essay examines the ways in which the *Santería* religion allows some Cubans to access the coveted Cuban foreign currency/*peso convertible* economy by entering into relationships with foreigners seeking religious knowledge, products, or status. While some of Cuba's folkloric ensembles have been presenting and selling Afro-Cuban culture on behalf of the government for years, I am particularly interested in how *Santería* provides Cubans unconnected with either the tourism industry or the Florida-dominated remittance market a means for entering the Cuban foreign currency economy. This chapter focuses on the specific ways some Cubans convert spiritual and cultural capital into financial capital, as well as the impact of this financial exchange upon the practice of *Santería* itself.

Following Bourdieu's (1984) concept of cultural capital, I use the term *spiritual capital* to refer to religious status: cultural capital accrued through esoteric religious knowledge, ritual status or title, the ability and authorization to perform rituals, and the perceived efficacy of one's ritual or religious actions. Of course, *santeros* (*Santería* initiates) always have valued religious knowledge and efficacy, and the services of expert practitioners possess local value within the community itself. I contend it is the growing foreign interest in Cuban *Santería* that often gives local religious practice international market value and the potential for Cubans to obtain highly coveted foreign currency. This may have significant ramifications for the religion, as some *santeros* worry that acquisition of foreign capital may become an overriding concern, pushing certain contemporary actions beyond the limits of acceptable practice toward a commercial existence harmful to the religion.

For purposes of this chapter, I refer to foreign visitors interested in Cuban *Santería*—tourists, travelers, students, scholars, and religious practitioners—collectively. This collective grouping of foreigners reflects my assertion that most students, performers, culturally minded travelers, religious practitioners, and scholars interested in *Santería* are influenced to varying degrees by widely held notions of authenticity and cultural authority, all desiring to move past the "frontstage" performance of Afro-Cuban folklore and tourist entertainment to genuine "backstage" regions where "real" culture bearers and their culture exist (MacCannell 1999). My inclusion of scholars and non-scholars in a generalized category also acknowledges the work that emerged from the crisis of representation and influence of postcolonial theory in 1980s anthropology, which interrogated both the power relations between fieldworkers and subjects, and the presumed rigid opposition between scholarly fieldwork and tourism, as well as between ethnography and travel writing (Marcus and Fischer 1986; Clifford and Marcus 1986; Pratt 1986). As pressures of the post-Soviet Cuban economy continue to plague Cubans and a twin-currency economy creates class division in a society accustomed to the egalitarian ethos of socialist rhetoric, I argue that all foreign visitors interested in *Santería* culture present Cubans with similar types of opportunities to gain highly desired foreign capital and social contacts.

While I argue that the unique economic circumstances of post-Soviet Cuba create an environment that greatly increases the likelihood of change and innovation within *Santería*, neither change nor economic concerns are radical or new to the religion. *Santería* is, at its core, a pragmatic religion, concerned not so much with life after death (which practitioners believe exists) as with living well on earth and realizing one's own potential and destiny. In interactions with ancestral divinities known as *oricha*, believers use the religion to overcome obstacles and achieve fulfillment, wellness, success, and happiness—goals that certainly would not exclude concerns of financial or material wealth. Change is a constant theme in *Santería* history as *santeros* have continuously adapted to social conditions, keeping the religion relevant and workable while persisting through slavery, religious syncretism, racism, persecution, republican and revolutionary repression, and folklorization. In light of this reactive and adaptive history, the current changes resulting from financial pressures are therefore significant in nature but not completely unprecedented.

What is new, I argue, is that the current change occurs not because of centralized, institutional repression or secularization, but because of patronage from individual foreigners that view *Santería* with positive interest. Indeed, this contemporary change in the religion follows not a sudden crackdown against religious practitioners or a generalized repression but Cuba's post-Soviet opening and official proclamations of religious tolerance, all of which have facilitated foreign traffic to the island, including visits focused upon religious activities. This foreign traffic is changing the local market value exponentially, in many cases pushing transactions involving the religion to levels of incredible wealth for those locked outside the Cuban *peso convertible* economy. In this vein, I contend that Cuba's growing economic inequality and the desperation it engenders has the greatest potential to create change in the religion today.

In the following section I trace the arc of *Santería* culture during the Revolution, noting the influential forces of repression and folklorization. In many ways, the professionalization of *Santería* performance through Cuba's folklore industry laid the groundwork for the capitalization of *Santería* performance that followed.

Social Change and Santería Performance in Revolutionary Cuba

The revolutionary government that came to power in 1959 sought to create national performance institutions that would reflect the Revolution's inclusive ideology. In this way, the Cuban state itself had a hand in the visibility of *Santería* arts, beginning with the formation of the Teatro Nacional in 1959 and Conjunto Folklórico Nacional in 1962, followed by other national ensembles. These talented troupes, particularly the Conjunto Folklórico Nacional, toured nationally and internationally, providing a professional face of Afro-Cuban culture different from the exaggerated caricatures found in popular entertainment of earlier eras (Moore 1997). These ensembles were prominent government showpieces meant to demonstrate to the nation and the world the inclusiveness and distinctive excellence of revolutionary Cuban society.

But while granting Afro-Cuban culture an unprecedented central position in Cuba's folklore industry and official national identity, the revolutionary government also began to view all religions negatively, first declaring itself a secular, then atheist, nation. The state took a contradictory approach toward *Santería* (and other Afro-Cuban religions), praising it as historical heritage and folklore while dismissing it as a superstitious religion. In the early 1960s, the Cuban government hardened its attitudes toward religion in general, forbidding anyone with any religious leanings from membership in the Cuban Communist Party and even positions of nonpolitical leadership. Restrictions were put on public *Ocha* (*Santería*) celebrations, which had to be registered with local authorities (a policy still in place today). Government agents monitored *Santería* communities; *Santería tambor* ceremonies—collective celebrations, also called *bembé* or *toque de santo*, using drums and songs to honor the *oricha*—were spied upon, and those who dared initiate children during this era were jailed. Over time, *oricha* worshippers adapted by altering their hours of ritual activity, modifying observance of their religion, and concealing their involvement when convenient or necessary.

Though *Santería* was regulated and its practitioners marginalized, the religion never came close to disappearing during the first decades of the Revolution and in some ways became more visible than ever. In a sense, the persecution of the colonial and republican eras meant that *santeros*, with their decentralized, private "house-temples" and secret rituals, were experienced and accustomed to practicing their religion under difficult circumstances.[3] From the mid-1960s through the early 1970s, a hostile and paternalistic attitude toward the religion on the part of the government set in whereby the religion was reluctantly tolerated as a holdover of an ignorant and primitive past, one that would ostensibly evolve into a benign secular folkloric tradition as *santeros* absorbed the educational benefits, secular ideology, and scientific rationalism of revolutionary Cuba. Even though these hostile attitudes were officially changed toward state acknowledgment and inclusion of religious believers in the fourth Congress meeting of the Cuban Communist Party in 1991, a sense of paternalistic tolerance of *Santería* on the part of the government and many Cubans still exists today in an officially secular Cuba.

Ironically, while the "superstitious" elements of the religion were derided during the first decades of the Revolution, the government itself provided a means of employment for a few expert practitioners. A select group of performers of Afro-Cuban religious traditions—especially drummers and song leaders, but also dancers—were offered state employment as performers in folkloric ensembles. The professionalization of folk and traditional arts under Cuba's revolutionary government brought unprecedented financial security to performers fortunate enough to obtain these coveted positions. These expert performers achieved a seemingly impossible status in the new Cuba, that of expert *santero and* good revolutionary citizen, a type of *Ocha*-Socialist double-consciousness success story.[4]

As government employees, these artists drew a salary in exchange for the study, creation, rehearsal, and performance of folkloric arts. To this end, they were also given training, instruments, rehearsal facilities, and, to varying degrees, scholarly guidance by cultural authorities. This system of patronage continues to this very day and has produced a large number of well-trained musicians with an extremely high level of technical proficiency and versatility. Moreover, their training under the revolutionary system is often broadly based; a master drummer of the sacred Afro-Cuban *batá* drums—learned traditionally through apprenticeship with master drummers—may also sight-read symphonic percussion scores, create experimental musical improvisations for a modern dance piece, and display knowledge of academic sources and concepts. This broad training, combined with international travel connections, exposure, and experience, often makes professional folkloric artists better prepared than non-folkloric traditional performers to teach foreign students and articulate cross-cultural concepts of aesthetics and performance.

In 1985, the government began operating a program for foreigners called FolkCuba, featuring workshops in Afro-Cuban drumming, song, and dance taught by the Conjunto Folkórico Nacional (Hagedorn 2001). After Cuba's opening in the 1990s, FolkCuba became a template for the expansion of cultural and even religious tourism as an economic enterprise. In the cash-starved Special Period, the Afro-Cuban traditions that previously had been folklorized and professionalized were increasingly capitalized. Some urban religious practitioners locked out of the foreign currency economy began to see opportunities as a result of growth in the foreign patronage of *Santería*.

Foreign Patronage and the International Trafficking of *Santería*

Though foreigners—including American citizens interested in *Santería*—never stopped visiting Cuba during the Revolution, the changes in post-Soviet Cuba greatly increased international tourism to the island. In this confluence of domestic economic need, increased visits by foreigners, greater traffic in foreign currency, social openness, and religious tolerance, Afro-Cuban folkloric expressions increasingly found value as cash-earning commodities in addition to being virtuosic expressions of national identity. As foreign capital became an influential part of everyday Cuban life, some liturgical performers and religious practitioners began to view foreign interest in *Santería* folklore and religion as an activity that added potential economic value to their everyday lives. Indeed, more than religious practice, the performative aspects of *Santería*—drumming, singing, dancing—were especially flexible products in the new Cuban market economy because of their ever-present status as entertainment and folklore above and beyond their traditional religious usage. This broad continuum of value, ranging from secular entertainment to sacred religion, attracted not only foreigners interested in religious activities but also a wide range of tourists, students, and artists in search of authentic Afro-Cuban performative culture. Imbued with an aura of authenticity and a deep connection to an African past and efficacious present, *Santería*'s performative culture began to be trafficked as a commodity of powerful tradition in the cultural capitalism market, allowing its culture brokers to participate in what Paul Gilroy (2000: 13) has called a "planetary commerce of blackness."

Aside from the religion itself, some foreigners view *Santería* as a window to an African culture that arrived on other American shores but did not survive intact in the present era. For many, *Santería*'s legacy of survival through the Middle Passage and slavery instills it with heroic emplotment, its music and song sonic signifiers of African power and survival. The antiquity of Cuban *Santería*, with its lineages of religious houses and drums reaching back into the 1800s, lends historical weight to the perception of Cuban *Santería*'s authenticity (and by extension, its power). Finally, framing this deep pool of *Santería* culture is Cuba, and the effect of Cuba's overall "otherness" (colonial architecture, old American cars, ubiquitous socialist slogan-art, etc.) upon many travelers enhances an overall sense of cultural, even exotic difference, contributing to the fulfillment of (touristic) desire for "authentic" experiences (MacCannell 1999). As the Cuban government expanded workshops and courses in Afro-Cuban folkloric music and dance in the 1990s, often with a primary focus on *Santería* performative culture, North American and foreign alumni began to set up their own cottage industries by offering themselves as guides for folkloric study in Cuba. Both state- and foreign-based tours offered packages of basic room, board, in-country travel, and a schedule of classes, performances, and opportunities to visit cultural sites and tourist nightspots. Some tours even incorporated attendance at a *Santería tambor* ceremony into their itineraries.

For some non-Cubans, as well as for Cubans born in exile to a non- or formerly *Santería* family, folkloric arts can provide an initial entry into a deeper involvement with the religion, one that may draw them to the island for further study. For most *santeros*, *babalaos* (divination experts), or *fundamento batá* drummers living outside of Cuba, the island is the origin of spiritual lineages that legitimize their religious status. As such, a visit to the island becomes a pilgrimage of sorts, a journey to the fount of the culture or religion they have been studying, or a visit to meet their elders/superiors (i.e., their godparent's godparent, or their *batá* teacher's teacher). For many foreigners, the religion and its performance traditions are believed to be "purer" or of a higher quality in Cuba than in other parts of the Americas. In Cuba, the age, depth, and breadth of established *Ocha* communities and expert practitioners typically prevent glaring incompetence or drastic innovation. Thus, many foreigners currently involved in the religion were first introduced to it through its performance element. This is a common entry for individuals who had no family or community ties to *oricha* culture or rejected it in their youth. Over time, performance students may develop a deep appreciation of *Santería* as a religious rather than as a purely aesthetic system. Should students desire more contact with the religion, their Cuban teachers may bring them to a *tambor* event, refer them to a divination expert, or provide a ritual service themselves. Consequently, the expert performer or ritual practitioner that initially escorts visitors to the "real" non-folkloric culture of *Santería* provides a valuable service that may end after a single contact or result in a lifelong relationship.

Foreigners may undertake a variety of religious ritual actions while in Cuba, including divination sessions; receiving protective amulets; undergoing Añá *batá* drummer initiation; receiving *oricha* accoutrements; and full initiation. Each ritual is also an opportunity for a ritual practitioner to earn foreign currency by providing those religious services. Every ritual action has a *derecho*: a ritual fee. The fee usually covers the ritual supplies and labor, and the greater the ritual action, the higher the *derecho*. An examination of the fees for the most important *Santería* ceremony—full initiation into *oricha* priesthood—illustrates the magnitude of financial capital involved.

Initiation expenses, which include ritual items and clothing, sacrificial offerings, specialized religious labor, and supportive labor, may vary considerably according to the *oricha* being "seated." An average cost for a Cuban to be initiated in Cuba, expressed in equivalent USD, would be approximately $500, a huge amount in a heavily subsidized economy where annual personal incomes in Cuban pesos average in the neighborhood of $125.[5] By contrast, in the United States, with its greater costs for materials and labor, scarce specialized ritual expertise, and higher levels of conspicuous consumption and display, an initiation often costs between $5,000 and $15,000, with initiations commonly exceeding $20,000. In fact, a common range of $5,000–$15,000 is an advisedly conservative estimate.[6] In California, I have heard of individuals taking out personal or home equity loans or second mortgages to pay for initiations.[7] Those consulted for this study commonly named $40,000 as a high-end estimate for initiations in California, while existing literature written by practitioner-scholars lists high-end figures of $45,000 and $50,000 (De la Torre 2004; Canizares 1993). As full initiations present a serious step for someone with experience in the religion, these estimates do not reflect additional costs associated with pre-initiation actions or *oricha* accoutrements, as well as follow-up rituals performed after the initiation.

While it is not surprising that initiations cost more in the United States than in Cuba, an interesting situation arises when foreigners, particularly Americans, travel to Cuba to become initiated. If an initiation for a Cuban in Cuba costs approximately $500, it might be reasonable to assume that the same religious actions and rituals utilizing the same expertise and items might cost the same for an American initiate, but in fact they do not. Paralleling the two-tiered admission policy of, say, Havana nightclubs—where a single performance venue might charge foreigners a higher entrance fee in convertible pesos and charge Cubans a lower amount in Cuban pesos—initiations in Cuba cost foreigners several times the amount it costs a Cuban, anywhere from $2000 to $5000, a huge sum in Cuba. Such difference is explained not so much by the cost of religious services and rituals as by their relative value. Foreigners tend to require much more organizational assistance, but such requirements, normally diffused in a favor-based economy, are countered by a foreigner's ability to pay for services and purchase required items either in Cuba or in their home country. Foreigners are charged far more money than Cubans because it is known they can afford to pay it and because, it is believed, the life-transforming step of becoming an initiate should never be something bought easily, done cheaply, or without respectful intent.

Foreigners are aware that they pay higher costs than Cubans for *Santería* objects and rituals. Conscious of costs back home, they often feel they are getting a bargain on an initiation they believe to be more authentic or more properly performed than one they could receive at home. While an observer could view this price arrangement as a foreigner paying tourist prices for local culture, or foreign capital buying (sub)cultural or spiritual capital, initiates are arguably more concerned that actions be performed properly given the spiritual magnitude of the rituals. Many foreigners also desire to help their godparents in the religion and the local religious community in general, viewing the higher costs as quasi-charitable acts that religious elders are entitled to by virtue of their expertise. Hence, foreigners may present the opportunity of a foreign currency windfall, one that generates enthusiasm on the part of all who benefit.

By organizing and directing initiations, Cuban *santeros* gain foreign *ahijados* (godchildren), and expand their religious "house" numerically, financially, and geographically. Hosts dole out money to various required participants, such as ritual and support laborers. In foreigners' initiations, unlike in those for most Cubans, participants might expect to be paid in hard currency. Again, the financial effects of an initiation might become longstanding as foreign *ahijados* may continue a lifelong relationship with their godparents, and may return with other foreigners who might also wish to undergo various rituals. Foreign scholars present a similar case, since they typically develop long-term relationships with their *santero* consultants: they represent a source of foreign currency as well as of social and educational capital, which bolsters the *santero*'s religious efficacy. Both well-situated scholars and highly motivated students might even work out opportunities for their teachers/ consultants to reach a larger audience, perhaps facilitating or sponsoring the production of instructional or performance audio/video recordings for sale, securing invitations to travel abroad, perhaps even paving the way to emigrate permanently. Because of the opportunities and income involved, such interactions hold the prospect of huge financial benefits and lasting consequences.

A single foreign client may enable an expert practitioner to increase his or her social and/or religious profile through the purchasing power of convertible pesos, enhancing the reputation and prestige of the practitioner, and attracting more clients and financial capital. *Santeros* with foreign clientele can afford better homes and furnishings, cell phones, jewelry, fine clothing, etc., which are highly visible items that index wealth, social connections, and success. When linked to religious practice, such success may be construed as evidence of religious efficacy, possibly generating even more patronage and capital. In addition to money spent on religious items (e.g., saint carvings and vestments, elegant tureens that house *oricha* objects, luxurious *oricha* offerings, display furniture) *tambor* celebrations can also be considered evidence of spiritual dedication and even spiritual power, therefore generating even more patronage and capital for these *santeros*. Indeed, such spending may be viewed as a business investment "in the maintenance of 'spiritual capital'" (Romberg 2003: 137). This type of consumption is all the more conspicuous in Cuba, where convertible peso-purchased goods or imported items stand out in comparison to the ubiquitous products Cubans purchase with Cuban pesos.

Not surprisingly, access to foreigners and their currency may lead to conflict or raise questions regarding motivations on the part of those who initiate foreign devotees, as well as to competition among practitioners for these clients—with certain practitioners insisting on their qualifications while deriding those of others. This type of conflict is built into the religion as it is compartmentalized, with each house-temple operating more or less independently, resulting in slight variations in practice between different houses. In a religion with no singular leadership, authority is based upon lineage, reputation, and testimonials of knowledge and efficacy. In such an environment, rivalry and envy may create gossip and suspicion, a situation further fueled by financial need and the monetary stakes involved. Therefore, it is not uncommon for rumors to circulate as to whether rituals for foreigners are short-changed or requirements are relaxed in the interest of profit or in order to provide a convenient and timely product for time-strapped and cash-laden visitors: "Did he give that scholar an amulet to impress him?" "I bet that *santero* told that Englishwoman she needed to become initiated immediately just so he could get another foreign *ahijado* in his house." "Did she offer that foreigner a cheap initiation just to get his *divisa*?" "How could that foreigner have prepared for an initiation in so little time...it must not have been done correctly." "How could he have sworn that North American to Añá drums? He could barely play." "She says her Californian *ahijado* isn't ready to initiate others, but I think she just wants the *ahijado* to bring her more foreigners to initiate." Such statements imply that certain religious actions involving foreigners are guided by money-minded *Santeros* rather than the wisdom of the *oricha*.[8] In a sense, these types of issues are really no different from the gossip of everyday life, a currency-fueled extension of the rivalry that may already exist between various major *Ocha* houses of worship in Cuba and abroad. The post-Soviet economic urgency felt by Cubans and the potential capital a foreigner represents seems to contribute to a competitive environment between rivals and a flexible and accommodating atmosphere for those performing initiations for foreigners who, after all, are spending a great deal of money.

In a lesson of free-market economics, some consultants in the Havana *Santería* community consider that foreigners are slowly driving up the costs of initiations by paying higher prices for ritual goods and services even though the two-tiered foreign/local prices remain in effect. For those Cubans locked outside of the foreign currency market, rising costs make full initiation into the religion extremely costly. They might therefore try to indirectly benefit from foreigner's initiations, for example, by arranging their own to coincide with that of a foreigner, or by making themselves useful to the poorly connected foreigner. Other ways of benefiting are less ethical, abusing the liminal or subordinate status of initiates to execute petty acts of *jineterismo* (hustling). One American that underwent a ritual initiation in Havana told me that he/she felt somewhat abused by excessive requests for money while ritually sequestered, commenting that he/she produced so many 20-dollar bills on command that he/she "felt like an ATM machine."

Foreign interest in *Santería* and other Afro-Cuban religions may also engender a variety of *jinetero* activities on the part of people at the fringes of the religion. For example, one might encounter an amateur tour guide eagerly offering contacts with religious performers or ritual experts, perhaps even an invitation to an in-progress *tambor* ceremony. Hoping to cash in on an interested foreigner by using the cultural capital of local insider knowledge, such relatively benign acts essentially transfer tourist referral services to the religious realm. But with *jineterismo* comes the potential for fraud, as self-described culture brokers may utilize the interests of novice visitors to traffic false items and information. Though exceptional, it is not unheard of for someone to return from Cuba to their native country having purchased a ritual object, participated in a *Santería* ritual, or even undergone an initiation, only to be told by local *Santería* authorities that their experiences or items were most certainly fraudulent. In addition, accounts exist of ritual experts performing fraudulent initiations on foreigners or bestowing upon clients new and previously unknown or suspect *oricha* (Ayorinde 2004; Ramos n.d.). For some observers, the penetration of the Special Period's hardships into *Santería* is symptomatic of the widespread and devastating cultural effects the Special Period has wrought upon Cuban society. In a 2004 article, Stephan Palmié describes an encounter at a *tambor* with what his Cuban companions referred to as a *"santo jinetero"*: a hustler *oricha* (or rather, a hustler *santero* pretending to be possessed by an *oricha*) that complains when Palmié (visibly a foreigner) offers a *derecho* in national rather than foreign currency. For Palmié's companions, the episode was an embarrassing intrusion of secular material need and self-interest into a sacred setting. In his subsequent description of *concentraciones* (organized demonstrations of public support for the Revolution) and the material enticements offered to encourage Cubans to attend, Palmié draws a subtle but damning parallel between the performance of the *santo jinetero* and the crowds at the *concentraciones*, implying that both parties, due to the deprivation and uncertainty they endure in post-Soviet Cuba, appear somewhat bewitched by the spectacle in which they participate, at least partially "faking it" for material reasons.

In this respect, Cuban observers have argued that this foreign involvement in *Santería* has contributed to a new type of Cuban practitioner, the so-called *diplo-babalao* or *diplo-oriaté*—both disparaging terms for Cuban ritual experts that focus their energies on foreign clients or on government-led foreign tour groups (Martinez Furé 2000; Ramos n.d.).[9] Rogelio Martínez Furé, a founder and advisor/consultant of the Conjunto Folklórico Nacional, as well as a scholar and performer, laments that the commercialization of traditional religion has led to "pseudofolkore" and "pseudocultural *jineterismo*" as "people who had neither respected [the religion] nor been part of its expressions were, when the time came, going to take it up in a commercial way" for personal gain (Martínez Furé 2000: 158–159). Railing against a "parasitic layer" of so-called expert practitioners who prostitute *Santería* for profit, Martínez Furé also warns that creating *Santería*/Afro-Cuban culture for "tourist leisure" threatens to turn the entire Cuban island into an exotic landscape and its citizens into natives, a superficial pleasure to be rented or bought by foreign visitors.[10]

While Martínez Furé speaks of individual Cubans cashing in on *Santería*, a larger player has entered the *Santería* market "in a commercial way": the Cuban government. Sensing the potential of *Santería*'s religious rather than folkloric economy, the Cuban government reportedly began offering package tours for individuals wishing to undergo *Santería* initiations in the early 1990s (Hagedorn 2001). These "*santurismo*" programs, also called "*Ochaturs*," are often regarded with suspicion by *oricha* observers who question where cultural outreach ends and personal/state finances begin. Such all-inclusive tours, which Hagedorn estimates cost a participant $6,000–$8,000, direct visitors to religious practitioners that work in partnership with the state, presumably in exchange for convertible pesos and favorable housing conditions.[11] Unlike model villages constructed in some countries to shield populations from the scarring effects of tourism (Smith 1989), this state-sponsored initiative is designed to keep to a minimum commercial transactions occurring outside state control. Combined with its sponsorship of the Yoruba Cultural Association (see chapter 8, this volume), the *Ochatur* programs position the Cuban government as a major institutional agent in the capitalization of *Santería*.

In the 1990s, African-derived religions rose to prominence in an unprecedented way. For a while, it seemed as if no *timba* group could resist giving a "shout out" to the *oricha*.[12] *Orichas* were the subject of dance tunes and rap recordings, and even were woven into films and *telenovela* storylines. Some prominent Cubans of predominately European descent appeared to publicly embrace the religion, causing resentment from some longtime Afro-Cuban *santeros* who suffered through periods of persecution during the Revolution (Benkomo 2000). Some Cuban youth also embraced the trappings of *Santería* culture (particularly real or imitation beaded *oricha* necklaces) in part to do what teenagers everywhere have been known to do: construct identity, accrue subcultural capital, and annoy their parents.

Without central authority or a singular tradition, how can *Santeros* ascertain that the encroachment of commerce and modern innovations brought on by Cuba's economic situation will not warp *Santería* beyond recognition? For believers, one key lies in the *oricha*, a "changing same" across oceans and centuries. Divination allows *santeros* to check and approve ritual actions with the *oricha*, while possession brings the *oricha* themselves to gatherings of their followers. Thus, rather than practice a modern hermeneutic mediation of an inflexible and historically distanced text, modern *santeros* continually interact with the *oricha*, the very subjects and authors of ancient cultural texts, who periodically return to earth at the behest of their children in a remarkable "fusion of horizons." Yet as new culture brokers on both sides of the Florida Straits—as well as the Atlantic—jockey for influence over believers and scholarly authorities, some seem poised to convert innovation into authority, and authority into capital.

Conclusion

This essay has surveyed how the financial pressures of post-Soviet Cuba impact *Santería* and has listed a few of the innovative and sometimes ambiguous ways that Cubans mediate the interaction between foreigners and the religion. Monetary concerns may increasingly cloud *Santería*'s already complex nature: simultaneously religion, subculture, national culture, pan-African diaspora culture, pop culture, subject of study, and commodity. The degree to which financial concerns affect the religion is variable and debatable. The examples cited here could be perhaps most charitably characterized as exceptional though not rare, not intrinsic to the religion but a way the religion is used to address material need and personal gain.

Well known to cultural insiders, this issue of religious commerce has been hiding in plain sight, and the growing financial division on the island will continue to present Cubans with the dilemma of balancing the sacred with material necessity. With the worst of *Santería*'s religious repression behind it, I believe Cuba's current two-tiered currency system and its resultant economic inequality have the greatest potential to create change in the religion today, more than the long-standing influences of state control, folkloric professionalization, or bias against religion.

Where might an increasingly commercialized and money-conscious *Santería* be headed? Here the examples of other Afro-American religions with possession by West African deities—Haitian *Vodou* and Brazilian *Candomblé*—may be harbingers of future *Santería* tourist commerce. When Haiti still had a viable tourism industry, tourist shows included actual possession rituals performed in dedicated tourist areas, while many *Candomblé* houses set aside seating at their house-temples for foreign tourists, allowing their actual *oricha* (*orixá*) celebrations to simultaneously serve as traditional religious events and cash-earning tourist spectacles.[13] While some scholars contend that such commodification may eventually empty cultural acts and products of their meaning, reducing them to expedient traditions performed for money, for others, publicly performed spirit possession—as opposed to folkloric recreations—may be just as genuine, and come to be seen as a public symbol of local identity. In many cases, commodification does not significantly erode authenticity, and *Santería* certainly continues to be a powerful and meaningful force in the lives of its practitioners.

The financial situation gripping Cuba today is not only the inescapable context for the religion but also for Cuban studies. Just as finances may cloud the moral vision of a profit-motivated *santero*, so can they distort the vision of one who visits the island interested in Cuban culture. For this reason I find it productive to return to some of the lessons wrought from anthropology's reflexive crisis of representation. The interrogation of presumed scholarly objectivity and the power relations between scholar and culture bearers lay bare the fallacy of neutral, omniscient ethnography and fieldwork, free from the influences of power, colonialism, race, class, gender, desire, and material need. Foreign researchers and students may arrive in Cuba deeply connected to their subject, and may share with Cubans sincere connections of commonality and friendship. But they/we remain foreigners; holders of passports, currency, and connections many Cubans covet. Our relations with Cubans may be close, but they are not equal.

Returning to the opening anecdote—to what "people in the street" made of my comings and goings in Matanzas—though I was then offended by their suspicion, I grudgingly concede at a certain level the correctness of their general assumption regarding commodity exchange. Aside from the sincere friendship I share with some individuals in Matanzas, the deeply moving and profound rituals I have experienced, and the communal rites honoring *oricha* and ancestors in which I have participated, work *was* done and money *was* exchanged as a by-product of my activities: rituals sponsored; *derechos* paid; lessons taken; gifts bestowed. I left Cuba with data, experience, and knowledge that I later fashioned into conference papers, lectures, written works (such as the one you are reading), and a doctoral dissertation—all markers of educational capital that enable me to procure academic work and its financial capital. Are the personal and the professional truly separable?

For a foreign scholar, paralleling the accommodating deference given to some foreigners paying for *Santería* initiations, more access may be given; more time, more patience, more tolerance, perhaps more answers—whether they exist or not—even secret ones that should not be spoken. Should the questioner (scholar, student, or tourist) make known what he or she is looking for, a respondent, influenced by social capital and material need, might be tempted to accentuate that which he or she believes the visitor wants to hear. Such obstacles to "real" relations, I would argue, are not removable and are best acknowledged and mediated. I say this not as someone above the messy realities of inequality, but as a North American scholar and drummer who, like any sensitive visitor to Cuba, finds himself surrounded by economic and social realities, constantly navigating the dynamic flow of *Santería*'s cultural and economic traffic.

This has been an unpleasant essay to write, one that intrudes upon the cultural intimacy of the *Santería* community, a community that has always endured negative stereotypes and social marginalization. Even amidst financial struggle, *Santería* continues on the island, unseen by most visitors, as a dutiful, unlucrative religious practice where devotion, service, reputation, and prestige are the main currencies of exchange. I have focused on the financial effects of Cuba's current economic situation on *Santería* because these effects exist. To pretend otherwise ignores the contemporary contextual reality of the religion and the innovative ways *santeros* adapt to the rapidly changing socioeconomic conditions within Cuban society. I also feel that simple mention, even in an oblique way, of the prominence of day-to-day finances in the lives of *santeros* is a worthy endeavor, for even though some *santeros* do not allow their financial needs to affect their religious practices, knowledge of such needs gives us a better understanding of their convictions vis-à-vis the difficult economic conditions of post-Soviet Cuba.

Notes

1. While *Santería* is not a universally applied term in Cuba, it is the most well-known term for the religion, particularly outside of Cuba. *Santero/a* and *santo* are more common, used to designate a male/female *oricha* initiate and *oricha*, respectively. *Ocha* is a contraction of the *Lucumí* word *oricha*, a deified spiritual being. Thus, *Regla de Ocha* translates as "Rule/law/way of the *Oricha*." The word *Lucumí* designates Afro-Cuban culture primarily of Yoruba origin, thus *La Regla Lucumí* translates as "rule/law/way of the *Lucumí* (*oricha*)." *Ifá* refers to a system of divination ruled by Orula, the *oricha* of destiny.
2. Many anecdotes and experiences cited in this essay were conveyed to me in Cuba during informal conversations rather than formal interviews. Due to the personal nature of religious practice and varying degrees of comfort in discussing it publicly, as well as the sensitive subject matter regarding opinions about practice, practitioners, appropriate religious standards, negative experiences, or opinions regarding the Cuban government, I intentionally avoid using named sources for many anecdotes in this essay.
3. "House-temple" is a literal translation of the Spanish *casa-templo*, a term that refers to *Santería*'s practice of using private homes as the main locale of worship.
4. These gains and successes were not without serious tensions along lines of race, class, authority, and culture. See Hagedorn (2001).
5. For initiation costs for Cubans in Cuba, my number is based on informal discussions with Cuban *santeros* in Havana and Matanzas, and with Californian *santeros* familiar with Cuban initiations. The general range given by respondents was $400–$1000 USD. For citations of initiation cost estimates for Cubans, see Mason (2002); Hagedorn (2001); and Ayorinde (2004).
6. Per capita income is difficult to determine in Cuba for several reasons. Salary statistics are scarce and always expressed in Cuban pesos, while foreign currency (as expressed in *pesos convertibles*) enters the economy in a variety of known and unknown ways and with uneven distribution throughout the economy. While administrators may

earn the equivalent of $180 USD per year, an illegal cab driver or a prostitute might earn more than this in a week from foreign clientele. An individual may also receive money from relatives abroad, skewing income estimates to an unknown degree.
7. This can be illustrated by surveying figures in scholarly literature that cite comparable figures even when not adjusting for inflation. In research undertaken in New York in the early 1980s, Gregory (1999) reported the cost of an initiation running from $4,000 to $10,000, while Murphy (1993) quoted a figure of $2,500 to $10,000 (with the higher figure considered abusive). Writing from her experiences from the 1970s and 1980s, González-Wippler (1994) cites a range for initiations in the New York area at $3,500–$20,000, the higher figure again considered excessive. In fieldwork conducted between 1993 and 1995, Julio O. Granda (1995) cited a range of $5,000–$20,000 for an initiation in Miami. A 1998 article in the *Miami New Times* quoted *oriaté* Ernesto Pichardo as giving a range for initiation costs from $7,000 or $8,000 up to $15,000 (Lantigua 1998). Hagedorn (2001) gives a general guide figure as one year's salary, as expressed by the range of $15,000–$20,000.
8. See Wirtz (2004) for an excellent discussion of *Santería*'s commercialization, and *doble moral*—the practice of publicly professing one set of values while behavingin a contrary way due to necessity. Wirtz (2004: 430) observes that many Cuban *santeros* "are quick to decry how others are out for a quick buck, even while they themselves could be accused of engaging in the very same practices."
9. Rogelio Martínez Furé used these terms in an interview with me in Havana, September 20, 2000 (see also Martínez Furé 2000), but the terms are much older. The prefix *diplo* dates from Soviet-era Cuba when *diplotienda* markets only accepted foreign currency and clientele. Florida-based *oriaté*, author, and scholar Willie Ramos (n.d.) also uses these terms in an essay "Diplo Santería and Pseudo-Orishas."
10. Religious secrecy and privacy present additional markers of change that is possibly attributed to foreign patronage. For instance, video recordings of *tambor* ceremonies, possession of devotees by *oricha*, and initiation rituals have circulated throughout the world, as well as on the Internet, though most Cuban *santeros* consider filming such rituals taboo. Their existence might point to shifting attitudes concerning ritual secrecy, but also to personal financial gain on the part of those allowing the recordings to take place. See Barber (1981) and Apter (1992) for discussion of the relationship between secrecy and power in Yoruba culture and the Afro-Cuban *abakuá*. See Nooter (1993) for a discussion of secrecy as African aesthetic. See Brown (2003b) for information on the *abakuá* secret society, including an historical accusation that its secrets were sold to white people purely for profit.
11. One authority of Afro-Cuban culture I encountered in 2000 (whom I shall not name) even developed a type of urban cultural "tourist bubble," bringing foreign guests to his home where they were given room, board, educational seminars, and religious activities in relative isolation. I was unable to determine the degree of governmental involvement (if any) in his enterprise.
12. *Timba* is a virtuosic and funky version of Cuban popular music that emerged in Havana in the late 1980s and early 1990s. See Hernandez-Reguant (2006) for a discussion of religious elements in *timba* music. See also Perna (2005).
13. See Goldberg (1983), Cosentino (1995), van de Port (2005), and Cohen (1988).

2

Plural Nation

5

Multicubanidad

Ariana Hernandez-Reguant

Havana, 1998

A young contemporary dance ensemble performs at a downtown Havana theater:[1] Six dancers, dressed in military uniforms, march in unison while following orders from a female officer. At one point, she blows her whistle and shouts, IDENTIDAD ("identity"). "What is *identidad*?" The dancers stand firm yet look confused. "*Identi...qué?*" asks one. "*Identi...quoi?*" asks another. "What is that thing...identity?" wonders a third. The officer slowly reiterates, "What is identity?" There is a long pause; a dancer shouts an eleven digit number. The others follow. It is the number of their national identification card. But that is not the answer. Under dim lights, the soldiers circle around in confusion. Then the stage lights up and a cacophony of sounds ensues. While one sings and dances to *Los Van Van*'s *timba* hit *Se Me Pone la Cabeza Mala*, another does so with the rap song *Amenaza*'s *No*, and a third with *La Macarena*. As they remove their uniforms to reveal colorful outfits underneath, one then proceeds to play a video game, while another one listens to music in his headphones, another types at the computer, and two others shout on their respective cell phones. Independently and differentiated from each other, they have found their self-expression. Yet they are alone.

The play resolved the conflict between individual needs and collective responsibility by proposing the withdrawal of the state, represented by the officer, from the private sphere. In the end, the dancers removed their colorful garments too, and, half-nude, danced with each other before lying down together. The message is clear: If only citizens could be left alone to express their individual creativity, they would then naturally find a balance between their need for self-expression and their contribution to the collective welfare.

This anxiety over self-identity filled the revolutionary government. Around that same time, state-owned Radio Rebelde unveiled a propaganda campaign to answer that precise question: "What is Identity?" It featured a series of spots that were broadcast several times a day for several weeks. One included the following dialogue over a background of early twentieth-century classical Cuban music:

> Man: On our unique culture....
> Woman: On the legacy of our forefathers...
> Man: On the education we all have the right to...
> Woman: Is our imprint, what makes us different.
> Man: National Identity: Five centuries of development. Enrichment. Endurance.[2]

Unlike typical propaganda messages, these radio announcements neither emphasized the need for civic action nor directly referred to socialism and revolution. Eight years into the Special Period, the constitutive facts of Cuban identity seemed to have little to do with political community. As developed further in this chapter, during these years of crisis public discourse sought to distance politics and the economy from national culture, and to that effect it redefined the latter. Differently from the standard revolutionary position, Cubanness was often presented as a matter of culture and heritage, rather than as an ideological commitment to Revolution. This discursive turn, which translated into specific cultural policies, stemmed from both the government's need for support and legitimacy during a period of extreme economic crisis and the need to reposition Cuba within a post-Soviet world regimented by capitalist regimes of value. This new emphasis in culture primarily had two aspects: the inclusion, however timid, of exiles into the nation's culture, and the reformulation of Cuban identity in tune with multicultural trends internationally in vogue.

In these years, many more discourses and events contributed to the visibility of a collective process of soul-searching. For the Cuban government, the disappearance of the Soviet bloc and the prospect of economic and cultural globalization caused a deep preoccupation with the future of socialism and therefore with its own hegemony. Like in 1961, when Fidel Castro first outlined the role of artists and intellectuals within the revolutionary process, culture was still considered a key vehicle for ideological hegemony.[3] However, if back then, cultural producers were required to adhere to revolutionary politics, in the post-Soviet world the Revolution was willing to compromise and tolerate a broader range of non-oppositional views. On the one hand, and as long as they did not openly oppose the Cuban government, cultural manifestations by expatriate Cubans were reclaimed as part of a nation now understood in diasporic terms. On the other hand, a certain degree of cultural diversity within Cuba was given visibility under a new framework of ethnic multiculturalism.

Since 1959, revolutionary nationalist discourse had been based on political community. The new government situated itself as heir to a long lineage of national independence struggles that were fought for a free *patria*—a notion in which nation, territory and self-determination converged. Revolutionary policies concerning education, the media, collective work, and political participation were intended to foster national unity and an emotional attachment to the *patria*.[4] Within this framework, leaving the national territory meant abandoning the *patria*, and that was considered an act of treason. Under revolutionary law, deserters had their property confiscated and were stripped of citizenship rights. In the 1990s, however, the disappearance of Cuba's socialist allies and the ensuing need for both income—in the form of remittances—and international support led to a softening of this position. Travel and emigration laws were relaxed, warmer relations with moderate expatriate communities were pursued, and culture acquired a central role in the nationalist discourse of inclusion.

A similar process had taken place in the former Soviet bloc countries, where political community had been a central element of nationality, particularly in multiethnic states.[5] In the post-Soviet period, national intellectuals in these countries often emphasized national culture and pre-socialist history as a means to redefine the connection among nation, state, and territory in nonpolitical terms. More generally, in the face of a crisis of political community, cultural nationalist discourses typically operate as an integrative factor, as they tend to polarize the social universe into two mutually exclusive categories: "the global" (formerly, "the foreign"), and "the local" (a category that promotes the identification of government and society in the defense of national particularity). As García Canclini (1999: 84) put it, such discourse only presents two options: either "to go global" or "to defend identity," the latter being the only morally viable position. In revolutionary Cuba, going global meant embracing capitalism, and that was not an option—at least not at the level of discourse. Instead, the emphasis on Cuban culture and history as constitutive of a contemporary identity offered a corrective to a nationalism primarily based on allegiance to a revolutionary project itself in crisis. If until then, national fervor capitalized on the collective construction of political society, now it also drew on a common bond that transcended past and present ideologies and celebrated cultural diversity.

In 1992, the Cuban Constitution was revised to allow for far-reaching economic and legal reform. The new version of the charter added the father of Cuban independence, Jose Martí, as the foremost ideological guiding force of the nation—ahead of Lenin, Marx, and Engels—and explicitly gave the state the duty to "defend the identity of Cuban culture and look after the preservation of the cultural patrimony," which included so-called intangible manifestations like stories, dances, and songs.[6] The Union of Writers and Artists (UNEAC) deemed Cuban culture in danger and in need of support to ensure its survival (Hernández 1994), and an annual holiday, National Culture Day, initially established to commemorate the birth of the nation as a political project during the First War of Independence, became an annual celebration of the nation's cultural melting pot (Bueno 1995).[7] Throughout the decade, conferences, publications, talks, research projects, and artistic works reflected anxiety over the nation's future, all proposing cultural community as key to an updated nationalism that could transcend ideological difference and social hierarchy.[8] Academic disciplines such as history, linguistics, ethnology, and social psychology were put to the task of linking cultural traits to national identity.[9] Early twentieth-century cultural nationalists like Jorge Mañach and Fernando Ortíz were recuperated despite their conservative political leanings, and their writings on cultural nationalism were reprinted and widely read.[10]

Fernando Ortíz, in particular, became a household figure. His theories were especially palatable to official intellectuals, not ready to do away with political community, but in need of a corrective that would ensure the survival of the national project. Ortíz placed the common experiences of migration and adaptation to the new environment as the sources of a shared Cuban cultural identity and as the propellers of a collective drive for self-government. He also formulated a model of cultural change, which he called transculturation, based on the simmering of an *ajiaco* or stew, where new elements might be constantly added, thus continually changing the taste of the dish (Ortíz 1996 [1939], Suárez 1996). Ortíz's (1936) notion of culture as a kind of *habitus* demarcated by social and material conditions, which he developed in his essay "The Human Factors of *Cubanidad*," was well suited for the troubled time of the Special Period. Accordingly, throughout the decade a renovated Anthropology Center within the Cuban Academy of Sciences and a new foundation devoted to Ortíz's legacy undertook research projects on Cuban ethnicity and cultural manifestations, such as traditions, material patrimony, cultural religion, etc. (Zito 2004). Along these lines, the 1997 National Social Sciences Prize was awarded to Soviet-trained ethnologist Jesús Guanche, whose research built on Ortíz's on the ethnic components of the Cuban nation. For Guanche, there was a single Cuban ethnicity which was multiracial and featured a shared culture and language, a common psychosocial personality, a national sentiment, a territory, a mode of production, and an aspiration for political and economic self-determination (Guanche 1996a, 1996b).

The redefinition of the Cuban nation as an ethnic and cultural community opened the door to two controversial elements. First was the disentanglement of nation from territory; effectively, the incorporation into the nation of the much vilified exiled community now refashioned as a "diaspora." The second was the discussion of race relations and the role of race in Cuban culture—previously taboo topics. The introduction of a discourse of multiculturalism, which allowed various communities to carve out a social and cultural space on the basis of ethnic heritage, necessarily entailed a redefinition of race vis-à-vis both culture and class. As detailed in the following sections, the very consideration of these two subjects, exile/diaspora and race, sought to broaden the basis for revolutionary support but also pushed the limits of revolutionary hegemony.[11]

A Diasporic Cubanidad

Before designing the aforementioned Radio Rebelde campaign, Frank Donikian attended a series of professional development workshops on national identity at the Communist Party School of Cadres. To stimulate discussion among participants, teachers used a certain "Test of Cubanidad," apparently devised to teach cadres new ways to think about what it meant to be Cuban. The test subsequently circulated around Havana, popping up at gatherings and parties for people's amusement, as seen at the end of the film *Nada +* (Cremata Malberti 2001). As soon as my neighbor Gustavo got a hold of it at work, he insisted on testing everyone. He gathered five of us at Hildita's kitchen on the ground floor and began firing questions: "At what time is the daily cannon blast in Havana?" "What do people sing when they die?" "At what time was Lola killed?" "What happens to the shrimp that falls asleep?" "Where are singers from?" "Where is 'the sinful corner?'" Excitedly, the two oldest women in the group, both over sixty, interrupted each other competing for the right answer. The younger ones were too slow to beat them, so we watched with amusement. Hilda, a normally taciturn woman consumed with the lack of produce in the bodega and her nonagenarian mother's health, cheerfully claimed victory (it must have been the first time we saw her laugh), having answered all hundred-plus questions right. Although Gustavo, in his forties, scored third, ahead of the younger contestants, he was upset as if he had lost. This was not a test that most people could pass, he complained; who could possibly know all those song lyrics, names of arcane bands, poems, proverbs and former street names from yesteryear? My neighbors suspected that the authors of the test were old people.

They were right. A group of middle-aged Cuban exiled men residing in North America since the early 1960s, who had formed an Internet newsgroup on Cuban affairs in 1994, created this test to assess their own degree of *cubanidad*. For these exiles, Cuban identity was located in prerevolutionary Cuba, and was not related to political allegiances or residence in the national territory, but to knowledge of traditional popular culture and music of their time.[12] The only trace of the exile experience in the test was precisely its generational quality.

A couple of months after the episode in my neighbor's kitchen, a large conference on cultural identity took place at the University of Havana. At the closing session—chaired by Minister of Culture Abel Prieto and literary critics Roberto Fernández Retamar and Ambrosio Fornet—the latter spoke about the uniqueness of Cuban culture, and offered as his core case a supposedly recent story about the Texas-Mexico border. As Mexicans were invariably caught and sent back, they began to claim Cuban citizenship—as U.S. policies toward Cuba guaranteed asylum to Cubans while deportation to Mexicans. It worked for a while; until the U.S. Border Patrol realized the scheme and began requesting those claiming to be Cuban to sing the Cuban national anthem, describe the Cuban flag, state the year of the country's independence, and name the Cuban president (all symbols of political community). As the word spread, Mexican migrants got Cuban schoolbooks, memorized them, and then successfully crossed the border. The U.S. patrol held a meeting. It was of utmost importance to differentiate Cubans from Mexicans, since the former could be allowed in while the latter were to be sent back. What could they do? They decided to hire a Cuban to devise a test that non-Cubans would always flunk, a test with questions that nobody could memorize, to which only Cubans could possibly know the answers. This was called the *Cubanidad Test*, continued Fornet. He then described the test in detail, as we know it. As an afterthought, he acknowledged that young Cubans would probably have to study as hard as the Mexicans in order to pass it. He went on to make his point: that most questions were related to popular music, which was evidence of the importance of music and musicality to the cultural identity of the nation.

Fornet did not know that this was in fact a test devised by middle-aged Cuban exiles to assess their own Cubanness, and although obviously apocryphal, his story was not far-fetched. Certainly, the *Cubanidad Test* was meant to distinguish Cubans from Mexicans, and other immigrants. But it was a test meant to be put to use *within* the United States itself, to establish other borders and border-crossings aside from that of "The Border" (i.e., the U.S.-Mexico border). As envisioned by its authors, the text would confirm the identity of Cuban migrants as *truly* Cuban, despite their extended residency outside the island. The veracity of this Cuban identity lay in the truth of lived realities; the test's answers could only have been imbibed through the everyday experience of a Cuban environment, of being exposed to forms of Cuban popular culture. The test, then, presumed that the central consensual marker of Cuban identity was participation in a popular culture shared by an "imagined community" in spite of other social differences.

However, as recognized by both Fornet and my neighbors, it was a popular culture in which young people had not participated. The test was grounded in the experience of an earlier generation of both revolution and exile. That was Fornet's own generation: a generation that was divided by migration and political cleavages, yet united in other ways, including race (white), education, and urban upbringing. If identity in exile was defined by opposition to the Castro government, identity on the island was similarly formulated by opposition and resistance to U.S. imperialism. This is why the *Test of Cubanidad* could be appropriated by older Communist Party officials as their own, without suspicion of its migrant origins, precisely because there was little difference between them and the exiles of the same generation in terms of social background and knowledge of popular culture.

The erasure of exile agency in Fornet's recounting of the test's origins further highlighted its core element: the importance of popular culture in the formulation of a cultural identity for an ideologically divided Cuban nation. The test showed two important trends: a wish to extricate nation from territory, and the implicit acknowledgement of other patterns of difference and distance, such as generation, upbringing, and race, which questioned the homogeneous experience of national identity. At a time when the Cuban government, in dire need of cash flow and international support, initiated a rapprochement with moderate sectors of the exile community, shared culture constituted the main vehicle for communication and understanding. Hence, while the flow of remittances from abroad was essential for the Cuban economy in the short term, the support of key intellectual and artistic Cuban-American figures was crucial in the long-term strategy to delegitimize the U.S. embargo against the island. To that effect, in the early 1990s the Cuban Ministry of Culture began inviting expatriate artists and intellectuals to visit the island.

In 1994, a few months before the summer crisis that would take 30,000 people to the oceans in the hopes of reaching U.S. shores, the Cuban government sponsored a conference called *La Nación y la Emigración* (The Nation and Emigration). The choice of words was careful and deliberate. "Emigration," as opposed to "exile"—which was more accurate—diffused ideological differences, as invitee Maria de los Angeles Torres (1995) pointed out at the time. At this time, moreover, a new emigration wave was underway that was not so much motivated by political dissent as by economic reasons. These migrants—said Carlos Aldana, then chief of the Communist Party Ideology Department—should not be considered deserters (Suárez 1991). The meeting brought together members of the Cuban government's cultural apparatus and mostly U.S.-based artists and intellectuals from the so-called one-and-a-half generation—those who left Cuba as children. At the conference, Abel Prieto, then UNEAC's president (three years later to become the Minister of Culture) gave an invited lecture entitled *Cultura, Cubanidad y Cubania* (Culture, Cubanness and Cubanicity) that established the government's official position on the issue of national identity vis-à-vis both culture and territory. Prieto did not completely disengage nation from state, but he did unhinge nation from territory. He saw the state as the culmination of the nation's form, and, following the official revolutionary line, linked national identity to a political project, and nationalism to patriotism. Predictably, he located the formation of the nation in the act of collective resistance during the battles for independence, *before* the creation of the state. But he added an important point: it was during that struggle for political independences that people from "multiple and diverse ethnic and cultural groups" bonded. Hence, the nation was not only a political project but also a cultural process. Nonetheless, he stated that a *cubanidad* not committed to a political project—the state—was "fake" or "castrated." Yet he conceded that just as a castrated *cubanidad* could be found on the island, there could also be "true" Cubans residing abroad. In the end, he acknowledged that culture was what was common to all Cubans, and therefore the arena where the nation could meet its emigrants. He then called for including émigré production within the national patrimony, which he promoted later as minister of culture (Hernández-Valdés 1997). Specifically, he gave the green light to the publication of debates on migration, Cuban-American literature, and the limits of the nation as well as texts by and interviews with writers and artists in exile in important journals like *La Gaceta de Cuba* and *Temas*.[13]

One year after *The Nation and Emigration* event, Cuban intellectuals from both sides of the Florida Straits came together again at a University of Havana conference on Cuban identity. Again, these meetings were conducted behind closed doors and access was highly controlled.[14] This time there was no disagreement: national identity transcended both national borders and ideological boundaries and was based first and foremost on a shared culture.[15] Cuban scholars had gathered evidence to show that a single cultural identity was shared by self-identified Cubans wherever they lived. For instance, University of Havana psychology professor Carolina de la Torre (1995) investigated the consciousness of national identity among Cuban children both in Cuba and in places like Iowa, which she was able to visit thanks to the academic exchanges just opening up with U.S. universities. De la Torre concluded that Cubans, regardless of territorial residency, shared mental representations of themselves—as a people—and of others. National sentiment was thus not just anchored on the existence of a homeland, but on a common culture, which included not only particular forms of social interaction but also a moral universe. Poet Nancy Morejón expressed it eloquently when she said, "no one can say Cubanness goes this far and not farther" (qtd. in Behar and Juárez 1994: 633). As Ambrosio Fornet (1997) later remarked, the unity of Cuban culture became the most discussed topic in all meetings between Cuban intellectuals from inside and outside the island.

Many research projects and artistic works were by then recounting for the first time in postrevolutionary history an all-inclusive cultural history of the nation.[16] In regard to music history, for instance, the second edition of Helio Orovio's (2004 [1992]) dictionary of Cuban music included, without distinction, exiled musicians who had been excluded from the first 1981 edition. Cuban music journals also timidly began to feature articles on expatriate musicians, as long as they had not been vocal opponents of the regime.[17] A transnational history of popular Cuban music was presented in the 1996 film by Rigoberto López, *Yo Soy, del Son a la Salsa* (I Am, from Son to Salsa), a documentary coproduced by the Cuban Film Institute (ICAIC), and a New York salsa label (RMM). The film chronicled the history of salsa music from its origins as *son* in the rural areas of the island's Orient in the early twentieth century; to New York, where it was refashioned as *salsa* by expatriate Cuban, Puerto Rican, Venezuelan, and other Caribbean musicians; to present-day Havana, where it culminated in the form of *timba*. While conforming to a nationalist musicological history that insisted on the Cuban origins of *salsa* and *son*, the film prominently featured the role of Celia Cruz, who not only lived in exile in the United States, but who over the years had taken every opportunity to chastise the Cuban government and was absolutely banned from the Cuban media. This unprecedented inclusion alone made the film controversial, and as a result it was only shown publicly at Havana's international film festival that year.

Conciliatory gestures toward the exile community had their ideological limits, and culture could not heal all wounds. But for a generation too young to have fought either for or against the Revolution of 1959, it could become a safe vehicle to build bridges between those on the island and those in the United States, who had often rebelled against their conservative parents and come of age in the rise of multiculturalism and Latino politics.[18] Furthermore, there was a younger generation of artists who, since the late 1980s, had settled abroad and did not consider themselves exiled. Like jazz pianist Gonzalo Rubalcaba, many left temporarily and with the Cuban government's blessing in order to further their artistic careers, as long as they did not publicly criticized the regime (see chapter 11, this volume). This group maintained close ties with the island, often returning without obstacle for short- or even long-term visits (Borland 2004). For this generation, scattered through Europe and the Americas, the usual paradigm of island versus exile was increasingly unsatisfactory. Eventually tropes such as "Greater Cuba" and "diaspora" became colloquial terms used to refer to this transnational Cuban community.[19]

The consciousness of transnationality, at times referred to as "postnational," as if to transcend the intimacy between nation and territory by abandoning the nation altogether, inspired a number of underground artistic and literary projects within Cuba, beginning in the early 1990s. One of these projects, which sought to subvert the official territorial and political boundaries of the nation, was a fanzine-like publication called *Memorias de la Postguerra* (Postwar Memories). Founded by artist Tania Bruguera, the project had a long-lasting influence despite the fact that only two issues were made and their circulation was limited and informal. There, Cuban artists and critics on the island and abroad reflected on the dispersal of Cuban culture, engaging in debate over what two young critics, then living in Spain, termed as a condition of "post exile" (de la Nuez and Ballesteros 1994). For all of them, the boundaries and differences between those on and off the island were no longer clearly delimited, and the parallels between an internal and an external kind of exile were considered as significant as the disjunctures between ideology and geography. To prove it, in early 1994 an alternative art space located at a private home, the *Espacio Aglutinador* (the Agglutinating Space), began presenting works by Cuban artists, some of whom lived abroad, while others lived on the island but were marginalized from institutional channels (Fusco 1994, Valdés Figueroa 2001). In a similar fashion, a poetry collective founded in 1993, and integrated by writers Carlos A. Aguilera, Rolando Sanchez Mejia, Pedro Marqués de Armas, and others, placed emerging literary experiments from the nation's margins within a larger literary context. Their name, as well as that of their samizdat-type publication, was *Diaspora(s)*, in the plural, in reference to a general need to deterritorialize literary culture.[20]

A more specific notion of *diaspora*, applied to Cubans' dispersal, was gaining ground among the Cuban-American "one-and-a-half" cohort; and it was their usage that would take hold in everyday speech to refer to Cuban culture at the turn of the century. While both Ruth Behar (1994), in her *Bridges to Cuba*, and Maria de los Angeles Torres (1995), in the journal *Diaspora*, used the term to refer to their own generation of expatriate Cubans, for their colleague Román de la Campa (1994) the defining framework was the larger Latino diaspora in the United States, of which Cubans were a part. This Latino diaspora was not defined by a mythical and common homeland, but by the country of adoption. Thus De la Campa's dynamic notion was firmly based on a multicultural United States and suggested that ethnicities take shape only in retrospect in the location of arrival. In contrast, for Torres, and especially for Behar, who was concerned about the intersection of the Cuban and Jewish diasporas, the reference to a homeland was vital, particularly since in the 1990s this original land was no longer mythic or imagined, but suddenly accessible. Many novels and films from this period explore emotional narratives of nostalgia and belonging, as in Cristina Garcia's 1993 novel, *Dreaming in Cuban*, where Cuba becomes the mythical homeland, and in the various homecoming documentaries of the one-and-a-half generation (Hernandez-Reguant 2004b). In these narratives, the notion of diaspora invokes roots that are both physical and spiritual and that have the potentiality to transcend ideological cleavages.

As Ambrosio Fornet (2002) remarked, by eluding the politics and economics of separation the term *diaspora* presented itself as a neutral alternative of inclusion. Furthermore, its assumption of an essential link among Cubans based on an ancestral yearning that occluded differences of race, class, and ideology, was consistent with the thinking of Fernando Ortíz and his acolytes, which made it acceptable in the intellectual climate of cultural nationalism in the 1990s. In addition, the "diaspora" trope debunked Miami as Cuba's oppositional capital, highlighting the rise of Europe as a preferred living destination for young educated Cubans, many of whom wished to extricate themselves from traditional exile politics. That, more than anything else, is what sealed the term's currency among the island's young intelligentsia. Their interaction with those abroad could continue without stigma as long as their departure did not signify an ideological stance against revolutionary politics (Fowler 1998). To leave the nation's territory did no longer necessarily mean joining, the enemy. This is not to say that there were no ideological limits to Cuban identity. Diaspora was, for many, still exile, especially since the Cuban government placed restrictions on return visits for those who had overstayed their exit visas or left without the proper bureaucratic requirements.

In the 1990s, Madrid became a center for Cuban diasporic culture, particularly as, on the one hand, new immigration laws in Spain made it relatively easy for Cubans of immediate Spanish descent to migrate there; and on the other, growing numbers of Spanish tourists visited Cuba and forged personal ties with Cubans whom they invited to visit Spain. Furthermore, since 1996, a conservative cabinet in Spain emphasized both business relations with Cuba and support for pro-democracy positions and dissident politics, which often meant strained diplomatic relations between the two countries. As a result, Spain became a magnet for both political exiles and economic migrants. With a relatively small and not-so-active older exile community, Madrid only became a thriving scene for all things Cuban thanks to the newcomers of the 1990s. It was in Madrid in 1996 that the journal *Encuentro* was launched immediately becoming the main journal on Cuban affairs and agglutinating what Victor Fowler called, fittingly, an "exile-diaspora." Indeed, *Encuentro* purported to sustain an inclusive notion of Cuban culture that would go beyond political polarization (Gaston Baquero 1996). Yet it not always succeeded: it emphasized "high" culture over popular manifestations, and critical positions of Cuban politics took precedence over offering a voice to marginalized sectors in Cuban society. The journal was banned in Cuba. According to writer Antonio José Ponte (2007)—later to become *Encuentro*'s editor in chief—the Union of Artists and Writers pressured its members against collaborating with it, going as far as threatening them with expulsion from the organization and canceling their salary and official status as state-sponsored artists and intellectuals. Inclusion had its limits both on the island and in exile; but a new consensus had emerged about an idea of the nation that was no longer bound to a specific territory.

In Cuba, the turn to cultural nationalism had meant more than support for "high" cultural manifestations, exilic or domestic. The emphasis on ethnicity meant highlighting culture in an anthropological sense, not so much for its aesthetic value but for its meaningfulness in the making of community. That entailed support for traditions and folklore —the intangibles of Cuban culture introduced in 1992 in the Constitution as integral to the national patrimony.

Most importantly, this resulted in a debate on the "other" diaspora, not one associated with the historical Jewish dispersal but with the so-called Black Atlantic. The redefinition of the relation among blackness, race, and culture came to the fore, and in that fashion, Cuban ethnology met U.S. multiculturalism, and island intellectuals entered into fraternal dialogue with their Afro-diasporic counterparts over the meaning of race in Cuban society.

Afro-Cubanidad and the Ethnic Cuban Nation

According to a news brief, Havana's 2006 Carnival was to celebrate Cuban national identity through highlighting the festival's Spanish, African, and Chinese elements (EFE 2006). This seemingly innocuous announcement actually followed months of debate, led by Havana's UNESCO office, on cultural diversity as a way to revitalize a critique-ridden Carnival.[21] The idea was to emphasize not only roots and tradition but live community. As agreed at a UNESCO forum, the Carnival would be a contemporary fiesta of annual renewal, but it should properly represent the ethnic components of the Cuban nation.

The Carnival was ultimately canceled due to Fidel Castro's illness, but by the 2000s the notion of a multiethnic nation had become commonplace. A massive and encyclopedic *Ethnographic Atlas of Cuba*, published jointly as a CD-Rom by the Fernando Ortíz Foundation, the Academy of Sciences, and other cultural institutions, systematically classified the island's communities and traditions under this multiethnic light (Alvarado Ramos 2000). During the 1990s, thanks to foreign support, the restoration of Havana's dilapidated Chinatown—even though most of its Chinese residents were long gone—and the revitalization of Spanish regional clubs were only some of the many projects in cultural preservation and community development that highlighted the ethnic components of the Cuban nation. Even the children of Cuban-Russian couples organized themselves in this way (see chapter 7, this volume). Slowly but surely, Cuba's ethnic communities (in plural) were helping to shape a sort of revolutionary multiculturalism in line with similar trends in the United States, Canada, Australia, and other countries.

Accordingly, like in the United States over a decade earlier, the "black" experience, or as referred to in Cuba, *la aportación del negro* ("the contribution of the negro"), began to be reconsidered in ethnic terms: African-derived cultural manifestations started to be addressed in some circles, and not without controversy, as Afro-Cuban, in a move that suggested a shift in emphasis from race to the less contentious notions of ethnicity and culture.

Just as with Cuban culture in general, this ethnicization of race allowed for its further dissection into previous ethnic components; in this case the various ethnic groups brought from Africa as slaves. For instance, numerous festivals, conferences, and events celebrated the Yoruba heritage (see chapter 8, this volume), like the annual Guanabacoa's Wemillere African Roots Festival, which celebrated the contemporary liveliness of African-derived musical and religious culture in Cuba, and featured a guest African country in every edition.[22] More recent immigrant groups such as Haitians and Jamaicans were similarly deserving of attention. Gloria Rolando's 1996 documentary *My Footsteps to Baraguá* garnered an audience in academic circles in the United States with its documentation of surviving West Indian culture, memory, and identity in rural Cuba—an account void of contemporary context or reference to revolutionary politics. This multicultural model of race relations was suitable to Cuban intellectuals reluctant to adopt the dualistic model of race relations still operating in U.S. society, which evidenced a correlation between race and inequality. Instead, an ethnic multiculturalist model, just like earlier socialist discourses of political community and social equality, to some extent eluded the thorny issue of race at a time, precisely, when increasing economic stratification made the racial gap more evident.

During the Special Period, manifestations of white racism intensified. On television and film, people of color only appeared in stereotypical roles, while depictions of interracial relations only took place as illicit affairs. One of the most popular soap operas of the period, *El Naranjo del Patio* (The Yard's Orange Tree), had the country glued to the television set with a story that resurrected the familiar myth of Cecilia Valdés, a 19th century mulatto woman who sought social advancement—unsuccessfully—through marriage to a white man. The series, similarly, focused on a conniving mulatto seductress who enticed respectable white men to destroy their families and fortunes. Yet, despite these very entrenched stereotypes, most people, white and black, denied the existence of racism, dismissing its manifestations as cultural ways that should not be judged through an imported lens. The ideology of mestizaje and its associated categories of syncretism, transculturation, and racial democracy were still powerful.[23] The Revolution, while initially purporting to eliminate racial inequality, left the problem to its own devises. The underlying theory was that race was a manifestation of class, and that taking care of class hierarchy would ultimately eliminate racial inequality. The social advancement of black Cubans under the revolutionary regime was undeniable, yet racial prejudice and racist attitudes did not disappear; they were swept under the rug. It was common for Cubans to reject foreigners' reproaches of racist behavior and speech by alluding to their cultural specificity and rejecting the importation of foreign models of race relations and interaction. Often, white-skinned people would claim a drop of African ancestry, invoking the saying *Quien no tiene de Congo, tiene de Carabalí* (Whoever does not have some Congo, has some Carabalí) in reference to two common African ethnicities among slaves. While in another context the same people would emphatically defend their racial purity and trace their ancestors on all sides to Europe, at other times, the strategic attribution of African ancestry sealed the claim of national co-ownership of the African past while denying the possibility of contemporary racial prejudice. Furthermore, by locating their drop of Congo or Carabalí blood in a remote past (distant great-great-grandparents were often invoked), whites were exonerated from further mixing in the present. A poll taken in urban centers in 1994 showed that over two-thirds of white Cubans opposed interracial marriage, and also viewed with disgust the possibility of mixed-race offspring (de la Fuente 2001).

A popular comedy film, *A Paradise under the Stars* (Chijona 1998), is a case in point. There, interracial sex was introduced in the context of workplace harassment at the Tropicana Cabaret between an aggressive black manager and his employee, a white married woman. She soon becomes pregnant, and then learns that her husband is, in fact, her half-brother. After delivery, the concerned families run to the hospital. As one relative leans over the crib to see the newborn, another asks, "Did she give birth to a monster?" in allusion to the parents' kinship. The other responds, "Worse! To a *negrita*." The baby's dark skin evidences that she is not the product of incest after all, but of an even worse aberration: interracial adultery. The newborn's grandmother is the first to accept her, reasoning that "in this day and age, a mulatta is great business," in reference to her value in the new transnational economy of love. The return of the myth of the sexually voracious mulatta (believed to be a prostitute at heart) and the criminalization of the black man (feared as a street hustler) became fixtures of the Special Period's iconography and literary representations (see chapter 2, this volume). Expressions of prejudice on the part of white Cubans were only emboldened as they reacted in bewilderment to the obvious fascination of European and North American tourists with blackness, as well as to the ubiquitous sight of biracial/binational couples on the streets, nightclubs, and beaches.

This increasing disenfranchisement of black Cubans led intellectuals and artists of color to push for a national debate on race, addressing it in terms of not only class and colonial heritage, as had typically been the case until then, but also in terms of culture. While the recuperation of African-derived folklore, music, and religion was not something new, the focus now was their public representation as well as their consideration as lived experiences, rather than as historical survivals. These Afro-Cuban intellectuals and artists were concerned with debunking racial stereotypes and fostering a constructive dialogue with the broader society, seeking to raise the general consciousness regarding a situation of racial inequality—something that even the National Academy of Sciences ended up acknowledging on the basis of careful research (Fernández 2001). Throughout the second half of the 1990s, several meetings, typically hosted by sympathetic cultural institutions such as the Center Juan Marinello (in 1995), the *Temas* journal (in 1996), the Union of Writers and Artists (in 1998), and the Fernando Ortíz Foundation (in 1998 and 1999), were held to discuss the need for positive depictions of blacks in the media, the introduction of Afro-Cuban history and culture in the school curriculum, the redress to employment discrimination, and the protection of Afro-Cuban cultural heritage. But typically, these meetings took place behind closed doors, with little public projection within Cuba. As a result, a few of these scholars and artists decided to abandon their institutional affiliations to express and address their frustrations more freely. For instance, all-black theater groups such as *Todo en Sepia* and *Teatro Negro* were formed as a result of black actors' frustration with their lack of opportunity (Cervera 2004). Others gathered around a new, and short lived, foundation created by Pablo Milanés, a popular singer whose international stature had permitted him to amass a small fortune by Cuban standards. In any case, however, they connected with foreign scholars invested in Black Atlantic and African diaspora models of cultural circulation, mostly in the United States. Academic and cultural exchanges taking place at the time led to the Cubans' higher international profile, as was the case for the aforementioned independent filmmaker Gloria Rolando, writer Nancy Morejón, and others who became regulars in North American academic circuits with their promotion of Afro-Cuban cultural identity.[24] Also artists who made Afro-Cuban culture and traditions the object of their work received at this time the attention of the international market.[25]

The discourse of some of these official intellectuals was at times self-defeating, as when scholars called for studying the role of *lo negro* (the black element) in Cuban culture, seeking to identify the Afro-Cuban substrata to all sorts of cultural manifestations.[26] At the other end of the argumentative spectrum was a position that claimed not the essential integration of African elements into national culture, but the impossibility of such occurrence. That was the position defended by Rogelio Martínez Furé (2000: 157), a renowned folklorist, disciple of Fernando Ortíz,

> [t]here is, of course, no homogeneous Cuban culture, which is why I also think it's a mistake to speak of a national cultural identity. There is no one national cultural identity. In all countries of the world, there are multiethnic, pluricultural identities. In all countries of the world, pluriculturalism is prevalent. What we must accept is the plural heritage, not homogenizing monomania. In Cuba there is no one cultural identity, there are diverse national cultural identities, or, to simplify, there is a multiethnic, pluricultural identity. A mulatto Cuban from

Baracoa, the descendant of Haitian émigrés in a coffee-growing area, is not the same as a black Cuban descendant of Arará from the province of Matanzas, a sugar-growing area, or a fair-skinned Cuban from Pinar del Rio, a tobacco-growing area, the descendant of Canary islanders. They are all Cuban, but there are differences in food, speech, psychology, religious beliefs, and phenotype. I believe it is important to accept plurality and free ourselves from that monomania, according to which we are all the same.

One might wonder, then, what would link these various Cuban types, what would make them "all Cuban," and whether Martinez Furé's position would not entail a return to political community as key to national integration; particularly, as he identified culture with heritage, in the form of food, religion, and the like, rather than with dynamic forms of interaction, value, and morality. Moreover, he then correlated culture—as tradition—with skin color, thus destabilizing the myth of the *mestizo* nation (one mixed race and one national culture), while opening the door to racial essentialisms. Was race a cultural construct or was culture a manifestation of race? In the end, Furé seemed to argue the latter, thus going against the grain of the official revolutionary position, which for decades saw racial difference as a manifestation of class—something that socialism was to eliminate. Yet his position ultimately claimed race as race, as a physical construct with social consequences, sometimes allied with class, sometimes with culture. One way or another, on the face of socialism's failure to bring about social equality, a new wave of cultural nationalists debunked revolutionary materialist views that equated difference with inequality, by denouncing the latter while claiming the former.

It would still take several years for the seminal and controversial work of Walterio Carbonell, silenced since its publication in 1961, to be reprinted. There, in "Cómo Surgió la Cultura Nacional" (How did National Culture Emerge), Carbonell (2006 [1961]) established the development of Cuban national culture as a product of colonial racial violence. Carbonell's heirs were not so much the established Afro-Cuban intellectuals but younger black, often disenfranchised, artists who made the problem of racial injustice central to their work. If the aforementioned group of artists and intellectuals exemplified a strand of Afro-cultural nationalism that Paul Gilroy (2002: 212) identified as "feminist, moralist, and bourgeois," normally seeking acceptance without upsetting the status quo, a second group was typical of a more subversive stance that succeeded in galvanizing the disenfranchised black youth. In Cuba, this was a trend represented by a younger generation, often lacking the customary institutional affiliation that transcended the elite walls of academe and cultural institutions and subverted the terms of the debate by rendering positive those assumptions previously held as negative.

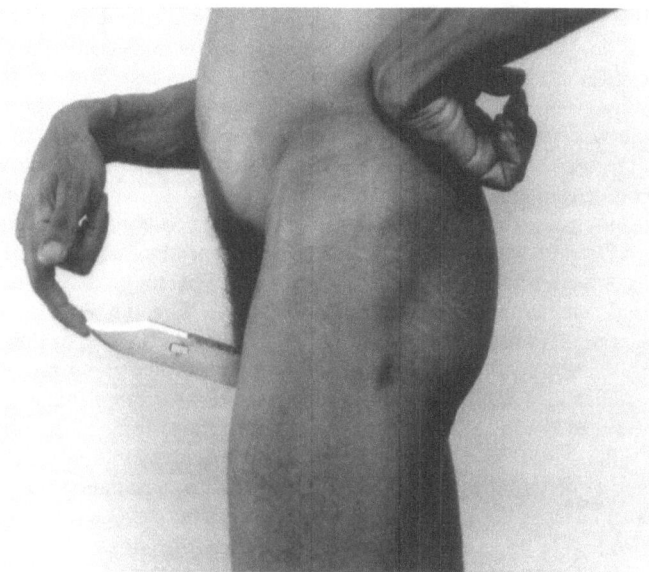

Figure 5.1   René Peña, No Title, 1994.

That is to say, this was a type of nationalism that Gilroy (2000: 210) described as "putatively street, working-class and habitually gendered male," and which became more powerful at the popular level by instilling pride in characteristics that had been subjected to scorn and shame, such as unrestrained sexuality, dark skin color, violent behavior, and so on. In Cuba, this aesthetic was represented to some extent by the photography of René Peña, as well as by *timba* music and later, rap, reggaeton, and their associated publics. (See Figure 5.1) *Timba*, more so than rap, and like reggaeton years later, typically situated black male sexuality at the epicenter of a new society structured by access to both women and hard currency, redefining blackness in cultural but also racial and sexual terms. *Timba*'s subversive power flickered along with the foreign indie labels that had sought to commercialize it. Yet, the popularity of its discourse hinged on the inseparability of race from gender, class, and generation—lines of segmentation that the culturalist approach tended to underplay.

Conclusion

In 2003, the tragedies of race, class, nation, and migration came to the fore during the concomitant trials of a group of dissident poets, journalists, and activists, on the one hand, and a group of boat hijackers, on the other. While the plight of the respectable middle-class dissidents garnered the sympathy of the Western world, the black and destitute would-be migrants were swiftly tried and executed with comparatively little protest. Some of the dissidents were eventually freed—the most famous among them, poet Raul Rivero, was allowed to move to Spain—but the hijackers were less fortunate. In their marginality and ultimate death, they would never join the "exile-diaspora" of the lettered email-using cultural elites. The diasporic ideal was not embodied in poor destitute migrants, but in jet-setting pop bands like *Habana Abierta* or *Orishas*, based in Madrid and Paris respectively, which, thanks to their apolitical stance, continued to enjoy a following in the island through recordings, media appearances, and live concerts. They inhabited a new space, a Greater Cuba. Just as importantly, this diasporic ideal that they exemplified was multiracial, multilingual, and multicultural, without renouncing to the essence (a *je ne sais quoi*) of Cuban identity—symbolized at its bare minimum by the insertion of traditional rhythmic patterns in their songs.

This generational and geographical transmutation of identity into culture and exile into diaspora allowed for the inclusion of intersecting perspectives and narratives of gender, sexuality, race, and ethnicity. In its complexity, *cubanidad* had never been a fuzzier notion, now closer to spirit than to reason. The *ajiaco* was boiling over, the pot was cracking, the ingredients were spilling.

Notes

* Special thanks to Gerardo Alfonso, Alfredo Alonso, Jorge Ferrer, Betty Gago, Lisa Maya Knauer, Ernesto Oroza, Kenneth Routon, René Peña, Georgina Torriente, and Ignacio Vera for their input and assistance.

1. Teatro Mella, **Compañía** Danza Abierta, "El Arbol y el Camino" (Dir: Marianela Boán), November 29, 1998.
2. Translation by author. In Spanish: Man: *En nuestra cultura única*…Woman: *En el legado de los próceres*…Man: *A la instrucción a la que todos tenemos derecho*…Woman: *Ese es nuestro sello, lo que nos hace diferentes.* Man: *Identidad Nacional: Cinco siglos de formación. Enriquecimiento. Permanencia.*
3. Toward the end of the decade, the government proclaimed the Battle of Ideas (*La Batalla de Ideas*) as an ideological struggle against globalization and imperialism to be waged largely on the cultural front. The *Batalla* was formulated by Fidel Castro at the closing of the 1997 Congress of the Union of Communist Youth to encompass five specific struggles: against U.S. imperialism, against economic crisis, for the freedom of five spies incarcerated in the United States, for peace, and for culture and education. Over 150 specific programs were subsequently developed under these different categories. See: http://www.monografias.com/trabajos16/jose-marti-ideas/jose-marti-ideas.shtml (accessed July 20, 2006).
4. Carneado (1986), Hennessy (1963), Fagen (1979), Hart (1983), Liss (1987), Medin (1990).

Multicubanidad   87

5. See Habermas (1989), Hutchinson (1992), Ong (2000), Verdery (1993), and Zhang (1998).
6. 1992 Constitution, Article 39.
7. Since 1980, Cuban Culture Day is celebrated every October 20. Established by Decree Law 74, it commemorates the liberation of the town of Bayamo by the troops of Carlos Manuel de Céspedes, on October 20, 1868, during the war of Independence. As they occupied the city, they sung a local song, *La Bayamesa*, which subsequently became Cuba's national anthem.
8. The first issue of a new intellectual journal, *Temas* (1, 1995), was devoted to this debate. While its director, Rafael Hernández, argued the centrality of revolutionary allegiance for Cuban nationalism, most other scholars emphasized culture as the element that could transcend ideology.
9. See, e.g., de la Torre (1995), Martín (1995), Martínez Heredia (1995), Ubieta Gómez (1993), and Valdés Bernal (1998).
10. For instance, in April, 1994, a special issue of the UNEAC's journal, *La Gaceta de Cuba* was devoted to Jorge Mañach, a conservative thinker who in the 1928 outlined the psychosocial traits that were part of the Cuban character. Likewise, Fernando Ortíz's anthropological writings were amply discussed; though in contrast, his multiple political commentaries, which expressed his liberal opinions, were not (Jorge Domínguez, personal communication 2000).
11. Also during this time, there was an opening toward other types of cultural diversity, including gay culture and identity. An examination of that aspect is beyond the scope of this essay. See, for instance, Emilio Bejel (2001) Gutiérrez Alea's internationally acclaimed film *Strawberry and Chocolate* brought attention to the new official position vis-à-vis homosexuality (see chapter 3, this volume; see also Quiroga 2000). Cuban-American author Emilio Bejel was on the jury of the 1997 Casa de las Americas award to U.S. Latino literature, which went to a Cuban-American author for a novella featuring gay and lesbian erotic affairs (Rivero-Valdés 1997). In Havana the book sold out immediately.
12. I am a cofounder of that newsgroup and a witness to the test's collaborative development and dissemination.
13. See, e.g., Padura Fuentes (1994), Fowler (1996), and Knauer (1997). Knauer's article on New York City rumba in *Temas* was in many ways pioneering in bringing to light the existence of just as "authentic" Cuban culture in the United States.
14. The meeting was sponsored by the University of Havana's Center for the Study of Political Alternatives (a think tank dedicated to study "the Cuban community abroad") and the Union of Writers and Artists (UNEAC). I was a visiting student at the University of Havana at the time, and it took a lot of pleading to be allowed to audit the sessions, which were by strict invitation only.
15. For instance, see García (1995).
16. For instance, in 1999, the state press Letras Cubanas published an anthology of Cuban poetry, which included exiled poets known for their vocal opposition to the Castro regime (Ferrer 2000). Just as unprecedented was the naming of a youth literary award after a literary character of the silenced writer Reinaldo Arenas. See http://lajiribilla-habana.cuba.cu/2001/n1_abril/015_1.html (accessed November 4, 2006). (I owe these two points to Jorge Ferrer.)
17. See, e.g., Padura Fuentes's 1994 article on exiled bass player Israel López "Cachao."

18. See Behar (1994) and Torres (2001).
19. Ana López (1996) used the term "Greater Cuba" in a similar way, in the context of chronicling expatriate Cuban filmmaking. López, however, still reproduced the dualistic model of island versus exile.
20. Between 1997 and 2002, the collective issued a periodic *samizdat* publication, printed abroad but distributed within the island, and which included Cuban and foreign writers who were banned from the state presses, such as Guillermo Cabrera Infante, Lorenzo Garcia Vega, Milan Kundera, and Hans-Magnus Enzensberger. The magazine also included images by underground artists both from the island and in exile, as well as miscellaneous essays by foreign theorists on the relation between intellectuals and the state, often with regard to the Eastern European and Soviet experiences. *Diáspora(s)*, like the other projects mentioned, was short-lived. The magazine was banned and its editors, often subjected to police harassment, finally migrated to Europe (Pedro Marqués de Armas, personal communication, July 30, 2006, and Carlos A. Aguilera, personal communication, July 30, 2006 and March 2, 2007).
21. See, e.g., Pérez Rivero (1998).
22. Like many other cultural festivals, this one began in 1988 during the Rectification Process but only gained in participation and media exposure throughout the 1990s.
23. See, e.g., Oliva Alicea (1998).
24. See, e.g., Perez Sarduy and Stubbs (1993, 2000).
25. Established artists like Manuel Mendive and Eduardo Roca Salazar "Choco" now received international attention. Many younger artists explored Afro-Cuban religious elements, like Belkis Ayón, Alexis Esqivel, and Roberto Diago. In music, the band *Sintesis* pioneered a fusion of rock and Afro-Cuban chants in the 1980s, acquiring a quasi-mythical status during the 1990s. Other musicians, like Nueva Trova singer Gerardo Alfonso, a "dreadlock" pioneer, used their song lyrics to expose racial prejudice. For instance, his 1991 *Tetas Africanas* (African Breasts) denounced the exoticization of blackness as a form of neocolonialism, while his 1994 reggae piece *Dicen* (They Say) protested the marginalization of blacks and their stereotyping as good runners, popular musicians, and thieves.
26. See Fernández Robaina (1990).

6

Preemptive Nostalgia and *La Batalla* for Cuban Identity: Option Zero Theater

Laurie Frederik

New artistic genres and styles are often born when a society is undergoing crisis and traumatic transformation; when desperate times force artistic minds to bend a philosophy, to adapt to the new social, political, or economic situation, and to paint a picture of reality from different angles. In theater and performance this type of creative surge is especially apparent, given the immediacy and ephemeral nature of the medium. Cuba's moments of political, social, and economic crisis have been frequent, and thus, theater has never fallen short of polemic or paradox. In Cuba, theater is an art that is said to live permanently in crisis. From the so-called Gray Years (1968–1976) to the Special Period in the 1990s, crises have provided artists with critical impulses. Diana Taylor (1991: 20) describes crisis as "the inchoate, confusing, contradictory nature of the transition (...) the turning point between life and death, regeneration and repression," and adds that the concept of crisis "represents a suspension, a rupture between two states." She then defines the accompanying "theater of crisis" as dialectical, exposing "the integrating theatricality of the social setting, the political shams and the rhetoric of legitimation that authority figures use to pacify the public" (ibid.).

In the Special Period, theatrical performance and artistic representation provide a rich milieu from which to look at how contemporary Cubans interpret and deal with crisis and social transformation, for it reveals dialogue, paradox, and contradiction at every level of production, effectively reflecting the complexity of the situation at hand. And in turn, as it is well known among the artists themselves, crisis drives creativity and gives social urgency and political meaning to art. The rupture-producing crisis between two states of perceived tranquility opens up a space for new meaning-making, as well as for the reinterpretation or recontextualization of old meanings. Since the Revolution, Cuba has been in a perpetual state of self-defined crisis, of *lucha* (struggle), and ideologically, this crisis is partially what has fueled the defensive stance so pervasive in the rhetoric of daily life.[1] Within the ongoing *lucha* are moments of intensity—moments that test the loyalty and endurance of the Cuban people. This article describes the creative bursts that emerged during heightened social stress and the ways in which the society has responded and attempted to reconcile the "breach" in the social drama.

Economic crisis in Cuba has led to an ideological crisis, one that questions belief in the viability of the socialist project. Once based on modernization and development, the events of 1989 altered the assumed trajectory of Cuban history. Cuban intellectuals returned to a national identity rooted in heritage and culture; a culture that included expressive and artistic manifestations as well as the routines of everyday life (see chapter 5, this volume). The Cuban state began to aggressively promote a *batalla* (battle) to defend its identity and to "rescue" cultural traditions thought to be its key components from the imperial enemy—an enemy that was no longer depicted solely by an antagonistic United States, but something that was broader, more evasive, and thus, more dangerous. The Cuban State sought to defend "true" Cuban culture from its perceived threat, and intellectuals were to have a crucial role.

Over the years, Fidel Castro has repeatedly reminded artists and intellectuals that they were responsible for the moral development of the country and the healthy maintenance of *Cubanía* (Cuban-ness). In 2000, Castro repeatedly proclaimed, "without culture, there is no development," while he reminded members of the National Union of Artists and Writers (UNEAC) that Cuba was immersed in a battle for spiritual literacy, and that they, as cultural specialists, were to combat neoliberal globalization: "Not long ago, we were terrorized when trying to figure out how we could save our identity. It is no longer a defensive fight, rather, a counter-attack. Culture has no value in itself, but rather as a formidable instrument of liberation and justice. This is the way to inculcate ideas and concepts."

However, what true Cuban culture was remained in a state of negotiation and flux, argued primarily amongst cultural officials, writers, artists, and other scholars, who championed the need to locate and rescue true *Cubanía* and the *pura cepa* (pure roots, stock) of Cuban culture. But true *Cubanía* and *pura cepa* were elusive concepts at a time of economic crisis and ideological change, agitated by a growing spread of global popular culture. A dialogue began about precisely which aspects of Cuban culture should be represented and maintained and which practices should be used to ward off external contamination. Urban residents claimed that Havana was the core of Cuban culture and that the countryside was "just scenery," while rural *campesinos* claimed precisely the opposite. Which was the "real" Cuba—country or city? Globalization notwithstanding, the search for pure *Cubanía* was already a complicated endeavor even within its own national boundaries.

Preemptive Nostalgia

Many of the preferred traditions thought to be particularly "Cuban," according to state intellectuals and officials, were characteristic of the rural peasant or *campesino* (rural peasant, farmer)—pure and humble, still unsullied, and often geographically isolated in rural areas. Many of the Cuban *campesinos* had played important roles in the history of the Cuban Revolution, not only fighting alongside the guerrillas, but also feeding and hiding them, risking their own and their families' lives. Following the Revolution, the initial successes of Cuba's agricultural transformation and the massive literacy movement were most apparent in the rural populations, which were largely destitute and uneducated before 1959. Therefore, the ideal *campesino* was not modeled on the *first* Cuban *campesino*, but rather, on the first *socialist campesino*—an image produced by early revolutionary crusades for literacy, education, and agricultural reform, which turned individual farmers into collective farm workers. When this particular prototype came into play on theatrical stages, in storytelling, and on painter's canvases, it was blended with individual creativity and artistic interpretation, which in turn channeled ideas back into the official versions of the ideal *campesino* as propagandized by the state.

In the 1990s, embodiment, enactment, and representation refashioned the twenty-first-century *campesino* into a modern Cuban image. Practitioners of community theater (Teatro Comunitario) revived a certain image of the Cuban *campesino* and its *pura cepa*. That is, these artists were rekindling the romance of rural culture and its traditions, and inserting them into an idyllic perception of what Cuban identity and the Cuban soul embodied. This idealized *campesino* did not desire expensive items or money and did not criticize the state. He was faithful to the Revolution, willing to fight to defend its honor and to continue to embody its values. He loved the land, hummed *son montuno* (variation of son music from the mountains) as he walked home from a hard day's work, and was serenely unaffected by the economic and ideological *batalla* occurring in the cities.

Nostalgia for the rural has been a long-standing trope in the development of Latin American identity: resisting colonization, cultural imperialism, and globalization through promoting the image of the humble and the authentic native, yet simultaneously wanting to appear progressive and modern. What was distinct in the Cuban case was that this nostalgic yearning was not simply nostalgia. It was not an issue of loss in need of recovery, but a reaction against the impending threat of loss.

Faced with the fall of the socialist block, the withdrawal of Soviet funding, the Special Period, the tightening of the U.S. blockade, and the subsequent opening to new capitalist markets, the Cuban government's reaction was not merely one of melancholy and longing, but one of self-righteous fortitude and a determination to endure. The counterattack was preemptive in nature and called up all its citizens to take part—not necessarily by giving up their urban lifestyles and hoeing fields themselves, but by buying into the mythology presented by cultural workers and the media. This defensive sentiment was directly imposed onto the Cuban population itself, especially in intellectual circles, where members were considered responsible for the expression and representation of the nation, as well as for the reproduction of its token symbols and metaphors.

Television, radio, and billboards, as well as a growing number of national conferences and cultural events disseminated a resurgent imagery of old men with straw hats playing *décimas* (rural musical form), while the media celebrated the accomplishments of provincial farmers in the Cuban countryside.[2] Actors and performers became a new revolutionary army or modern *brigadistas* (brigade members), setting out on crusades to find and rescue the noble *campesinos*, to remind them of their national value, of their pure souls, and of the national importance of maintaining a humble lifestyle. Performance groups emerged to represent and rescue the *campesino*, deploying a romantic imagery inspired by the Cuban countryside. In the process, they made a name for themselves in professional theater, won regional and national awards, and secured resources from the State for their exemplary revolutionary work.

One must question whether this cultural movement was really a nostalgic attempt to repossess the past, as it first appeared, or was it rather an attempt to construct some kind of imaginary, metaphysical "real"—an officially sanctioned *bricolage* of past and future, of all the most distinctive and desirable social attributes that state officials sought to preserve? By examining theater groups in rural Cienfuegos and Guantánamo, I researched how the conditions of the Special Period, along with notions of *crusade* and *rescue*, motivated and guided the development of theater projects and how the cultural politics of Cuba's past and present influenced the creative process. As the capitalist market became an inescapable influence in the late 1990s, I looked at how the commercialization of the Special Period's paucity turned into profit and created a predicament that even the most devout revolutionary could not resist.

New Cuba, New Man, New Theater

The evolution of contemporary Cuban theater has hinged on five pivotal historical moments in history, each moment propelling cultural policy along a distinct path, and each contributing to the role of theater in Cuban society. The 1959 Revolution initiated the sequence, at which point the drive for education and progressive development, especially in an underdeveloped countryside, created a national subject based on socialist politics. Artists and performers were given a prominent status in the new society and were promised full support, including playwrights and theater groups, as long as their art remained within the confines of revolutionary ideology. In 1961, Fidel Castro uttered the famous words: "Within the Revolution, everything Against the Revolution, nothing," which set the tonal boundaries of creative freedom under socialism. In the early years, most theatrical productions were modeled after European and Latin American classics—the proscenium stage intact. Social polemics and confrontational jabs at the system were not necessarily innovative in theatrical style. Yet a new social goal had been initiated: the development of a "revolutionary consciousness," a political concept that would dominate state propaganda and artistic creation for the next 40 years. Cooperation, sacrifice, struggle, political loyalty, and dedication to revolutionary narratives became the backbone of national identity and revolutionary metaphors permeated ideological and popular discourse—in large part through their integration into theater and art.

A new theatrical movement, called *Teatro Nuevo* (New Theater), emerged in the late 1960s during the crisis of the Gray Years. Cuban society was undergoing drastic renovation, as Che Guevara's concept of the *Hombre Nuevo* (New Socialist Man) was being built into the growing revolutionary consciousness. Cuban artists took on a privileged role in national politics when a small group of highly reputable actors and playwrights from Havana ventured out into the Escambray mountains to form a type of theater that was new in Cuba—one using anthropological methods to gather information about local culture, and giving voice to a previously unrepresented population, the *guajiro* (hillbilly), or in more acceptable postrevolutionary terminology, the *campesino*. The method privileged the audience and was more concerned with dialogue than with a finished, dramatic product and text.[3]

This vanguard group, called *Teatro Escambray* (Escambray Theater), intended to "cultivate" the *campesinos*, to expose them to professional theater, music, and the arts, and show the importance of their voice in public discourse. The actors remained in the Escambray Mountains for several months, interviewing and learning about the perspectives of the area *campesinos*, and ultimately wrote a play informed by their collected accounts. Their first and most famous play, *La Vitrina* (The Showcase), in 1971, discussed the pros and cons of the incorporation of *arrendamiento*, a form of collective farming at one point introduced by the new revolutionary state. The play was groundbreaking in its method, and illustrated how theater could be used to educate and empower. *Teatro Escambray* wrote the *campesino* into national scripts, and subsequently, into the national dialogue.

By calling its method *Teatro Nuevo*, or new theater, Grupo Escambray aligned itself with Guevara's idea of the *Hombre Nuevo* (new man) and the burgeoning national ideology. Their method inspired other theater groups. Flora Lauten, one of Escambray's founding members, began her own *Teatro Nuevo* group in the early 1970s, called *Teatro La Yaya* (Theater of La Yaya), and another Escambray alumnus, Albio Paz, founded *Teatro*

Acero (Steel Theater), a group formed within a Havana steel factory. Likewise, in Santiago de Cuba, the *Cabildo Teatral* (Cabildo Theater) produced plays about Afro-Cuban culture and social issues. Such *Teatro Nuevo* groups became models of revolutionary theater as well as blueprints for bringing illiterate *campesinos* and other marginalized populations into the public sphere as conscious political subjects. Cultivating once illiterate and unworldly populations and transforming them into socialist subjects saturated the motivations of many of these ensembles.

For the next 20 years, Cuban theater prospered. Urban theater was very different from *Teatro Nuevo* and community theater projects, but all theater remained an important aspect of socialist education and communication. With ticket prices costing a mere one peso (10 U.S. cents or less), anyone could attend a performance, and not just the wealthy.

The Special Period and Option Zero Theater

After the fall of the socialist bloc and the loss of billions of dollars in aid from the Soviet Union in 1989, Fidel Castro warned the Cuban people of the difficulties to come. Even more frightening than the predicted hardships was the regime's plan for the potential occurrence of a total blockade and aggressive attack of the United States. This last-resort strategy was named *Opción Cero* (Zero Option). *Opción Cero* called for a total evacuation of the urban areas and a retreat to the countryside. Without fuel, there would be no electricity, transportation, or communication, and the population would be forced to live entirely off the land and its natural resources. People were told it would be a truly revolutionary situation. Just like the original guerrilla fighters from the Revolution, they would sacrifice everything and fight for the *Patria*.

Although the plan was never published in state newspapers or mentioned in Fidel Castro's speeches, rumor and gossip worked their magic throughout the country and *Opción Cero* became a mythological "what if?". Years later, Cuban residents still spoke of Option Zero with unease, and in 2005, one theater group produced a play reenacting the national anxiety of the era. Luckily, Cuba never had to resort to *Opción Cero*, although it did slip into a distinctly "special period." With an extreme scarcity of resources, many cultural traditions and artistic endeavors were set aside, were considered peripheral to daily survival—especially when the last remaining spotlight burned out, the last canvas and paints were used up, and strings for musical instruments had deteriorated and snapped.

In mountain *pueblos* (villages), many *campesino* traditions were abandoned, such as the *corrida de cinta* (skill activity with horses), the *palo de grasa* (greased pole climbing), baseball games, cockfights, and the *altares de cruz* (altar of the cross rituals). Amateur musical and theater group activities were also suspended, since *campesinos* were too busy just trying to survive. Their days began before dawn, working fields with ox-driven plows, caring for farm animals, washing clothes in the river, and collecting wood for cooking. A hurricane in the early 1990s destroyed the meager crops that had initially made the countryside a potentially better place to live during the crisis. Cultural traditions were further threatened when many rural youth fled to the cities, or fled the island altogether. Urban residents joked about the rural migrants flocking to Havana; police from *Oriente* (eastern Cuba) were teased for their ignorance of city ways and were disrespected behind their backs—perceived as uneducated hillbillies who could be easily fooled and eluded. The geographical exodus was said to cause a threat to *campesino* identity and empathy; a threat to *campesinos'* common *alma de guajiro* (*guajiro* soul or soul of the land). Rural communities dwindled in number and the mountains retreated into a more profound silence than ever before.

Yet, just as some traditions appeared to be dying out, a new one was rising up from within the crisis. In the early 1990s, a new type of theater emerged with a method and philosophy that was directly shaped by the economic predicament. This new theater rekindled the model of *Teatro Escambray*; its mission was to bring theater to the community and to utilize local people in its creation. However, instead of a radical transformation of political consciousness and a shift to socialist modernity, this theater and its *teatristas* (theater people) sought to preserve the old, to rescue dying traditions, and to restore a sense of beauty and spirituality into the lives of the Cuban people. In the countryside, they searched for the *pura cepa* of *Cubanía*, for the noble inner core of the Cuban soul, still optimistic about the future of their struggling society. The new theater to emerge looked very much like the *Teatro Nuevo* of the 1960s and 1970s, which, except for *Teatro Escambray*, had died out completely by 1984 (Martin 1994). To avoid a dated reference, the revival was loosely called *Teatro Comunitario* (communitarian theater).

"Theater for the community, in the community, and by the community" became the mantra of *Teatro Comunitario*, echoing similar cries in popular theaters throughout Latin America. As expressed by a member of one of these new groups, *La Cruzada Teatral*, "Art for art's sake is ridiculous. The artist has to live and laugh with his community. He has to leave behind the bouquet of flowers and jump into the waist-high mud."[4] Indeed, *Teatro Comunitario* was celebrated as a moral contribution to the Revolution at a time of crisis, touting the values of cooperation and the value of the artistic experience for both actor and audience. Its style also fit in with the logistical restrictions of the economic crisis. Like *Teatro Nuevo* years before, *Teatro Comunitario* groups often took their theater out to marginal areas where residents had little or no access to formal cultural performance. Anthropological investigation supplied information and inspiration for their productions, and local residents acted in the productions. Unlike *Teatro Nuevo*, these ensembles were subject to the scarcity, pessimism, and desperation of the Special Period, yet their artistic zeal precisely originated from these very hardships.

Teatro Comunitario often focused nostalgically on what was fading away, celebrating the humble and uncontaminated elements of Cuban culture, and privileging the role of rural dwellers in the rebuilding of the Cuban spirit. The primary character in such representations was the *campesino* as yet untouched by the contaminants of the urban "areas of consumption" and the growing obsession with dollars. While *Teatro Nuevo* in the 1970s sought to showcase the *campesino*'s transformation and progression into the *Hombre Nuevo*, the *Teatro Comunitario* that emerged during the Special Period aspired to safeguard and preserve the old, the traditional, and the unchanging ways found in rural Cuba. *Teatro Comunitario* groups aspired to "rescue" the *campesinos*—not from their primitive lives in the countryside, rather from the modern contaminants that threatened to change them. Producers of *Teatro Comunitario* did not want to showcase the modernization of the *campesinos*; they wanted to defend their distinct identity and protect their long-standing traditions.

Teatro Comunitario groups were considered "professional" according to Ministry of Culture guidelines. They worked in both urban and rural areas, but they were considered the more "authentic," the more remote their location. These groups were determined to bring theater to the farthest reaches of the island, to those isolated places where *campesinos* still lived off the land and had no reliable electricity, radio signal, or transportation: in short, where an implementation of *Opción Cero* would not have required any change from their daily lives and where the theater project itself embodied the return to the supposed simplicity and primacy of nature. Rural *Teatro Comunitario* groups searched for "virgin" audiences that could provide them with an organic appreciation of the cultural spirituality and enlightenment they had to offer, away from critical and elitist intellectuals in the cities who would bemoan their lack of cultural refinement, or far from ordinary theater-goers, burdened by their own hardships (lack of transport to theater space, frequent blackouts) and popular expectations of "good" entertainment.

Approximately six of the most "authentic" theater groups emerged in 1991.[5] These groups embodied the spirit of the Special Period, and, to a great extent, *Opción Cero*, as their projects were fueled and inspired by the very scarcity that waylaid so many others. Sacrifice and selflessness defined their artistic mission, and the harsh conditions defined the reason for their existence. From the broader category of *Teatro Comunitario*, this smaller cohort, which I call "Option Zero Theater," was the focus of my research. After several years of fieldwork, I defined the criterion for an Option Zero Theater group along three axes. First, the group should have retreated to or resided in rural areas of difficult access (also called "zones of silence") as part of their working philosophy or principle. Second, they should embrace the scarcity and hardship and join together to spread theater, storytelling, and music to isolated communities, otherwise without access to artistic endeavors. And finally, they should follow the *Teatro Escambray* model—utilizing some form of social investigation with the local community and communicating the perspectives of those people. In the small town of Cumanayagua in Cienfuegos Province, I worked with the group *Teatro de los Elementos* (Theater of the Elements). In Guantánamo I worked with three different groups: *La Cruzada Teatral* (The Theater Crusade), *El Laboratorio de Teatro Comunitario* (Laboratory of Teatro Comunitario), and *Grupo de Lino Alvarez Realengo 18* (Lino Alvarez Theater Group of Realengo 18). *Teatro de los Elementos* will be highlighted here, since it was the most established and dedicated to returning to the land, and focused on the representation of what they believed to be the essential core of *Cubanía*.

Teatro de los Elementos: Theater of the Elements

Teatro de los Elementos comprised six actors and a director. It was located in a village called Cumanayagua, just one hour south of the artistic commune of the famed *Teatro Escambray*, in the foothills of the Escambray Mountains. *Los Elementos* worked with the local *campesinos*, collectively wrote original plays, and then brought the finished product to stages in larger cities, such as Cienfuegos, Santa Clara, and Havana. Actors also produced solo pieces and children's plays, which were performed locally. The group's director, José Oriol González, aspired to reinvigorate *Teatro Escambray*'s model and reformulate it according to Special Period conditions. José Oriol would proudly tell the history of *Los Elementos*—to reporters, theater critics, and foreign investigators—describing it as a tradition created through hardship, without resources, and necessarily returning to the purest elements of human existence. "The Elements" referred to water, air, earth, and fire, and were considered to be the foundation as well as the transcendence of sociality and politics.

In 1990, José Oriol began the group by taking several of his students at Havana's National Art School to a marginal neighborhood called Romerillo. There, the actors paraded through the *barrio* on stilts, dancing and singing, using patios and homes, and engaging the neighbors in the performances. Taken away from the daily drudgery of finding food, washing their clothes by hand, cooking over kerosene stoves, and waiting long hours for buses in the blistering Caribbean sun, the Romerillo residents were transformed, and, according to José Oriol, their spiritual selves were vivified in the midst of the crisis. The group continued to work in Romerillo for four months, slowly gaining the trust of community members, working with local children, and getting to know the problems and particular concerns of the locale. They performed for Romerillo musically, acrobatically, in short skits, monologues, always incorporating the particular flavor of the neighborhood, its legends and its personalities, using masks, costuming, fantastical imagery, and metaphor. In January of 1992, then minister of culture Armando Hart attended one of the performances. With Hart's subsequent support, José Oriol and his actors were finally considered "serious" and were approved to receive state funds and be officially recognized as a professional theater group. Now they were trusted not only by the community, but also by the authority that had the power to either promote or destroy their efforts.

Throughout the 1990s, *Teatro de los Elementos* prided itself on its ability to make theater in a time of extreme scarcity. The group was proud to infuse a new sense of beauty and cultural identity into a tired nation. Members discussed the unique disposition of the group as collective—one in which members worked together, without hierarchy, each with equal power and voice. In the absence of the technology that theater groups typically depend upon, they developed a working philosophy based on a nostalgic yearning for living off the earth and the representative image of a noble *campesino*. They performed in outside spaces, in forest clearings, on the rocky ocean banks, on grassy hills, and on front porches of the *bohios* (huts) of the *campesinos*. They spoke of the purity of the Cuban soul as one that was "uncontaminated" by the banality of the outside world.

In 1999, the *Los Elementos* traveled to an area in the Escambray Mountains called Hanabanilla, which had once been home to a *pueblo* called Siguanea. Siguanea's land was purchased by a Canadian-American hydroelectric company in 1958 and inundated by a man-made lake. The members of *Los Elementos* went to investigate the life and culture of Siguanea's previous inhabitants, still residing in the hills above the lake after having been forced to relocate 40 years before. I lived with *Los Elementos* in Cumanayagua, traveled with them to the mountains, and took part in the creative process of this new play.[6] Four months of interviews and information gathering in Siguanea and other rural areas resulted in heated theoretical discussions about *campesino* identity in contemporary Cuba and long nights of improvisations and rehearsals. The actors discussed whether the *campesinos* living in Hanabanilla were "real" or "*nuevo*" (new) *campesino*s. *Nuevos campesinos* had at one point been given rural land in an attempt to attract urban Cubans to move back to the countryside. According to the actors of *Los Elementos*, they were *campesino* in appearance, but they had been contaminated by living in the city and did not have the same "pure soul" as those who had always lived there. They knew how to "hustle" and thus had "capitalist hearts."

What eventually emerged from the creative process of investigation, research, discussion, improvisation, and script writing, was a mystical, romantic play about the lost village and the beauty of *campesino* culture. The play was named *Ten mi nombre como un sueño* (Remember my name as if a dream), taken from a *décima* line sung to us one afternoon by an eighty year-old *campesino* named Macías. In the play, the actors represented both the community's past and present, revealing the conflicted relationship between them in their attempts to recover the memory of the lost town. The story's moral was that their generation (born post-1959) should not forget or forsake their true heritage. Director José Oriol González explained that inundation was the fundamental metaphor of the play, representing "a submerged land, and the people that remain, without a soul, wandering." For him, Siguanea was a metaphor for the whole of Cuba and the imminent "inundation" of its distinctive culture. It was a symbol for what Cuba would become if it surrendered to the flood of globalization, and warned of the *desarraigo* (uprooting, sense of being lost or out of place) that threatened to ensue.[7]

The play showed Cuba as a dream, a fading dream that had to be revived and made real. It was presented on stage with muted and fanciful lighting, live *guajiro* music, guitar, *guiro* (a percussion instrument), and flute. In Siguanea, as in previous projects in Romerillo and rural Santiago de Cuba, *Teatro de los Elementos* had set out to rescue a set of disappearing traditions—disappearing, but still within reach of salvation. It was believed that the natural soul of the pure Cuban resided in these quiet and uncontaminated areas, which, with effort and determination, could be protected. José Oriol stressed the necessity of "returning to the land" in two senses: physically, becoming self-sufficient during the crisis of the Special Period, and metaphorically, returning to the land as the symbolic roots of Cuban identity. However romantic and utopian this return to nature was, its actual sustainability was a more difficult endeavor. After several years, the actors, like the rest of the Cuban population, were tired of living with extreme daily hardships, and producing theater under such conditions was even more of a strain. When the U.S. dollar was legalized and foreigners began to visit the country, expectations began to change.

Cultural Front Lines: The Massification of Culture

By the late 1990s, the extraordinary enthusiasm Fidel Castro originally incited for *La Revolución* was wearing thin, and traditional keywords such as sacrifice, struggle, and *Patria o Muerte* (Fatherland or Death) were no longer sufficient to rouse national patriotism and solidarity. "Culture" became a renewed focal point for *Cubanía*—an alternative beacon of faith to take up the slack left by a political ideology once buttressed by a superpower—the USSR—but now left virtually alone in the world. Quotes by Lenin and Marx were replaced with those of the nation's most famous nationalist and poet, José Martí, and upholding favored cultural traditions became akin to political allegiance. As one cultural critic stated: "It is not gratuitous that Cubans grant culture a place of preeminence in the middle of such hard times. To defend culture is to defend what we are. What we were. And what we will be" (Sánchez 2000). Responding to the new threat to Cuba's cultural integrity, Abel Prieto, the minister of culture since 1998, along with Fidel Castro and other prominent intellectuals, condemned the production and consumption of "pseudo-culture" and professed the need to protect the *pura cepa* from its capitalist invaders. Speeches to UNEAC members and conference attendees, as well as discussions on television roundtables, put the idea into both intellectual and popular discourse.

A turning point in the discussion was marked (as is much of recent Cuban history) by one of Fidel Castro's speeches. Once again addressing UNEAC, Castro (2000) announced the implementation of a new campaign called the Massification of Culture, "a crusade to expand the population's cultural horizons," especially in the most secluded places on the island. The campaign provided support for artistic groups to travel and perform more extensively around the island. It also promised to reopen the Schools for Art Instructors, which had been closed down, and to provide much needed supplies to the local *Casas de Cultura* (Houses of Culture). Abel Prieto (2000) described the Massification of Culture as a development program geared to avoid and confront the "avalanche of frivolity, foolishness, and fetishes" brought about by unethical market and mass communications practices typical of capitalism. At issue was the maintenance of "real values versus fictitious ones," and the fight against a pseudo-culture that was "banal," "frivolous," and "without history."

Coinciding with the Ministry of Culture's battle cry, artists' salaries doubled in 2000 and state money was pumped into a massive cultural mobilization or "massification of culture." Historically, official artists and intellectuals had been responsible for the dissemination of revolutionary consciousness and Cuban culture, and, therefore, it was only natural that they would resume their role of ideological educators during the latest crisis. Theater artists were to be especially important in this new campaign, since they were the least effected by the global market, unlike their colleagues in other arts. Cuban theater was a relatively unmarketable, un-exportable cultural medium, and thus was indispensable to the government's new national propaganda.

In this new campaign, the archetypical *campesino* was central. Now he was not solely a representation of the past, but was coupled with an eye on the future—on what he was to become after the teachings of the Massification of Culture campaign would take effect. The future *campesino* would be fully literate, educated and *culto* (cultivated). He would be able to recite Martí's poems by heart, read Cuban literature, play and appreciate both traditional and classical music, make and attend Cuban theater, use a computer (even in the zones of silence), and discuss international politics. Thus, the real *campesino* and the seed of the real Cuba was, in these views, a combination of past and future images.

The Massification of Culture campaign coincided perfectly with the objectives of *Teatro Comunitario*, and especially Option Zero Theater. While artists, in their ultimate quest for creativity and originality, were perturbed by the term "massification," they usually agreed with the underlying premise of the campaign. Certainly the common folk—the nonartists and nonintellectuals—believed the Massification of Culture to be a good cause, for the development of the project promised benefits for both performer and audience. Yet, the question remained: Who was distinguishing Cuba's "real values" and "worthwhile classics" and who would be the ones to perform them for the masses? Who would be writing the modern narrative—the *campesinos* themselves or the professional artists who had the microphones and were fully funded by the Cuban state?

From Zero Options to Many Options

A *campesino* revival in the popular imaginary and the cultural authority of *Teatro Comunitario* practitioners in Cuban politics were evidenced, in part, by television broadcasts showcasing *campesino* culture (including performance clips of Option Zero Theater groups), new national dance troupes highlighting *guajiro* styles (typically rural styles of music, dance, and costuming) in Havana theaters, and also in the increase of interviews sought from those artists now recognized as "cultural specialists." *Teatro Comunitario* was more popular than ever, although the scarcity that had once driven the movement was no longer so acute. In addition, as the artistic reputation of these artists grew, so did their demands and desires for recognition and material rewards. Rewards often consisted of better artistic support, better housing, rights to a telephone and car, and travel opportunities, as well as a higher position in the intellectual structure; one with a higher degree of cultural authority and status.[8] By 2000, Option Zero Theater had become a theater of many options. Like *Teatro Nuevo* decades earlier, *Teatro Comunitario* emerged during a particular crisis—the political economy creating a distinctive artistic imaginary that forged a new niche into Cuban history, but one that was likely to be destined to pass, or lay fallow until the next moment of social distress.

Some of these groups persevered, but abandoned their Option Zero characteristics. Themes of nature, tradition, authenticity, purity, scarcity, and sacrifice, which began as artistic premises and points of creative departure, were later used for political and economic gain, responding to the same stressful factors of the Special Period that had initially inspired its drive toward a nonmaterialistic purity. The return to the *pura cepa* ultimately became a marketing tool for soliciting additional state funds or to lure interested *extranjeros* (foreigners) who could help to fulfill their dreams. *La Cruzada Teatral*, based in a non-tourist-attracting location, was not marketable internationally, but they were able to secure thousands of dollars from national sources after winning an esteemed award for their devotion to the Revolution and for their *Teatro Comunitario* work. Actors, whose participation in local Guantánamo groups were otherwise forgotten and snubbed by prominent Havana intellectuals, were recognized as members of *La Cruzada* and thus were respected as artists with a national mission. Ecological groups and third-world development organizations from Canada and Europe became interested in the sustainable agriculture of *Los Elementos'* farm project and their focus on *la naturaleza* (nature). These same foreign groups would also eventually invite *Los Elementos* on a European tour and inadvertently seduce several of the group to emigrate, so that by 2003 only two of its original founding members remained. "*Somos un barco*" (We are a ship), José Oriol said, smiling sadly, after most of his group had "sailed abroad."[9] The group's fame, attained from their devotion to humility and socialist principles, had provided personal opportunities that tested their political convictions. Using the authentic native as the national tool of resistance was proving a precarious project in Cuba. Ironically, the very thing that Option Zero Theater represented—the local and the *pura cepa*—was what sold best on the global cultural market.

The Comedy and Tragedy of Twenty-First Century *Cubanía*

Cuban political ideology and the national imaginary is saturated with the classic dichotomy of purity and contamination, past (traditional) and present (modern), yet it is, in fact, a much more complicated, and often paradoxical scenario than it first appears. What was once the New Man—progressive and modern—is now obsolete, while the new ideal is an impossible fusion of humble austerity and cosmopolitan refinement. Community theater groups such as *Teatro Escambray* that first crusaded into the countryside to enlighten primitive and illiterate peasants, bringing modernity and progress, later reemerged as crusades to rescue a dying past, the same past the Revolution had once endeavored to transcend. Cuban artists cherished the *campesino* as virtuous and humble, but also criticized him as backward and brutish—in the end, still *inculto* (uncultivated)—even as he represented Cuban nationality.

The preservation of a particular heritage is partly in the hands of these official culture producers, who strive for innovation and individuality in their work while also feeling responsibility and loyalty to the national collective. As Nestor García Canclini (1995: 110) has stated, "[T]he dramatization of the patrimony is the effort to simulate that there is an origin, a founding substance, in relation with which we should act today." Yet what that patrimony is inevitably changes over time in any social context. In Cuba, the actual dynamic of this process became evident as intellectuals negotiated what true patrimony was and what was included in its "repertory of symbolic goods." Both modernizers and Traditionalists combined forces during the Special Period to teach the noble, and now famous, *campesino* the contemporary version of *campesino-hood* in order to fulfill his new national role. The successful theater groups must prove that they have played a part in the campaign for national cultivation—a cultivation based on a kind of preemptive nostalgia for a figure supposedly dying out, yet paradoxically one that never really existed.

Teatro comunitario, or more specifically, Option Zero Theater, may be considered a "theater of crisis," but in Cuba, artists cannot unveil the political sham or undermine its rhetoric without risking their livelihood and their freedom. Instead, the theater and its *teatristas* appropriate politics and use it to their own end in a more subtle and sometimes unconscious act of subversion. The State welcomes artists' apparent revolutionary loyalty and dedication to maintaining the integrity of socialist morality, while many in the population still want to believe that such a simple form of beauty and humility exists in confrontation with the hardships they endure 18 years after the onset of the Special Period. There is both a public and private mask, which must be maintained.

What remains to be seen is where the next *batalla* will lead the Cuban people and Cuban artists who represent them. When nostalgia can no longer bolster up, or hold back, the troops, where will Cuba turn? And how will its artists respond? Perhaps the preemptive battle to save *Cubanía* will be victorious (as in the motto *Hasta la victoria siempre*, till victory forever), and the crisis will someday end, but it is also possible that the wishful *hasta* (until) will be forever instilled into Cuba's nationalist battle cry.

Notes

1. For writings on the development of Cuba's consciousness of struggle (in Spanish: "lucha") see Guevara (1968), Fagen (1979), and Bunck (1994).
2. Although *campesino* imagery was not new in Cuba, it always had an important part in cultural and identity discourses, as evidenced, in part, by a long-standing television program called *Palmas y Cañas* (Palm Trees and Sugarcane), which showcases rural and traditional culture through music, dance, and performance. However, a distinct resurgence of the *campesino* image in the 1990s was displayed in new forms and with increased intensity, especially in the theater.
3. Methods of social investigation included interviews, collection of narratives, participant observation, and extended residence with subjects of study. *Teatro Nuevo* and *Teatro Comunitario*, also known as the "theater of conscientization" or Latin American Popular Theater, was blossoming in many Latin American countries in the late 1960s and 1970s, largely stemming from the work of Brazilian educator, Paulo Freire (*The Pedagogy of the Oppressed*, 1970), and later applied to theater

by fellow Brazilian Augusto Boal (*The Theater of the Oppressed*, 1985). See also de Costa (1992), Weiss (1993), and Risk (1987).
4. Emilio Pérez, *La Cruzada Teatral*, Maisi, Guantánamo. Interview with author.
5. This number of so-called authentic groups changes—depending on which institution or cultural official is judging the level of authenticity. *El Consejo Nacional de Artes Escénicas* (National Theater Board) had six professional *Teatro Comunitario* groups listed in its 2000 statistics.
6. See Frederik (2000 and 2005) on the group's creative process.
7 Jose Oriol González. Interview with author, Cumanayagua 1999
8. Professional actors are tested and categorized on levels from one to four, level one being the highest and thus best paid. Level One actors were making more than medical doctors in 2000, as the State increased salaries of police and artists before those of other professions.
9. José Oriol González. Interview with author, 2003.

7

Wandering in Russian

Jacqueline Loss

A brief anecdote sets the stage for future investigations: It was in 2001 when I accompanied a Cuban colleague who lived in the United States and his Spanish-speaking Russian wife to the Old Havana home of a couple of his friends who remained on the island, a theater critic and a painter.[1] After a bit of rum, the linguistic world switched to Russian and in the last thirty or so minutes of the dinner, I was left out; there was laughter and little translation. While the function of Russian was no longer vital to international transactions on the national sphere, I was not convinced that it was entirely useless. All four then reconciled their behavior, explaining to me that, in fact, they had in common this phenomenon of longing for certain elements of the Soviet Union, to which they had all traveled years before for the purposes of study. What had become clear to me was that although Russian was no longer the principal language of international affairs, it did function as a foil in my presence, and for these Cubans who were born in the 1940s and 1950s and had studied in the Soviet Union, that evening at least, Russian, if ever so slightly, continued to defend Cuba against *la yuma*.[2] Such a resort to Russian is complex. Cubans' memories of their experiences in the Soviet Bloc are often filled with disillusionment, and it is likely that the language switch that occurred at the gathering is wrought with that sensation.

Nostalgia for the Soviet Bloc is increasingly a force with which politicians, social scientists, and cultural critics contend. The ironic, pop-cultural film *Goodbye Lenin!* (2003), which tragicomically depicts a son's efforts to preserve the memories of his convalescing socialist mother, has become emblematic of this phenomenon that has many variants including the leftward political trends in Central and Eastern Europe and the business of selling Soviet and GDR memorabilia. The immense value inherent in recollection is a topic already being examined by post-Soviet memory studies.[3] However, one post–Cold War society whose collective memorialization of the Soviets that has hardly been considered is Cuba.

The way in which artists convert the leftovers of the Soviet Bloc into the experience of contemporaneity is poorly represented in sociopolitical categories and reports. Creative attempts at reckoning with the Cuban-Soviet union translate a very Cuban reality that escapes commitments to transitions. The collective filter of the world that the Soviet Union provided Cuba has disappeared, but just because the Soviet Union has disintegrated, does not mean it has departed from the imaginations of Cubans. In its very disintegration, the Soviet Union has begun to expand and morph in contemporary Cuban culture. In the absence of the material presence of the USSR, Cubans are referencing its traces. Those who studied in the Soviet Bloc possess an immediate, up-close inheritance that includes the Russian language. The cultural workers/politicians recast the Soviet legacy, isolating those elements that are most oppressive and bureaucratic while vindicating others.

For nearly three decades, the Soviet Union subsidized the island economically and intervened in military matters. In the wake of the Soviet Union's disintegration in 1991, food, electricity, and gasoline were scarce. Cuba faced the necessity for change: it revised paradigms of law, culture, and economy. In 1992, the Cuban Constitution was modified; references to Marx and Lenin were balanced by additional references to the Cuban national hero José Martí, and the phrase "fraternity with the Soviet Union" was erased. In 1993, the legalization of the dollar signaled the beginning of a dual economy. Amidst this social upheaval, it is not surprising that almost immediately after the Soviet Union's dissolution, many Cubans claimed to have inherited next to nothing from the Soviets. Many Cuban and foreign intellectuals blamed the revolution's most repressive measures on Soviet influence, while the majority of Cubans not only preferred U.S. music, but U.S. refrigerators, radio, and TV sets. Nevertheless, in the past decade, many Cuban writers and artists are beginning to account for the Soviet impact.

This is not to say that, in the aftermath of drastic food and petroleum shortages, most Cubans yearn for the USSR or for its offerings—rather that there exist many, largely parodic, reflections on this lost empire within political discourse, oral testimony, and artistic production. This chapter considers the sociopolitical and cultural residue of the Cuban-Soviet Bloc internationalist union within a yet-to-collapse authoritarian regime and how it metaphorically interrupts an apparently unidirectional flow of Cubans into a capitalist transition. Cuban writer Ernesto Hernández Busto (2006) speaks to the necessity of such a critical account:

> While the Cuban experience in the United States can count on various emblematic essays … Cubans' Russophilic experience awaits the essay that details the hidden spaces of this cultural shock and returns the "palavina" (in Russian, "medio": an appellative with which Cubans

described a hybrid being, originating from a Russian mother and Cuban father, or vice versa) his or her honor that was lost on account of Criollo chauvinism.[4]

In this regard, that which is so-called authentically homegrown or indigenous—*criollo*—contrasts with the artificial, superimposed Soviet realm, generally perceived by Cubans as unappealing. Hernández Busto counterposes such an examination of the Russian-Cuban to the Cubans' "natural" experience of hybridity coined by Gustavo Pérez Firmat (1994) as "life on the hyphen."

One of the only texts that directly engages this topic at any length is surprisingly not by a Cuban but by a North American. In Martin Cruz Smith's detective novel/quasi-anthropological study of transnationalism, *Havana Bay* (1999), the Russian detective Arkady Renko travels to Cuba to reckon with the mysterious death of a colleague, as well as the remains of the Soviet Union in Cuba. As a parallel to Smith's novel, the essay, "Lo que dejaron los rusos" (What the Russians Left), by the Cuban science-fiction writer, Yoss (2004), is a brief, nontheoretical compendium of Soviet traces within contemporary Cuban culture. With the exception of a few fascinating texts among which is *El diseño se definió en octubre* (1989, Design Was Defined in October), a reflective and prophetic work in which Gerardo Mosquera considers the integration of arts into society, from the standpoint of the experiences of the Russian avant-gardes as opposed to the didactic art characteristic of the 1960s, critics of the Special Period have yet to reveal a truly mixed bag of affirmation, disdain, critique, empathy, and yearning.[5] I contend that mining these traces serves to complicate our understanding of the *transition*, a term that generally focuses on Cuba in relation to its future; a future with the United States in a central position. It casts aside Cuba's past relationship with the Soviet Bloc, as well as Russia's and Cuba's current interest in each other, in the arts and economically. It is important to illuminate a triangle, rather than a linear path from Castroism to capitalism. Americanization and Sovietization need to be understood in relation to one another, as well as in relation to other spaces such as Cuba.[6]

Although Fidel Castro remains in power, now in his role as elder statesman, the last decade and a half in Cuba has been characterized by transformations that are discussed throughout the present collection. While the economist Javier Corrales (2004) has argued that Cuba's 1993–1996 opening of new sectors to direct foreign investment (FDI), liberalization of farm markets, legalization of the possession of U.S. dollars, and new forms of self-employment reforms were not exactly the onset of an across-the-board transition, but rather led to the rise of a gatekeeper state, there are many others who actively describe Cuba as living through a transition. The distinction between description and prescription is slight. Jorge I. Domínguez (2004) marks June 23, 1990 as the start of Cuba's economic transition when the

Political Bureau of the Cuban Communist Party declared that foreign investments and joint ventures did not clash with the socialist system. The extent to which the entire nation has since moved unilaterally toward both market economy and a consistent practice of individual rights (of the sort that the transition-makers desire) is debatable.

The culture industry articulates a different aspect of the debate. Some Cuban artists today are playing with the leftovers of the Soviet Bloc, and in so doing, they challenge the consequences of the life of this nation in "transition," by questioning the limits of an historically ideological authoritarianism and pervasive neoliberalism. While the panorama for this discussion of how Cubans speak to their nation's relationship to the Soviet Union is vast, this chapter focuses on four different expressions that are characterized by (1) what Svetlana Boym (2002) calls "restorative nostalgia," realized through the sociopolitical vindication of Russia's pre-Stalinist revolutionaries for the sustenance of the Cuban Revolution; (2) the necessity of Russian-Cuban biculturals documenting themselves; (3) the parodic gaze toward cultural importation from the Soviet Bloc in dialogue with U.S. popular culture; and (4) an artistic collage between Russians and Cubans, emphasizing, once again, Russia's pre-Stalinist revolutionaries.

We Don't Dance Like Russians!

News reports on the 2000 visit of Russian president, Vladimir Putin, the first to make a visit to Cuba since that of Mikhail Gorbachev in 1989, suggest that none of this other culture actually stuck. A Russian acquaintance who lived 13 years in Cuba stated: "Cubans and Russians are people with such different cultures and idiosyncrasies that their fusion was impossible and influence minimal." A Cuban similarly discounted the penetration: "Nothing remained, we don't dance like Russians, we don't eat like Russians, and we don't even drink vodka" (García-Zarza 2000). What these reports did dare to convey about the remains of the marriage were the number of Russian names on the island—Boris, Yuri, Vladimir, Aliuska, Niurka, and even Lenin; cautiously nostalgic declarations by Cubans of missing the good deals on products that they were sometimes able to swindle at the Russian stores; the Russian president's experience of speaking in his native tongue about literature with several Cuban representatives; the presence of Lourdes, the Soviet's electronic radar station that not even one year after Putin's visit had plans to be shut down.[7]

To imagine the day after—what will happen after Castro dies—perhaps we do not need to look so far. With the legalization of the dollar as a means to cope with the consequences of the collapse, a conspicuous simultaneity is enacted.[8] As Fowler-Calzada (2001b: 43) observes, the "after" to Fidel Castro's regime will resemble very little the experience of Germans after the collapse of the Berlin Wall in which "thousands of citizens of the East [were] walking through the streets of capitalism, contemplating, awed by the store-windows that were filled with things that they dreamed of or heard about but never saw." The dual economy has meant that Cubans grew accustomed to the appearance of capitalism. While, to a large extent, the urban space, until November 2004, was divided, according to dollarized and nationalized economies, the store-windows are visible to even those whose salaries cannot permeate their stocks.

These divisive economics take us back to the 1970s when, in the wake of the failure of the 10 million ton sugar harvest of 1970, Cuba relied more heavily on the Soviets. The Padilla Affair and the First Congress on Education and Culture in 1971, Cuba's entry into the Council for Mutual Economic Assistance (CMEA) in 1972, and Cuba's involvement in the liberation efforts in Algeria, Guinea Bissau, Zaire, the Congo, and Angola throughout the decade can be seen as markers of this Sovietization. Whether Cuba was acting out its own ideological motivations for internationalism or was a pawn of the Soviet Union in these battles is frequently debated.[9] The status of Cuba's trade relations with the Soviet Union combined with Cuba's brief and limited acceptance of entrepreneurship meant that, at least, at the beginning of the 1980s, the island was experiencing an economic wealth that it had not previously within the revolution. Thus, Cuba's current economic disinheritance from the Soviets can only be understood in light of the fact that the highpoint of Cuba's trade relations with the USSR was as recent as 1985 when "trade between the Soviet Union and Cuba reached almost 10 billion pesos" (Bain 2006: 4).

Soon after, with the arrival of glasnost and perestroika to the Soviet Union, Cuba stopped receiving Soviet newspapers and magazines as a means to sustain the ideological rhetoric of its revolutionary nationalism. As Castro introduced a period of Rectification in 1986, aimed at reestablishing the ideological purity of the nation, many were left stranded without the likes of Soviet media—*Novedades de Moscú*, *Tiempos nuevos*, and *Sputnik*—that had begun to serve Cubans as a guide through which to navigate their own difficulties and emerge on the other side, not necessarily within a transition toward democracy or capitalism, but actually within a reformed socialism. This moment in the media was intense, as described by George Black (1980: 378) in an article that appeared in *The Nation* in 1988: "[Cuban bookstores have] the sad look of dumping grounds for Progreso Publishers' remainders, with yellowing piles of old Bulgarian party statutes and textbooks on bovine tuberculosis, Gorbachev's book, *Perestroika*, also arrived in huge quantities and sold out in no time. The inability of the newsstands to keep *Novedades de Moscú* (Moscow News) in stock has become legendary."

Rubén Zardoya Loureda, a professor of Social Sciences in Havana, provides some rationale for this sentiment: "The influence of this media on Cuban public opinion turned out to be much more powerful than that exercised by hundreds of hours of counter-revolutionary radio propaganda that came to us from the U.S.A." (Zardoya Loureda 2002: 36). While Black's statement glamorizes decay and collapse, through its tragic tone, Zardoya Loureda's commentary reinforces the Soviets' ideological state apparatus for the purpose of encouraging Cubans to continue defending themselves in the face of Yankee aggression.

Such a gesture toward restoration cannot be viewed without also mentioning the sorts of obligations and policing representative of the 1970s, a decade that is characterized by the degree of oppression and pervasive Sovietization. A copy of a list of fifty-two slogans that Comités de Defensa de la Revolución (Committees of the Defense of the Revolution) were supposed to shout at manifestations in the 1970s were mimeographed by the diasporic writer Juan Abreu (2004: 1) to illustrate the extent of Sovietization experienced by Cubans. Five slogans on the list pertained directly to the Soviet Bloc: "Viva el invencible campo socialista" (Long live the invincible Socialist camp), "Viva la Flota Soviética" (Long live the Soviet Fleet), "Saludamos la Flota Soviética" (Let's salute the Soviet Float), "Viva el Marxismo Leninismo" (Long live Marxism-Leninism), and "Viva Lenin" (Long Live Lenin). This is to say that the openness reflected in the Soviet Bloc media of the mid-1980s contrasts sharply with the obedience of the Sovietized government manifest in these slogans of a previous decade.

More than any other singular work, the song "Konchalovski hace rato que no monta en Lada" (Konchalovski hasn't rode in a Lada in a while) by the troubadour Frank Delgado may be considered the anthem of leftovers for the Soviet Bloc. Delgado was born in 1960, and like many of the artists explored here, in his 1970s' youth he was fed a Soviet Cuban cultural diet. In the aftermath of the imposition, he experienced both longing for certain aspects of the diet and the relief for the ability to critique ideology. The song title refers to Andrei Konchalovsky, an acclaimed Russian film director whose films are no longer the paradigm of what is seen in Cuba. However, while he is not symbolically riding around in his Lada there, it is interesting to note that the audiovisual magazine *Miradas* did publish a translated interview with him in 2004. At least, some Cuban film critics are still concerned with his vision (Mijailkov-Konchalovsky 2004).[10] Delgado's *trova* (ballad), which is so explicit that it hardly requires interpretation, revels in the ability to have an opinion about Marx. The song's principal and repeated question and answer—"did you read *Capital*?, Yes, but I didn't like it, because the heroine dies at the end"—marks the fall of socialism from occupying the space of a singular master narrative to becoming a minor fiction that Delgado is now able to say that he does not like. Nevertheless, Delgado's eyes burn as he observes the new world order/disorder and identifies his place in it through what he knows so well—references to his Soviet cultural past.

An overview of Cubans' reactions to my own research elucidates the extent of the Soviet presence in the Cuban landscape. Cubans claim to have had varying degrees of contact with the Soviets, depending on their employment and neighborhoods in which they lived, but enough of a dimension such that the Cubans coined them *bolos*, alluding to their Othered appearance, what they perceived as an awkward and clumsy physicality that mimicked bowling pins. Many Cubans tend to ascribe the limited contact that they had with Russians during the Soviet Period to separate living quarters and business establishments. Before delineating particular modes of memory, let us rehearse the more general, oft-heard remarks by Cubans about the Soviets. Much like it had been throughout the Cold War Era in the United States, in Cuba, there is some confusion around the categories of "Russian" and "Soviet." Russians were not only Russians, but also other members of the Soviet Bloc. They may reminisce about experiences with Russian individuals then and now. They may speak about the public imposition of a foreign language and pedagogical strategies as well as codes of conduct, and then suddenly become cautiously nostalgic about such programs as "El idioma ruso por radio" ("The Russian Language by Radio"), about certain films by Soviet and Eastern European directors, or even about Russian cartoons. The fact that the masses go to the ballet and to the theater is sometimes remembered, however erroneously, as a Soviet leftover. My interest is not in verifying such memories against a construction of objective reality, but rather in considering these traces of the past within a reinscribed present in which even old partners, such as the Russians, are finding a new place.

Lenin Park

For Svetlana Boym (2002: 41), "Restorative nostalgia puts emphasis on *nostos* and proposes to rebuild the lost home and patch up the memory gaps ... [Restorative] nostalgics 'do not think of themselves as nostalgic; they believe that their project is about truth. ... Restorative nostalgia manifests itself in total reconstructions of monuments of the past.' "

As is it is in the rhetoric of diverse nationalisms, "restorative nostalgia" is constitutive of a certain bent of contemporary Cuban rhetoric, and in "De lo efímero, lo temporal y lo permanente" ("About the ephemeral, the temporal and the permanent") by Fernando Rojas, ex-editor of *El Caimán Barbudo*, the official publication for Cuban youth, and the current vice minister of culture, it is especially so. Rojas (2002) defends the Cuban revolution's Leninism and its socialist survival in a post-Soviet world. Furthermore, the anthology in which the article appears peaks in favor of those Cubans "that do not look for the outside and after ... they play out life on the inside and now" (Ubieta 2002: 5). The collection's editor, Enrique Ubieta Gómez, yearns for an imaginary, whole Cuba, and it is in this vein that Rojas recollects his childhood experiences of drinking cheap milk in the early 1960s in a recently inaugurated Parque Lenin in a section of his essay appropriately entitled "Requiem por el lácteo y otras reminscencias" ("Requiem for Milk and Other Reminiscences").

Memory becomes the point of departure for linking the Cuban Revolution's early years to its future. Rojas (2002: 15) writes: "The unknown Leninist tradition recognized the priority of a politics of absolute solidarity with national liberation movements, and something of that remained (...) within the heart of the Soviet bureaucracy, and most of all, in the people of *that tremendous country*."[11] Cubans, however, according to Rojas, developed that aspect of the tradition even further than the Soviets. In "El triunfo de Stalin," published in *El Caimán Barbudo* in 2004, Rojas evokes a similar phrase. Speaking of the 1930s in the USSR, he states: "[T]he paradox resides in the very excesses of principles of the decade that helped *that great country* resist and conquer."[12] Allow me to take Rojas's words a step further. If, in fact, such a Leninist tradition was unknown, it is difficult to envision how it left its marks on the Cuban people and government, both cited by Rojas as under its influence. Taking Lenin Park to be the founding myth for a narrative that refuses to take as a failure Cuba's alliance with the Soviet Bloc, Rojas also bitterly rejects the notion that Cuba was a pawn of the Soviets and affirms that Cuba sustained its alliance with them on shared ideological grounds.

An especially controversial moment within Rojas's reflections on the Soviet Union occurs when, in "¿Porqué cayó el socialismo en Europa oriental?" ("Why Did Eastern European Socialism Fall?"), a debate published in *Temas* in December 2004, Rojas ponders the extent to which the Soviets could have defended themselves against the Nazis "without the forced industrialization, without the agricultural cooperativization, and without the unity of the nationalities—that we know how they were achieved" (Brown et al. 2004: 99). When the journal's editor, Rafael Hernández, asks whether Rojas is suggesting that the Soviet Union could not have withstood the Nazi invasion without Stalin's authoritarianism, Rojas warns against conflating those programs with Stalin, but confesses his own quandary over this period.

Rojas is not the only Cuban cultural worker/politician who relies on Lenin for the future of Cuba. By returning to the October Revolution of 1917, and especially to other thinkers who the Cuban Revolution cast aside, some Cubans today such as Celia Hart (2003), and Ariel Dacal and Francisco Brown Infante (2006), are attempting to rescue socialism from bureaucratization.[13] In "La bandera de Coyoacan" ("The Flag of Coyoacan"), Hart (2003) urges Cubans and internationalists alike to embrace the tradition of Leon Trotsky. Hart, the daughter of Cuban revolutionaries, Armando Hart and Haydée Santamaría, vindicates Trotskyism from the oblivion beset it by the horrors of Stalinism. While Rojas's tone is defensively nationalistic and hardly admits errors, referring to the 1960s as "the epoch of the best Havana nights, almost completely banished the squalor that shows, for instance, in scenes of *P.M*" (Rojas 2002: 14), Hart is critical of Cubans having silenced particular thinkers.[14] Yet, both Rojas and Hart have in common the insistence upon capturing distinct "lost" moments in order to sustain the future of the Cuban Revolution. Like the popular perceptions with which I began this conversation, these perspectives represent another level through which the artistic gestures need to be interpreted.

Koniec

To the question of what remained of that alliance, Jesús Díaz, author of works that take place in the Soviet Bloc, responded "not much" (Elmundo. es 2002). Yet, like Hernández Busto (2006), he recalls those children of mixed Russian and Cuban marriages. Those "children" are closely watched in several Cuban short stories and novels, such as Antonio Álvarez Gil's *Naufragios*, where their hybridity is almost sexualized: "The Russian girl was pretty and conscious of it. The mix of blood had favored her a lot. At once she had the enigmatic beauty of the Russian women and the salsa of the Cuban girls" (Álvarez Gil 2002: 74).

In May 2005, in Havana, a group of young Russian Cubans organized a symposium entitled "Las otras herencias de Octubre" ("The Other Inheritances of October"), where, in fact, Hart presented her "La bandera de Coyoacan." The group's project, *Proyecto mir_xxi_cu*, is invested in transnationalism, as opposed to the consolidated nationalism envisioned by Rojas. Their name—the Spanish word for "project," followed by the Russian for "peace," "world," or "community," then by the Roman numerals for twenty-first century, with the final "cu" suggesting a world wide web domain—indicates a virtual Cuban experience. Promoting the descendents of Russians in Cuba, whom they claim are the second greatest minority within Cuba after the Chinese, is one of their principal goals.[15] While the articulation of these minority politics is comparable to that of Chinese Cubans and Jewish Cubans, the Russian Cubans' project has distinct implications given that it was specifically revolutionary politics that brought the Russians to Cuba. This group of Russian Cuban artists and intellectuals is affiliated with the state-sponsored Hermanos Saíz Association, the organization to which young artists may belong before joining the UNEAC, the national union of writers and artists—a fact that is interesting if we consider institutional support as a marker of the extent to which the Soviet-Cuban occupies a space within the public sphere.

Proyecto Mir's founders are Polina Martínez Shvietsova (born in Camagüey in 1976) and Dmitri Prieto Samsonov (born in Moscow in 1972) who, in March 2004, collaborated on their first annual event entitled "Koniec" in Sancti Spiritus, Cuba. With the word "Koniec," meaning "end" in Russian, they resign themselves to pronouncing their predicament through transliteration, and in so doing, allude to both an ending and a symbolic return to an empire that for more than half of their life they called home. In the following passage, Martínez Shvietsova (2004) delineates the scope of the encounter.

> *Koniec?* was the first event where they proposed to analyze and investigate the influences of the Euro-Asian imaginary in Cuba: the traces that they left on various generations of Cubans, the almost totalitarian presence of intelligence of the extinct USSR, bringing together for the first time several young artists and intellectuals who are *aguastibias*[16]... Koniec? is not the end as the chosen title for the event indicates. Koniec? is the beginning and the continuity of a rescue of traditions of our Russian mothers, of the best scientific and artistic works that the ex-Socialist countries left for thirty years.

While the aforementioned explanation rests on both genealogy and the act of converting an epithet into a powerful signifier of union, another essay written by both Martínez Shviétsova and Prieto Samsonov (2005) provides a theoretical reflection on the necessity of a geopolitical demarcation that demonstrates these authors' investment in archiving their histories within Cuba. The article's title—"RecUrSO al Ser en CUBA"—is the point of departure for an exploration of their parents' attraction for the Other that led to the very existence of these Russian-Cubans. While their writing emphasizes the importance of upholding what is "theirs" and of the link between loss and creation, it is also contingent upon making contact with individuals who are similar to themselves—part Cuban and part ex-Soviet Bloc, and upon assuring the continued assistance of Russian players in the Cuban sphere.

Prieto Samsonov's poem, "Jurel en pesos" ("Yellow Tail in *Pesos*"—a rereading of Virgilio Piñera's 1943 "La isla en Peso" ("The Island's Weight")[17]—expresses the poetic subject's dissatisfaction with capitalism, with his positioning in Cuba, and with his inability to reclaim a homeland, using the characteristic Cuban motif of national identity—food. For those familiar with literatures by ethnic minorities in the United States, the tone and motifs of Prieto Samsonov's poem will hardly be new:

> The damned circumstance of the dollar everywhere
> is as if I can't breathe any further than
>   [the reefs
> in which fifteen years ago my body was all tangled up.
> ...
> But still, with its price in pesos
> it will never be like that *selyodka*[18] with onions
> that I used to try at my grandfather's
> when we ate meat, and fish,
>   and again meat.
> ...

> The village of theirs has become an expensive
> [and absurd place
> and again absurd
> that is called the black market. (Prieto Samsonov 2004: 49–50)

The utopic island experiment that is Cuba can no longer satisfy the Russian fruit of this experiment, but neither can the other half; the poetic subject has been betrayed by his forefathers' dreams for solidarity and ends up asphyxiated by the dollar.

While it would be inaccurate to read this poem as the product of *Proyecto Mir*, Prieto Samsonov's disparagement is crucial to identifying an aspect of the zeitgeist of that project that can be seen within the poem's generational markings, provided through spatial categories. It is obvious that "El pueblo de ellos" ("the village of theirs") is distinct from Rojas's "great country" of Lenin. The disjuncture upon which these verses remark suggests that the poetic subject is the child of those who constructed the union. Unlike Rojas, the poetic subject is someone for whom Batista only existed in textbooks.[19] The present can only be compared to the superimposed past that, in "Jurel en Pesos," was almost organic.

Koniek

With that same word Koniek, K-O-N-I-E-K, mispronounced and uniquely transliterated from Russian into Cuban Spanish, an initiation occurs simultaneously with an exit. K-O-N-I-E-K appears in capitals at the end of the 2002 video by the Cuban alternative punk rock group Porno para Ricardo. This visual initiation and exit is immersed in the aftermath of the territorial encounters of the USSR in Cuba. The fact that it forms part of the same generational epoch of the *Proyecto Mir* is evident in the allusion to Soviet Bloc cartoons that ended with the word Koniec. The cartoons have become an important marker for this generation of Cubans born in the late 1960s and early 1970s. Although some members of that generation articulate that they never truly liked those cartoons, they still serve them as symbolic glue in today's world. In Miami, "Russian cartoons" have been stockpiled. Even though the first waves of Miami Cubans felt that their world was destroyed by the Soviets, in more recent years, successive generations of immigrants transform Miami, and in the absence of Cuba, they utilize *los muñequitos rusos* as a resource to reconstruct their youth and homeland.

In the case of Porno Para Ricardo, musicians who congregated around the Playa neighborhood of Havana, a distinct version of a familiar photo album is toyed with, in the eclectic punk style of lead singer Gorki (his real name). The band finds an acerbic plenitude of expression by combining references to the U.S. punk/metal band of the early 1990s called Porno For Pyros, Lou

Reed, the Communist International, and Russian cartoons. Putin's official interlocutors are not the only ones who can communicate in Russian. At least, on some imitative level, so can the members of this band whose very name threatens to destabilize the national codes of conduct with its admission of pornography. Porno Para Ricardo's song entitled "Los músicos de Bremen" ("Bremen-town musicians") plays with the 1969 Soviet cartoon adaptation of the Brothers Grimm fairytale, delivered punk-rock style in the language of this other idiosyncratic people.

The homage involved in parody does not escape either their music or videos. On par with the vintage aesthetic of the music are the videos of director Ernesto René whose "Los músicos de Bremen" is filled with images of all that journalistic reports insisted Cubans were excited to see go—Soviet pedagogy, red stars, as well as hammer and sickles.[20] At the beginning of the video, which in 2002 was nominated for the national music video awards, *Premios Lucas*, rapid clips ground spectators in television cartoons. The camera zooms in on a map of the Soviet Union in a classroom where the musicians pose as unusually nerdy-looking Cubans. A great *descarga* (celebration) takes over in the video, once the band members get out of their school uniforms from the *pre-universitario* Lenin, the Russian school, the *primaria*, and the *secundaria*—reflecting an *imperfect* uniformity reminding us of a 1960s *aesthetics of hunger*—and refashion themselves as both tourists in history and modern-day citizens of Havana—in a Havana that belongs to the world.

As if in an ideological and aesthetic flashback, the musicians splatter red paint on their rehearsal room. Run-down Lada automobiles—those same Ladas of the news reports of Putin's visits—are captured by the camera. Male subjects digging up the urban streets jog the Cuban memory of the 1970s' sugar harvest in a uniquely warm and empathic manner. This approach, perhaps somewhat startling to outsiders who are more familiar with the human oppression of such desired agricultural outcomes, can be explained partially by the temporal distance, but also by the last decade's less than sanguine experiences of a dual economy. The resulting differences between the haves and the have-nots undoubtedly temper these artists' recollection of their youth and of the universal, Soviet-style idealism in which they were inculcated. The gaze of its director reflects an element of insane harmony in the strange, collage-like experience. The video humorously concludes with a display across the screen of, among other words: "Pashiva" (Thank you), "Stonia," "Croacia," and finally "Koniek."

This is not to say that the video does not treat more critically the residues of this transnational union as well as the current state of affairs on the island. The abandonment and isolation that emerges out of an experience of insularity as well as out of the restrictive governmental policies toward travel are easily read. In contrast to the more quaint beginning of the recorded version of the song, sounds of static introduce the struggle to get reception. The video's principal female protagonist stands on a rooftop talking on a cordless phone as she watches cartoon figurines of airplanes and birds fly away. Then she points the antenna toward the planes desperately begging for a signal to communicate with the world, reminding spectators of the video's initial static. It is clear that travel, let alone communication with the outside, is restricted. At once, she labors to traverse the city. Although there is an exaggerated, almost cartoon-like quality to her movements and appearance, one of the most pressing socioeconomic problems facing Cuba today, transportation, takes center stage. In the past, the Soviet Union was an important vehicle through which Cubans accessed the world. It is certain that, as Zardoya Loureda's statement about counterrevolutionary radio stations suggested, American stations could be always heard in Cuban territory. Nevertheless, the aforementioned Soviet and Eastern Bloc publications, the possibility of travel abroad for study and professional reasons, or even as an award of travel granted to hardworking Cubans that the island's connection to the Soviet Union provided, had an importance that cannot be underestimated. The removal of these possibilities, as "Jurel en Pesos" suggests, entails a sincere sense of isolation. An aesthetic counterpart to the ideological imposition is the superimposed images within René's video (2002) that allow the cracks in the system to be seen. Sociopolitical impositions are alluded to aesthetically through the video's superimpositions of cartoon-like figures that convey a field beyond the actual filmed video. They point to an expansive temporal framework as well as to the "cracks" within the legacy of history on the present.

While stagnancy and immobility, thematic staples in representations of Cuba, are concerns of this three-minute video, so are cultural movements, in a way that contrasts with the imposition of capitalism implied in the term *transition*. The bubbly red and white letters that dance across one of the final segments of the video declaring "esta guitarra es rusa" ("this guitar is Russian") clearly suggest the principal trade relations with the Soviets. While this may be a sign that soon the Russians will dance off the stage entirely, it is important to archive this seemingly minor detail wherein actual disguises transform the 2002 Cubans into a 1960s Soviet-Cuban experiment.

Mayakovsky Again

The metaphor of the family photo album is particularly useful for examining the Soviet residue in Cuba. Such albums helped us conceptualize "Los músicos de Bremen" as a portrait of 30-something-year-old Cubans in their attire from their youth—a conversion of real-life musicians into their longed for, but not necessarily "preferred," cartoon characters. In a comparable fashion, other Cuban visual artists render a different part of this same album, by parodying the *heroic rhetoric* of the Soviet-Cuban unions in outer space. For instance, in a July 2003 art installation called "Héroes de Baikonur" that took place in Old Havana, Tonel (Antonio Eligio Fernández) inserted his grandfather, named Antonio Fernández, into a fascinating assemblage of objects, photographs of an international team of scientists, and etchings. The narrative says that he led a team of international rocket scientists who, between 1962 and 1970, from a modest house in the neighborhood of Nicanor del Campo of Playa, investigated traveling to the moon and back to the Soviets' space launch facility, Baikonur, now in Kazakhstan, but previously called Leninsk, in the USSR.

In Tonel's "Los heroes de Baikonur," (see figure 7.1), we see Vladimir Mayakowsky, along with—from the top left, clockwise,—Trotsky, Lenin, Rosa Luxembourg, and finally, Antonio Fernández. In the previously referenced debate on the collapse of Eastern European socialism, Desiderio Navarro, the Cuban critic and translator (from among other languages, many Slavic ones into Spanish), remarks that within the Soviet Union critiques from the Left within were silenced. He refers specifically to Vladmir Mayakovsky's case, a poet known in Cuba since the 1920s, and whose censored poems were delayed publication in the 1980s.[21] Frank Delgado's provocative *trova* that we have come to know already also references Mayakowsky. Mayakowsky—the poet of the workers—was visible in postrevolution Havana, meaning Tonel is not drawing from an archive of the "ignored" (recall Hart speaking of Trotsky) or "unknown" (Rojas's vision of Lenin). Nevertheless, Tonel's personal union of his grandfather with these Russian revolutionaries does nuance this historical quest for progress and makes spectators feel almost

Figure 7.1 "Los héroes de Baikonur"

as if they were traversing a family photo album inextricably linked to fading moments in national history. It familiarizes the History by substituting first names for surnames, and makes it seem as if the Soviet exploration in outer space was the culmination of the October Revolution.

What is the point of this memory in today's world? Why not just bury it within the annals of foolishness? Tonel unfastens the logic of History, recasting aspects of it in the manner that he deems fit. In one of the texts that forms part of the same installation entitled "La novela es el género...," ("The Novel Is the Genre..."), Tonel fortifies the union between his grandfather and Mayakowsky even further by suggesting that the latter met his grandfather on a streetcar in 1925, which made possible the translation of his grandfather's poetry into many languages. Tonel ridicules the links between family and national pride, rendering humorous his grandfather's entrance into Soviet internationalism: "Fernández would become the first Spanish poet of his generation to be translated into Russian, Kirguiz, Tartar, and Armenian (of all these first editions, copies have been saved in the family archives)." In a collage that highlights absurd personal alliances within the international union, frivolity and play are important. These categories, predominantly cast aside by socialist realism in the 1970s, are the mainstays for Tonel's humorous and dramatic rereading of the twentieth century.

Conclusion

What we do know about transitions of the late twentieth century, whether from fascist regimes in the Americas or from communist ones in Central and Eastern Europe, is that the old battles do not disappear from the playing field for very long. While some may be focusing on the Comandante's death, he has not yet retreated from being a forceful global player. This fact makes an examination of the leftovers of the Soviets in Cuba a particularly precarious task. North Americans are continually reminded of the symbolic weight of vintage—from period pieces to retro fashion to old-time automobiles. The velocity of the production of nostalgia is outstanding. The vintage aesthetic of Cuban culture is so compelling because it weaves together distinct fields. Cuba calls to mind the vestiges of a prerevolutionary past when hookers were hookers (not physicians), when Cadillacs were really Cadillacs and not hybrid testaments to the creativity of Cuban survival, when Havana, we are told by some, was glorious as it is so frequently portrayed. It paradoxically recalls a different, more parochial period of U.S. American dominion, when American cars and not Japanese SUVs were the admired monsters. There is both a comfort and curiosity about the island's decay. Cuba suggests an ideological world when the Cold War could clearly delineate enemies; that is, when they did not hide in caves as did the new enemy Saddam Hussein. Cuba has become a more accessible outpost for travelers and tourists who themselves suffer from socialist nostalgia.

The Russian-Cubans' children of mixed marriages insist on documenting and inscribing themselves, politically and culturally within Cuba, so as not to be finalized and misread like the "Russian cartoons." Porno para Ricardo only observes and offers opinions, like Frank Delgado's song, yet critiques harshly *from within*, utilizing the Cuban experience of a Soviet imaginary to propel themselves into the future. Tonel defies the teleology of grand narratives in his collage of Soviets and Cubans, and in so doing, intimately recasts an historical vision. Many of these memories desecrate the inheritance at the same time that they convey consternation in the face of disinheritance. These memories reinforce a nationalistic rhetoric at times, and at others, shelter Cubans from what is truly unknown—the future.

I am not projecting onto Cuba a facile nostalgia for the ideologies of the Soviet Union, of the sort that, according to Miguel Saludes (2005), could be witnessed at the February 2005 Feria del Libro (Book Fair). He said that delegations from Germany, Austria, Spain, Australia, and the United States, made it seem like the *Feria* was in a time machine. According to Saludes, "[O]ne could see the nostalgia for the glorious past of the defunct socialist governments of Eastern Europe." I do not perceive such nostalgia, but I do believe it would be remiss to discount the exponential memories of the presence of the USSR in Cuba. Rather, the pain and consternation of disinheritance seen within this parodic production necessitates questioning the degree to which we may envision Cuba as involved in a teleological passage toward capitalism.

Notes

1. This essay expands vastly from a six-page article entitled "Vintage Soviets in post-Cold War Cuba" (Loss 2004). I am grateful to many settings for allowing me to "workshop" parts of this presentation, including Wellesley College Departments of Spanish and Russian, University of Connecticut Humanities Institute, University of California in San Diego Department of Communication, University of California in Riverside Department of Hispanic Studies, and The Cuban Studies Working Group at New York University. I am also grateful to Raul Aguiar, Víctor Fowler Calzada, Polina Martínez Shvietsova, Ernesto Menéndez Conde, Jorge Miralles, José Manuel Prieto, Dimitri Prieto Samsonov, Desiderio Navarro, Antonio José Ponte, Reina María Rodríguez, Armando Suárez Cobián, Yesenia Selier, and Esther Whitfield, who all have been critical interlocutors. The errors here are my own. Image of "Héroes de Baikonur" is provided by the artist, Tonel.
2. *La yuma* is Cuban slang for foreigner, most frequently, someone from the United States.
3. There is expanding body of works in different disciplines on the condition of memory and the post-Soviet Bloc. Svetlana Boym's *The Future of Nostalgia* (2002) on nostalgia and the Soviet Union and Central Europe is particularly illuminating.
4. All translations are my own.
5. See Víctor Fowler (2001b) and Yoss (2004). Since 2004, Yana Elsa Brugal, a Cuban theater critic who received her Ph.D. in Arts and Sciences in San Petersburg, Russia, has organized the annual "Stanislavski siempre" conference, and she is currently examining the Russian influence in Cuban theater. Aurora

Jácome's muñequitosrusos.blogspot.com must be credited in drawing attention to the significance of the Soviet Bloc-Cuban solidarity in recent cultural production. The February 2007 international symposium "Cuba-USSR and the Post-Soviet Experience" that I co-organized with José Manuel Prieto brought together writers and artists around this theme, and over the past year, the topic of the sociocultural impact of the Soviet-Cuban union on the present has been explored more extensively. See Rafael Rojas's "Souvenirs de un Caribe soviético" (2008) as well as various blogs, including those of Jorge Ferrer, "El tono de la voz"; Ernesto Hernández Busto, "Penúltimos Días"; and Yoani Sánchez, "Generación Y," among many other spaces. In November 2007, in Havana, the "Vostok" exhibition took place, and in February 2008, the Torre de Letras organized "Tres Jornadas dedicadas a la literatura rusa en la literature cubana." The permanent research group "Revolución Bolchevique historia de la URSS y Cuba. Análisis crítico socialista desde el siglo XXI" was initiated in May 2007 in Havana.
6. I am addressing the following related questions in my manuscript "Dreaming in Russian: The Politics of Memory in Post-Soviet Cuban Culture." How do collective/artistic memories of the Soviet-Cuban union evolve in a society whose government remains socialist? To what extent can Cubans be active agents in a reification process of these utopian symbols? How does this particular experience of hybridity wherein imperialism and leftist politics converge challenge existing frameworks of identity politics within and outside of Cuba? How should we problematize the category of "transition to democracy" when we consider the current memorialization of the Soviet Bloc in Cuba?
7. See Bain (2006) for a discussion of Lourdes.
8. As of November 8, 2004, the dollar was no longer accepted in Cuban stores, although its possession was not criminalized.
9. See Black (1988), Erisman (2000), and Gleijeses (2002).
10. The full lyrics are reprinted in Yoss (2004: 144).
11. The italics are mine.
12. The italics are mine.
13. See Francisco Brown Infante's and Ariel Dacal (2006), which purports to analyze the reasons and the consequences of the fall of the USSR. In his preface, Allen Woods (2006) reminds readers of Russia's backwardness before the revolution and of the discrepancies between Marx and Engel's vision and the actual Soviet experience, as well as the problem of the USSR's isolation, signaled by Lenin and Trotsky. He concludes by calling for the destruction of bureaucracy, "the terrain wherein the pro-bourgeois tendencies could put down roots and grow." For Woods, Venezuela is a lighthouse for a future in which Cuba is less isolated.
14. *P.M.* (1961), directed by Sabá Cabrera Infante, was a short film that featured the nightlife of Havana. It was censored and the cultural supplement edited by Sabá Cabrera Infante's brother, Guillermo Cabrera Infante, *Lunes de revolución*, was subsequently shut down. This controversy resulted in Fidel Castro's 1961 "Words to the Intellectuals," the most memorable part of which is frequently quoted: "Dentro de la Revolución, todo; contra la Revolución, nada" (Within the Revolution, everything; against the Revolution, nothing).
15. The number of Russian-Cubans in Cuba is estimated to be around ten thousand (Sequera 2000).
16. *Aguastibias* is the term that Cubans used to refer to Russian-Cubans.

17. In Spanish, the word peso means "weight." It is also the name of the Cuban currency as well as that of other Latin American countries.
18. In Russian in the original. It means "herring."
19. Batista was the dictator overthrown by the 1959 Revolution.
20. This video can be seen on youtube at the time of this writing [www.youtube.com/watch?v= lkqDDlUFPMo].
21. As Alejo Carpentier affirms, "Soviet literature had an early diffusion in Cuba. First the poets Yeset and Mayakowsky were known and already read by 1924." In fact, Mayakowsky's impressions of the racial and monetary inequities in Cuba located in the poem "Black and White" (1925) are often considered a reference for Yevgeny Yevtushenko's part of the script for *Soy Cuba* (Mikhail Kalatozov 1964). According to Desiderio Navarro, in the mid-1980s, he and Tatiana Gorstko compiled and translated a collection of Mayakowsky's poems, the majority of which were previously unpublished in Spanish. While the editors were paid for their work by the Cuban publisher *Arte y Literatura*, the volume, *Poesía censurada en nuestra lengua Vladímir Maiakosvki (1893–1930)* (Censured Poetry in Our Language, Vladimir Mayakowsky [1893–1930]), did not see the light of day.

8

The "Letter of the Year" and the Prophetics of Revolution

Kenneth Routon

In January 2003, a group of over 800 *babalaos*, or Ifá divination priests, gathered together in Havana, Cuba, to read the "Letter of the Year," an annual divination ceremony that forecasts the social, political, and economic climate for the coming year. The group of both Cuban and foreign diviners was organized by the Miguel Febles Padrón Commission (CMFP), which, since 1986, has united a number of otherwise independent divination priests to annually carry out the ceremony. Although it has been performed intermittently beginning with the first generation of Cuban *babalaos*, knowledge of the ceremony was until recently largely confined to the island's Ocha-Ifá (i.e., Santería) communities. Since the late 1980s, however, the Ifá oracle's prophecies have attracted the attention of the larger Cuban public, as well as the international press. The annual divination ceremony's increasing public visibility and contested political meanings became clear in the CMFP's 2003 reading. Aside from the usual predictions of natural disasters, social ills, and war, the CMFP's reading made what some believed was a cryptic reference to Fidel Castro himself with one of the year's slogans, "The king turns in his crown before dying." The proverb not only underscored the danger of talking about Fidel's death but also turned heads given the fact that the CMFP is an opposing faction of *babalaos* in the struggle over control of the ceremony, at odds with the government-funded and directed Yoruba Cultural Association (ACY). Although members of the CMFP went to great lengths to stress that the proverb was in no way a reference to the nation's *comandante en jefe*, claiming instead that it referred to "all of humanity," the incident underscored the volatile political role of popular religion in contemporary Cuban society.

This essay critically examines the increasing public visibility of *babalao* prophecies and how this relates to popular conceptions of power, value, and national identity in contemporary Cuba. I begin by outlining the early history of Ocha-Ifá with a particular emphasis on the *babalaos* and their self-described status as the "high priests" of this religion, a factor that helps explain why the current regime has selected them to be the official spokesmen for this religious community. This is followed by a discussion of the pivotal role played by one particularly controversial *babalao* in opening up the priesthood to accusations of commercial exploitation, which is at the heart of the rivalry between the two main factions competing for control over the annual divination ceremony. After describing the current regime's role in the commodification and institutionalization of Ocha-Ifá cults, I explore the power struggles and infighting that have characterized the annual divination ceremony and discuss its impact on the national imaginary in contemporary, late socialist Cuba. I argue, in particular, that attempts by the current regime to reinvigorate grassroots political support for the Revolution and attract badly needed tourist dollars in part by harnessing popular religions of African origin to the ideological agendas of the state have only exacerbated existing tensions within the *babalao* priesthood.

The crisis of late socialism is characterized, above all, by the emergence of competing regimes of value. In Cuba, this crisis has been marked not so much by paradigmatic shifts in value systems, but by the hesitant flirtation with "novel ways to value labor, property, leisure and cultural production, as well as to experience and express social identity and citizenship" (Hernandez-Reguant 2002: 5). After the collapse of the former Soviet Bloc and the withdrawal of massive foreign subsidies, the Cuban government began implementing a series of liberal economic reforms in an attempt to save the sinking national economy. As a result, socioeconomic differences emerged between a small minority of Cubans with access to dollars and remittances from abroad and the majority who turned to the expanding black market to meet their daily needs. In this situation, commodities, services, bodies, and labor became valued in new and sometimes conflicting ways by both individuals and the state as an older ethos of *compartir* (sharing) faced an emerging ethos of *resolver* (resolve), *conseguir* (get), and *inventar* (invent); that is, making ends meet through wheeling-and-dealing, hustling, and individual resolve (Hernandez-Reguant 2002: 6–7).

Despite significant efforts by the revolutionary government to eradicate race- and class-related disparities, the crisis of the Special Period has had a more devastating impact on the Afro-Cuban population. Afro-Cubans are far less likely than white Cubans to have family abroad to send dollar remittances during economic hard times and also to have fewer ties to the dollar economy generated by the growing tourist industry (Pérez Sarduy and Stubbs 2000). Moreover, this situation is further complicated by the increasing commodification and exoticization of Afro-Cuban religions and expressive culture marketed for foreign tourist consumption (Hagedorn 2001; see chapter 4, this volume). The marketing of Afro-Cuban religions for foreign consumption was obvious during my fieldwork in Havana between 2003 and 2005. After trying to keep Afro-Cuban popular religions in the shadows for several decades images of Ocha-Ifá, Palo Monte, and *Abakuá* ritual specialists and devotees suddenly stepped into the limelight of public marketing campaigns beginning in the 1990s. Most foreign visitors to the island will readily recognize the image of an Afro-Cuban *babalao* performing a divination ritual as depicted, for instance, on bottles of Santero *aguardiente*; the crude depiction of a dark-skinned *palero* standing before his *nganga* complete with human skull and secret ideographic script on bottles of Ta' Francisco cologne; the tourist posters with photos of dancing *íreme* masquerades belonging to the *Abakuá* societies; or the pictures of happy-go-lucky female devotees of Yemayá and Ochún smiling on billboards promoting foreign tourism. These images, along with token visits to regime-friendly *babalaos* that are frequently included in foreign tourist packages, are just some examples of the more recent commodification of Afro-Cuban popular religions. Afro-Cuban expressive culture and history has also been forced to the forefront of national politics, not only raising questions about the intermingling of secular and spiritual power but also leading to intense debates on how to define national identity.[1]

One of the most significant obstacles the revolutionary regime has faced in this regard is the increasing globalization of Cuban Ocha-Ifá religion and the potential threat it poses to national identity. Beginning in the early 1990s, intellectuals, academics, and state officials began placing more of an emphasis on national identity rather than political community (i.e., the revolutionary project) in order to diminish the threat that globalization and neoliberalism posed to the nation's sovereignty and self-determination (see chapter 1, this volume). This has had rather direct implications for the Ocha-Ifá community. As the numbers of foreign visitors to the island interested in going through Ocha-Ifá ritual initiation continue to rise—an expensive endeavor that costs anywhere from $2,000 to $8,000 by some estimates—a power struggle has emerged between practitioners, intellectuals, and state officials as they attempt to use the religion for widely divergent purposes (Ayorinde 2000). In the past, the absence of an overarching institutional authority among Ocha-Ifá cults contributed to their survival in Cuban society.[2] Now, given the increasing international popularity and economic importance of Ocha-Ifá, "there is no obvious representative among *santeros* and *babalaos* for dialogue with the state," and, "[a]ttempts to create unifying organizations, such as the Yoruba Cultural Association, have been undermined by jealousy among rival groups of practitioners" (Ayorinde 2000: 79). The rivalry between competing Ifá ritual specialists has been most intense in the struggle over control of the annual divination ceremony, with heated exchanges and emotionally charged accusations of *interes* (i.e., economic and political exploitation) coming from both sides of the divide. The existence of rival groups of Ocha-Ifá priest-healers and their links to political power, however, are not solely the result of recent socioeconomic conditions in Cuba; they have a history that goes back to at least to the turn of the twentieth century.

In the following, I briefly describe the organizational structure of Ocha-Ifá religion and, in particular, the *babalaos*' claims of ritual authority as the "high priests" of the religion. Ifá divination priests, as I show, claim rank over Ocha priest-healers (*santeros*) due to their mastery and control over the purported "foundational" texts of Ocha-Ifá religion. I then turn to a discussion of the historical struggle over ritual authority within the Ifá priesthood itself, a struggle characterized in part by disagreements concerning the proper control and distribution of sacred ritual objects. The purpose of this section is twofold. First, the *babalaos*' self-representation as the "high priests" of *santería* may explain why the government has chosen to recognize them as the cultural ambassadors of Ocha-Ifá cult houses on the island rather than others. Second, endemic rivalries and accusations of economic exploitation of the religion within the Ifá priesthood are not unique to the Special Period. Rather, they have characterized Ifá ritual politics in Cuba for decades and have only recently become more intense and public.

Ritual Politics and the Commodification of Authority

The popular religion of Yoruba origin in Cuba known as Regla de Ocha-Ifá, or Santería, revolves around the worship of several *oricha*, or divinities. Through a ritual economy defined by sacred forms of exchange and spirit possession, devotees enter into reciprocal relationships with the *orichas*, honoring them with praises and sacrificial offerings in exchange for health, well-being, and spiritual protection. Ocha-Ifá temple-houses comprise ritual families linked through initiation by a common ritual godparent, a knowledgeable elder who oversees the introduction of new devotees into the religion. Although they share a common belief system, cosmology, and similar ritual practices, Ocha-Ifá temple-houses are not organized into a hierarchy ruled by an overarching authority but exist relatively independent of one another. Although their relative autonomy allows for some minor variation between groups, Ocha-Ifá cults, nonetheless, share a fairly standardized set of religious beliefs and practices. The establishment of standard ritual protocols and common procedures for the handing over of sacred, authority-affirming ritual objects, however, did not emerge without struggle. Conflict between rival groups competing for power and prestige has, in fact, been common throughout the religion's history in Cuba.

The organizational structure of the religion popularly known as Santería in Cuba actually comprises two somewhat distinct priestly branches: La

Regla de Ocha and La Regla de Ifá. The organizational separation of Ocha and Ifá cults is based primarily on differences in the division of ritual labor to which each lay claim. The officiating priests-healers and diviners of Ifá, called *babalaos*, an exclusively male priestly title, control the rich and complex divination system known as Ifá, initiate devotees to a single *oricha*, Orula, and carry out the annual divination ceremony known as the Letter of the Year. The priest-healers and diviners of Ocha, referred to as *obá oriatés* (or *santeros*), a role open to both men and women, perform a less elaborate system of divination called *dilogún* and initiate devotees to numerous *oricha*. Whereas the Ifá cults appeal to only one spiritual authority (i.e., Orula) and attempt to monopolize spiritual power and authority through a hierarchy of heterosexual male divination priests, the Ocha cults tend to decentralize spiritual authority by appealing to the numerous and sometimes competing interests of several *orichas* in a diffused network of both male and female ritual specialists (Brown 2003a). Although there is more cooperation between these groups than there is tension and conflict, there has been, nonetheless, some notable power struggles both within and between the two groups throughout the religion's history on the island.

Much scholarly and popular opinion has it that the Ocha cults were derived from the Ifá cults, positing Ifá as an entirely separate religion.[3] They argue that African-born *babalaos*' knowledge of divination verses formed the structural and spiritual basis for Lucumí religion in Cuba (e.g., Murphy 1981).[4] Among some Ifá devotees, this linear, diffusionist narrative of the religion's historical origins in Cuba often carries with it an implicit engendered ideology of ritual politics. Here, the male *babalao* plays the most influential regenerative role by symbolically fertilizing a dormant spirituality with his ritual knowledge and expertise. His authority not only derives from this "symbolic birth event" but also from his devotion to the level-headed, restrained, and just figure of Orula as opposed to the unpredictable, selfish, and assorted character of the *orichas*, a distinction reflecting common perceptions about the essentialized qualities of masculinity and femininity on the island (Brown 2003).

Although more than 10 African-born *babalaos* are acknowledged in ritual invocations and oral histories in Cuban Ifá temple-houses, there are five that stand out as the most significant given the fact that they left behind powerful and influential ritual families that continue to exist today (Brown 2003).[5] Despite the fact that they are credited with the founding of different branches of Ifá it appears that there was a high level of cooperation among them. This first generation of *babalaos* soon established themselves as the ritual high priests of Lucumí religion in Cuba, which they partly achieved through claims of ritual authenticity and through origin narratives that, more often than not, stressed historical continuity. The *babalaos*' appeals to the control over ritual power and prestige were also pursued through the controlled and strategic distribution of ritual objects known as *olofin* that serve to authenticate their spiritual authority.

Between the late nineteenth century and the first decade of the twentieth century, there were around forty *babalaos* in Havana (Brown 2003). By 1948, their ranks, according to William Bascom's estimates, had grown to around two hundred (Bascom 1952). After the deaths of the first generation of conservative *babalaos*, who zealously guarded their *olofin* by limiting their distribution and severely restricting the entrance of new Ifá devotees in order to monopolize their power, the number of Ifá divination priests grew rapidly between the 1950s and the 1970s (Brown 2003). It is believed that the head *babalao* of each major *rama* had an *olofin* and that their distribution was governed by strict rules. These formal ritual procedures, however, were often contested. Although the first couple of generations of *babalaos* guarded their *olofin* to maintain their hold on power and authority, by 1945 this would all come to an end under the leadership of a powerful Havana *babalao* by the name of Miguel Febles y Padrón.

Miguel Febles y Padrón and Francisco "Panchito" Febles del Pino were the sons of the older and well-respected *babalao* Ramón Febles Molina. When their father passed away in 1939, his *olofin* went to its rightful heir, his eldest son Panchito. Shortly afterward, however, Miguel Febles stole the *olofin* from his brother who later conceded. Febles soon came to be regarded as a powerful *babalao* by the end of the 1940s for his mastery of Ifá divination, his predatory use of *brujería* (sorcery) to undermine his rivals, and through the fabrication, distribution, and control of his *olofin*. Febles first began manufacturing and distributing his *olofin* to his colleagues and godchildren but soon started producing and selling them in mass quantities. Febles's most profitable period came after the triumph of the Revolution during the 1980s when he expanded his influence abroad in the United States and Colombia. This would be the case despite the abundance of rumors that accused him of fabricating and selling many sealed *olofin* "cans" that were actually empty and, therefore, devoid of magical power. As an authority-affirming ritual object, the *olofin* confers great symbolic capital on its owners but by mid-century in Havana it had become "a 'commodity fetish' with a fluid 'exchange value' in the hands of Miguel Febles" (Brown 2003: 88–99).

Miguel Febles's actions are indicative of deep riffs in Havana's *babalao* community, creating a crisis of spiritual authority that would continue to resonate well into the "Special Period." The emergence of rival groups of *babalaos* and their struggle for control over the annual divination ceremony have become one of the major lines of contention defining the articulation and expression of national identity in contemporary Cuban society. As the cultural significance and role of Ocha-Ifá in the public debate regarding national belonging becomes ever more contested, state officials have not hesitated to step into the fray, attempting to capitalize on the divisions and infighting among different factions in order to serve official ideological agendas. This has, perhaps, been most clear in the current regime's support of the ACY, an organization attempting to nationalize the island's Ocha-Ifá community and establish themselves as the only legitimate authority for control over the annual divination ceremony.

Decentering Ritual Authority?

In order to better understand the current controversy surrounding the Letter of the Year ceremony and the government's support of the ACY, a brief discussion of the revolutionary regime's relationship with the Ifá divination priesthood is necessary. Despite initial attempts by the postrevolutionary government to repress Ocha-Ifá religion on the island—having local police deny permission requests to hold religious parties (*toques*), barring devotees from membership in the communist party, or through media campaigns that disparaged practitioners as criminals or social deviants etc.—the current regime could not resist weighing the religion's potential political value in providing continuing popular support for the Revolution and its potential in attracting hard currency through tourism (Hanly 1995).[6] By the late 1970s, according to Cuban ethnographer Natalia Bolívar, Castro's regime began promoting several regime-friendly *babalaos* as folkloric attractions for foreigner tourists and diplomats who paid in hard currency. These so-called *diplo-babalaos* charged in U.S. dollars for their services, just as the government "*diplo*-stores" that sold imported consumer goods to foreign diplomats and tourists. The government took most of the money, ranging anywhere from the 15,000 dollars a Spanish television station once paid to film a half-hour ceremony to at least 2,000 dollars that *babalaos* often charge to initiate foreigners. According to Bolívar, the *diplo-babalaos*, "also put on special 'ceremonies' for foreigners, including some with bare-breasted women dancers who went into 'trances,' and eventually drew strong protests from serious believers" (qtd. in Tamayo 1998). The government then, according to Bolívar, has played a significant role in the exoticization and commodification of Ocha-Ifá religion.

By the early 1990s, after the demise of the former Soviet Bloc and the end to massive flows of subsidies, tapping into Ocha-Ifá's secret ritual economy became not only an economic but a political necessity as well. Given the grim economic forecasts of the late 1980s and the threat of economic collapse in the 1990s, it became crucial for the revolutionary government to reenergize grassroots political support, which meant appealing to the social base that formed the core of support for the Revolution—namely, the black population and the working poor. One way to do this was by tapping into the social resources of Ocha-Ifá and ensuring that the prophecies of the *babalaos* did not fuel anxieties about the future. The result was a government-sponsored media campaign that promoted Ocha-Ifá as national folklore and the creation of a special government office on religious affairs, which some of the regime's critics believe attempted to recruit *babalaos* to work for the regime's internal security apparatus (Oppenheimer 1992). Although these accusations are almost impossible to confirm, several of my informants do in fact believe that Fidel Castro turned to the counsel of regime-friendly Ifá diviners when making difficult decisions, often jokingly referring to the "army of *babalaos*" that allegedly advise the regime as the "Ministry of Orula" (also see Cabrera Infante 2000; Gutiérrez 2002).

The most obvious indication of the revolutionary regime's desire to garner the support of the Ocha-Ifá community and the *babalaos* in particular, however, came in 1987 when they extended a formal invitation to the Oni of Ife, the official *babalao* of the sacred Nigerian city of Ile-Ife, to visit the island. Although his visit was preceded that same year by other African dignitaries, including the Asantehene of Ghana and the Nigerian writer Wole Soyinka, the Oni of Ife's visit was the most anticipated of these visits by both the regime and the Ocha-Ifá community. Earlier that year, according to some interpretations, "the Ifá oracle...announced that Castro would die unless the Yoruba 'king of kings,' the 'great Ooni' of the *babalaos*, traveled to Cuba and kissed the ground" (Valdes Figueroa 2001:226). The Oni of Ife's visit was arranged by Jose Carniedad, an Afro-Cuban specialist on African religions that Castro assigned to head the Party's Office of Religious Affairs in 1984. The Yoruba religious leader, attended to by top government officials, including Castro himself, reportedly urged Cuba's *babalaos* to cooperate with the regime when he met with a government-selected group of them in a special ceremony at Havana's Casa de Africa (Ruiz 1987; Moore 1997: 231). His visit, however, was not without its fair share of controversy.

Some prominent Cuban *babalaos* complained about their exclusion from the event, which they were forced to watch on the evening news rather than witness in person (Fernández-Robaina 2001). Others questioned the entourage's spiritual motivations by calling attention to the disproportionate amount of time they spent striking economic agreements as opposed to attending to religious matters (Fernández-Robaina 2001: 90–91). But the most controversial moment of his visit came when the Oni commended Cubans for having retained what he claimed was 80 percent of the religion and declared Cuba's Ocha-Ifá community to be "a subsidiary (*subsede*) of Ile-Ife," a comment apparently embraced by the ACY (Ayorinde 2000: 79–80). The Oni's statement infuriated some Cuban *babalaos*. "He was saying that we are missing things," the late Cuban *babalao* Lázaro Marquetti told me, "but the [Cuban] Lucumí religion is a total religion; it isn't lacking anything." Marquetti went on to mention how flamboyant he thought the Oni of Ife appeared, "with his forty wives and army of attendants, he was only really concerned with getting rich." Marquetti, at the time of my interview, had only recently resumed his activities as an Ifá divination priest. He had stopped for three years in protest of what he referred to as the "commercialization" of the religion.

Two workshops followed the Oni's visit to Cuba; one at the Casa de Africa in 1992 that hosted a debate about a return to Africa and fears of ethnic division, and another called "The International Workshop on Yoruba Culture," which held discussions on the *"yorubización de la santería"* and the return to ritual orthodoxy through the purging of syncretic elements and placing the religion under the dictates of the Oni of Ife (Ayorinde 2000). These have been increasingly divisive issues within the Ocha-Ifá community since the Oni's visit. Fernández-Robaina, for example, notes three major tendencies and concerns within the Ocha-Ifá community in the past couple decades. First, is the desire on behalf of some to organize new associations, such as the Asociación Hijos de San Lázaro, La Sociedad San Antonio, and the ACY. Second, there have been attempts to recuperate older ritual practices of which there are two main variants; the first seeks to rescue ritual forms typical of the colonial and republican era by limiting initiation to those in need of healing an illness or for material and spiritual improvement. This mode of selecting eligibility for initiation is intended to limit the increasing commercialization of the religion, which has led to a dramatic rise in what some believe to be unnecessary initiations. The other variant suggests the adoption of the Yoruba mode of initiation in Nigeria, which only involves "seating" one oricha in the head of an initiate rather than several as is done in Cuba. For example, Victor Betancourt's Ifá Irán Lowó society, who also happens to be the youngest ranking member of the Miguel Febles Commission, has recently begun performing the head-and-foot initiation style characteristic of early initiations on the island and believed to be of African origin. Fran Cabrera and Taiwo Abimbola, the son of Yoruba *babalao* and writer Wande Ambimbola, founded the Ile Tun Tun society. "[A] reborn Ilé Ifè homeland on Cuban soil," Brown notes, "[m]embers wear African clothes and conform to hierarchies and rituals believed to organize the Ifá order of the Ifè kingdom" (Brown 2003a: 162)

Finally, some advocate forming schools and academies in order to insure the "proper" transmission of ritual knowledge and practices. Others reject institutionalization altogether, arguing that this is a matter that should be handled by the *padrino* and his or her *ahijados* or initiates (Fernández-Robaina 2000). As Ayorinde notes, the attitude of *"en mi casa mando yo"* (I rule in my house) has worked against institutionalization and unity (Ayorinde 2000: 79). Apparently, only a minority of Cubans have shown an interest in institutionalization, ritual orthodoxy, and "re-Africanization," and it appears that the majority of these have been *babalaos* who like to stress the distinction between Ocha and Ifá by arguing that the latter (Ifá) is more African because of its ritual purity and the former is more Cuban because it is more syncretic (Ayorinde 2000: 81). This contestation over the relative Africanness and Cubanness of Ocha-Ifá religion has had serious implications for the articulation and expression of national identity in Cuba: "If African-derived cultural practices are to reflect and validate a *national* identity (which they do), then the importance of Africa cannot be allowed to predominate. This could lead to transnational ethnic identification which could be potentially threatening to national unity" (Ayorinde 2000: 83).

The revolutionary government has responded in part to this threat to national identity through the licensing and funding of the ACY. Yet, paradoxically, it is the ACY, among others, who appear to advocate transnational ritual identification with Ile-Ife, which seems to contradict efforts to promote a singularly Cuban national rather than transnational identity.

The Battle over the "Letter of the Year"

Since the onset of the so-called Special Period, the annual Ifá divination ceremony known as the "Letter of the Year" has attracted the attention and curiosity of the larger Cuban public as well as the international community. Popular interest in the ceremony's annual prophecies has come to rival if not eclipse the significance of the government's own socialist slogans for the year. In an era of uncertainty and scarce resources the *babalaos*' annual prophetic pronouncements—e.g., "Some Would Give Up an Eye to See Another Go Blind," "Contradictions Bring the Light Out of Its Hiding Place," "The King Turns in His Crown Before Dying" etc.—offer more provocative metaphoric fat to chew on than official socialist slogans for the same years— e.g., "2006—Year of the Energetic Revolution in Cuba," "2005—Year of the Bolivian Alternative for the Americas," "2004—Year of the 45th Anniversary of the Revolution," or "2003—Year of the Glorious Anniversaries of Martí and the Moncada." But the existence of multiple prophecies and infighting among various factions of *babalaos* has not only led to a crisis in ritual authority and threatened to undermine the integrity of the annual ceremony but has also been further complicated by the political opportunism of forces outside the religion. As a result, Ocha-Ifá religion has become a veritable battleground of contested political meanings in contemporary Cuban society.

Although the government officially covers the reading performed by the ACY on national radio (Radio Progreso), most Cubans hear of the annual predictions through *radio bemba*, or word of mouth. Some take the prophecies seriously while others express only mild interest. During my fieldwork local interpretations were almost always dire. In January 2004, for example, one of the rumors circulating the streets was that the *babalaos* were distressed after the annual ceremony because, as one friend put it, "they don't know who is going to govern the country this year," suggesting that a change in political leadership was imminent. Local interpretations of the prophecies for 2005 were equally ominous in tone; the dead (*los eggun*), my informants warned, would rule over the coming year, ensuring that the immediate future would continue to be marked by an atmosphere of uncertainty. In 2006, some interpreted prophetic warnings that "the road toward neighboring lands would grow even longer," as indication that immigration accords between Cuba and the United States would be threatened, a situation that could not only undermine the chances of those planning to emigrate to the United States but further alienate family members separated by out-migration. I should note that these interpretations of the annual prophecies were not necessarily circulated by those who opposed the revolutionary government. Most of them came from people who, like most Cubans, temper frustrations with the country's socioeconomic difficulties by noting the success of the revolutionary government in areas such as race relations, medical care, and education. The point here is that attempts on behalf of Ifá divination priests to manage local interpretations have been hindered by the existence of multiple prophecies by various rival groups. The most significant factor plaguing the annual ceremony's credibility are the multiple readings performed by these competing factions. In 1999, for example, there were at least six ceremonies performed by different groups and at least one more was carried out in Miami (Guerra and Loureda 1999).

After the first generation of *babalaos* passed away, the tradition of performing a single, annual divination ceremony was lost. As early as the 1950s, prominent devotees were complaining about the crisis in ritual authority that Miguel Febles's actions had precipitated and attempts were made to revive the institution. Just prior to the Revolution, between 1950 and 1959, Bernardo Rojas brought together various factions and for almost a decade the ceremony was carried out by a single, unified group of *babalaos*. Soon after the Revolution, and after Rojas passed away, however, these groups splintered into competing factions once again. In 1976, a group of *babalaos* came together to form an association known as the Ifá Yesterday, Ifá Today, Ifá Tomorrow Association but eventually dissolved after the government rejected their request for a state license. Another attempt was made several years later under the leadership of the *babalao* Manelo Ibañez, who renamed the organization the ACY of Cuba. In 1991, during the early years of the Special Period, the association was officially licensed and began receiving both media and financial support from the state, a decision I examine in more detail later. Today, according to the association's president, Antonio Castañeda, the ACY has some 7,000 registered members, 1,000 of which are *babalaos*, and claims that the eldest *babalaos* on the island make up its Cuban Council of Elder Ifá Priests who are responsible for its annual divination prophecies.

The government's decision to support the ACY may have been due, in part, to the existence of a rival group of *babalaos* whose prophecies are seen by some as less politically sensitive to revolutionary vulnerability. Since its founding the CMFP has united hundreds of *babalaos* within Cuba and abroad during its annual Letter of the Year ceremony. Soon after being licensed by the state, the ACY began performing its own annual divination ceremony to compete with the CMFP's annual prophecies. By officially recognizing an association of Ifá diviners interested in institutionalizing their priesthood, the state benefits in several ways: state recognition ensures more direct access to and information about (e.g., statistical, sociopolitical, and financial) this somewhat secretive religious community, marginalizes those groups that are not interested in institutionalization by making them appear to be against the virtues of religious unity, guarantees some measure of control over how their prophecies and activities are interpreted, provides for the appearance of religious tolerance in a country once officially declared atheist, indicates the state's commitment to its historically marginalized and largely black communities by elevating their cultural heritage to the level of an officially sanctioned public institution, and generates hard currency in attracting religious pilgrims and foreign tourists with a thirst for the "authentic" Cuba, to name just some of the potential factors influencing the government decision to formally recognize this aspiring association.

The existence of various annual prophecies and competing factions has been increasingly politicized by different groups both on and off the island. Indicative of the ceremony's increasing political significance in contemporary Cuban society are the recent flurry of scholarly articles on the subject published in Cuba and abroad, including a large section of a recent issue of the University of Havana Review.[7] Local reaction to this coverage in recent years has been mixed with some *babalaos*, such as the CMFP's Victor Betancourt, denouncing such coverage as opportunistic sensationalism. Though Betancourt (2003) addresses his comments to the international community his criticisms of the "opportunism" that characterizes the interests of those outside the religion, whether at home or abroad, can easily be read as a veiled reference to government itself. Nonetheless, interpretations from abroad, especially in the Miami exile community, have certainly complicated matters for the CMFP. Rumors on the streets of Miami had it that the commission's letter for 2004, Baba Eyiobe, was the same one that appeared when Castro came to power in 1959 and that reappeared in 1989 when the commander of Cuban troops in Angola, General Arnaldo Ochoa, who many exiles believed was the only person capable of organizing a successful coup on the island, was shot and killed. Many Cuban exiles in Miami believed that the CMFP's 2004 letter predicted a major political shakeup on the island. The CMFP, of course, emphatically denies these interpretations.

Although both factions of Ifá divination priests on the island have been preoccupied in recent years with managing public interpretations of their prophecies, the majority of their public relations efforts have continued to focus on discrediting their rivals. Today, the CMFP and the ACY are the two main rivals struggling for control over the annual ceremony. The differences in the ritual protocols followed by these two groups appear minor. For the former the youngest ranking member is the one who takes out the letter (i.e., ritually determines which sign will rule the year) whereas for the latter it is the oldest *babalao*. For the former the ceremony should be performed on the first day or during the first week of the new year whereas for the former it should be performed during the morning hours of December 31. They also differ on what kinds of ritual sacrifices are appropriate for a successful ceremony.

Some argue that the sacrifices should always be the same every year whereas others argue it depends on what Orula orders to be done, which is revealed in divination (Argüelles 2003). Despite differences in ritual procedures it is fairly obvious that the more important lines of contention between these two associations center around contestations over their respective claims of the power and authority necessary to control the annual ceremony. Although the conflict between these two factions is often represented as a contest between competing claims of spiritual or ritual authenticity, the struggle has increasingly been articulated in terms of economic exploitation and morality.

The sometimes heated rivalry and tensions between these two major factions of Ifá divination priests has included a number of seething rhetorical attacks designed to undermine the spiritual capital of the other side by claiming that more than just religious concerns motivate their organizing efforts. The CMFP, for example, accuses the ACY of submitting to political manipulation by the government in exchange for the perks of state sponsorship (e.g., a restored mansion in central Havana to serve as the association's center, state-sponsored media coverage and financial support, the sociopolitical capital that comes from state recognition etc.). The ACY, however, counters these charges by accusing the CMFP of exploiting the religion for profit, a particularly thorny issue since the onset of the current economic crisis. Similar accusations of economic exploitation and political manipulation have also hindered efforts to unite *babalaos* across the political divide between Havana and Miami (Correa 1997). Antonio Castañeda, president of the ACY, for example, wearing a suit and tie and sitting behind a large office desk in his second-floor office, appearing more like a businessman or politician than a divination priest, had the following to say regarding the rivalry between the two groups:

> We have been fighting for unification for several years.... Today, some want to go to battle over the letter of the year.... They say we [the ACY] are being manipulated by the government. But what we do has nothing to do with politics or influence. I'm still driving the same car I had before I became president of the association. I don't receive any special favors. The truth is they [the CMFP] want to exploit the religion to get rich.

Accusations of *interes* (profiting from the religion), however, are often a matter of interpretation. After we concluded our conversation, Castañeda apologized for having postponed the interview a week before. I had been waiting to interview him for a couple of weeks. "I was in France," he boasted, "attending to one of my ritual godchildren [*ahijados*], a wealthy French businessman who paid for the entire trip and even treated me to a brief vacation."

The ACY's allegations of spiritual transgression, which denounce those who use the religion as a vehicle for profit, are thinly veiled attempts to dismiss the CMFP's *babalaos* by implying their participation in the illicit economic activities associated with *jineterismo*. Like *jineteros*, Castañeda deplores rival *babalaos* as purveyors of the entrepreneurial spirit that has come to define the informal economy since the withdrawal of massive foreign subsidies that began in the early 1990s. The informal economy lies outside formal state control and presents a challenge to revolutionary morals by allegedly promoting the materialistic and individualistic values associated with capitalism. The claim that the CMFP embodies the legacy and infamous reputation of Miguel Febles spiritually discredits its members by accusing them of commodity fetishism with respect to the religion, thereby shaming them by insinuating that their economic activities are contrary to the values of socialism. The CMFP has responded in part to charges of economic exploitation with their own counterclaims of spiritual transgression. They note that they, unlike the ACY, have refused to be co-opted by the state, which they describe as a kind of spiritual coup that has essentially enabled the government to usurp the powers of Orula for both financial and political reasons.

Exploiting the religion for profit was perhaps the most salient concern of my informants in Havana and Matanzas. Many complained that this not only represented an act of spiritual debauchery that threatened established ritual protocols but was also causing unnecessary harm and suffering and angering the *orichas*. Yoel, a popular *santero* in the province of Matanzas, complained that tourism in Havana coupled with the financial disparity of its residents was exposing the religion to unprecedented forms of greed and corruption. Those who turned to the religion with the intention of making money by initiating tourists, he argued, were not only inflicting harm on unsuspecting tourists but were also threatening to alienate the *orichas* from their devotees on the island:

> [I]n Havana, they bring in saints (*orichas*) that are not known here.... Songs don't even exist for those saints. Everything they do is for commerce. There's this Spaniard *impresario* that came to Havana and received the *mano de orula* and made saint. Afterwards, the guy lost his business; one of his legs swelled up and now he has heart trouble. You know what people are saying? That he's waiting until he can come back in order to kill the person that did that to him and he has his reason. They made him a saint that wasn't necessary. He was supposed to receive Changó but instead they made him San Lázaro because it's the most expensive.... There was also this Spanish woman who made the wrong saint and, afterwards, she went bald. They talked about it on the radio in Spain. They were criticizing the religion. The woman destroyed all of her ritual belongings and now is half crazy.... Notice that the saints do not come like they did before.... They don't do the same things that they did before. They make their exceptions.

The current regime's role in the commercialization exploitation of Ocha-Ifá is indisputable, the most obvious indication of the state's role in the commercialization of Ocha-Ifá religion occurring in December 2005. As mentioned earlier, it is common to see Ocha-Ifá images on commodities such as *aguardiente*, perfumes, and tourists' novelties sold in stores that only accept hard currency (i.e., the convertible peso used as a local substitute for U.S. dollars and euros). During my field research, I never came across any of these religious images on products sold in stores that charge in pesos, the massively devalued currency that the state still uses to pay citizens' salaries. In a local hard currency store (*chóppin*) in Guanabacoa, a simulated Ocha-Ifá altar (*trono*) had been arranged alongside discounted fans, toilets, lamps, clothes, and food. The altar had been set up as part of a store-wide end of the year sale. In front of the altar, a folklore ensemble performed dances for the *orichas* (or Ocha-Ifá "saints"). One *babalao* in Guanabacoa was incredulous: "What do the *santos* have to do with the sale of commodities?" he fumed. "How embarrassing," he complained as he threw his hands up in resignation, "... it's an outrage!"

These examples of both alleged *jineterismo* and "official" state commercialization of the religion was addressed in one of the collective *rogación*, or purification/healing ceremonies, that I attended earlier in January 2004 organized by one of the ranking *babalaos* of the CMFP. The ceremony had been necessary and, indeed, urgent after the annual divination ceremony had revealed one of the most ambiguous signs of the Ifá corpus, Baba Eyiobe, one forecasting either prosperity beyond imagination or hopeless tragedy and destruction. As the ritual cleansings were performed on the back patio of his temple-house in Central Havana, the *babalao* suddenly interrupted the proceedings with an impromptu speech. Citing an Ifá text, the presiding *babalao* told the story of how an entire African village had suffered from famine because the ports had been closed, an obvious reference to the American blockade or embargo. He then offered what very well may have been a reply to the ACY's charges of spiritual transgression through the illicit practices associated with *jineterismo*: "We Cubans...we're all hustlers [*jineteros*]! We have no other choice. The *santeros* and *babalaos*...they're all hustlers. We're all hustlers by necessity! And the government...the government's the biggest one of them all!" His comments are significant for two reasons. First, he explicitly calls attention to what has remained a public secret on the island for several years—namely, that hustling has become an integral if not vital economic strategy in the new culture of *resolver*. For the state-sponsored *babalaos* of the ACY to pretend otherwise or to take the moral high ground by claiming their nonparticipation in the informal economy, in his view, amounts to hypocrisy. Second, he not only implicates the government in the economic strategies associated with *jineterismo* but also suggests that they too are exploiting Ocha-Ifá religion for profit and that the ACY has remained complicit in these exploits. His intention was not to advocate the commodification and economic exploitation of Ocha-Ifá religion. Rather, he was simply calling attention to the current socioeconomic reality of scarcity that defines daily life on the island and the fact that no one in Cuba can claim moral purity with regard to the new hustle economy. Everyone is implicated.

After the *babalao*'s impromptu speech, everyone present, their heads and faces still wet from the herbal water and the goats' blood, walked down to the oceanfront with offerings to Olokún. Despite the police presence, the defiant *babalao* insisted on completing the sacrifices in public along the Malecón in front of the port of Havana, although he had not received prior permission. There, in front of the tourists, *jineteros*, lovers, and police, he sang the praises of and offered seven roosters and a duck to Olokún, the mysterious *oricha* of the profound depths of the sea, the impenetrable and dark abyss. According to a Cuban friend of mine who accompanied me to the ceremony, the whole question of spiritual corruption was precisely why the collective purification ceremony had been necessary in the first place. It was intended to ritually "cleanse" and, therefore, protect devotees from any possible mystical repercussions associated with the morally ambiguous actions at play within the religion in an age of scarcity, a problem related to both the U.S. embargo (hence, the ceremonies' proximity to the port of Havana) and the deteriorating domestic economy.

Conclusion

The government's decision to support the ACY has important political and economic implications. In part, it reflects an attempt to tap into the secret ritual economy of Ocha-Ifá. This has contributed significantly to the increasingly commercialization of the religion through international marketing campaigns designed to attract foreign tourists to the island. Of course, the ACY is not responsible for those who choose to exploit or otherwise violate ritual protocols in the interests of profit. But their association with the state has only fueled allegations of their complicity with regard to the government's marketing of the religion for foreign tourist consumption. What is perhaps most perplexing about the government's support of the ACY is that it appears to be encouraging an association that promotes what some refer to as the Yorubaization of Ocha-Ifá religion on the island and advocates, according to Ayorinde (2000), decentering local ritual authority in Cuba by placing the religion under the dictates of the Oni of Ife in Nigeria. It is not entirely clear what is behind such a decision, which appears to contradict the government's desire for a unified national identity as it encourages identification with a transnational ritual authority. There are, however, at least two possible implications of the government's current support of the ACY. On one hand, it reflects the government's desire to cast these religious cults as cultural "survivals" from a remote African past, a move that attempts to displace the local foundations of ritual authority by claiming that the religion's roots lie elsewhere. This certainly fits well with the government's efforts to represent Ocha-Ifá as a kind of quaint national folklore, which acknowledges the entertainment value it has in the form of myths, songs, and dance but implicitly rejects its contemporary vivacity by representing it as an essentially "dead" practice to be valued only as an historical curiosity.

On the other hand, through its support of the ACY the government appears to have, at least with respect to the Ifá community, sidelined the issue of national identity for the time being in exchange for the political guarantees that the control of the annual divination ceremony may bring. The "official" *babalaos* of the ACY will always come up with a politically correct *letra*. The use of Ifá divination to bring competing factions under one authority is not without historical precedent. In the mid-eighteenth century, for example, a Dahomean king used the Ifá divination of his Yoruba neighbors, "in order to centralize the kingdom's oracular authority by delegitimizing and controlling the dangerously 'centrifugal' and subversive tendencies of the country's multifarious *vodun* possession oracles" (Brown 2003: 115–116). The government's investment in the struggle over control of the annual divination ceremony is not only a political strategy designed to create the impression that it respects the religious faith of its citizens but is also intended to mend the frayed edges of the body politic by encouraging the unification of multifarious religious factions and ensuring that their prophecies do not contradict the state's agenda. After all, ritual identification with a transnational religious community may appear to be less of a challenge to the legitimacy of the state's power and authority than a politically charged prophecy that reflects negatively on the nation's leadership.

My effort in this essay has been to show how the Letter of the Year ceremony and infighting among various factions of divination priests struggling for control over the ceremony was initially a relatively esoteric conflict without much relevance to those outside of Cuba's Ocha-Ifá community. What was once a matter of local ritual politics, however, was suddenly forced to the forefront of nationalist politics after the state became involved in the conflict, as well as by the increasing global presence of the religion facilitated in part by the development of the tourist industry. As a result, Ocha-Ifá religion has become one of the most visible battlegrounds on which struggles over how to define national identity and the politics of value in contemporary Cuban society is waged. This battle over the prophetics of revolutionary society not only exemplifies the government's attempt to place more emphasis on national belonging rather than political community (i.e., the socialist project) but also calls attention to how the new culture of *resolver* is characterized as much by struggles over value as it is by economic strategy.

Notes

1. For specific examples of narrative describing the intermingling of secular and sacred power in Cuba see Bascom (1951: 17), Brown (2003: 84–85), Carbonell (1993: 198), de la Torre (2003), Díaz Fabelo (1974), Lachantañeré (2001), Melgar (1991), Miller (2000), Orozco and Bolívar (1998), and Valdes Figueroa (2001).
2. I am using the term "cult" here in the strictest sense to refer to the acephalous nature of a number of relatively small but interrelated ritual families.
3. West African antecedents more than likely had some influence on the animosity that developed between the Egbado and the Oyo and their competing ritual systems in Cuba (see Ramos 2003).
4. The Ifá-centric accounting of many scholars is largely due to the fact that their main informants were *babalaos* (see Brown 2003: 147; Murphy 1981; and Cabrera 1980 [1974]).
5. The founders of these principal *ramas* or branches were Carlos Adé Bí, Remigio "Adechina" Herrera, Joaquín Cádiz, Oluguere Kó Kó, and Francisco Villalonga (see Brown 2003).
6. Religious believers were banned from the Cuban Communist Party until 1993 when the government officially welcomed believers into the party (see Benkomo 2000; Selier and Hernández 2004).
7. See de Rey Roa (2002), Sigler (2005), Argüelles (2003), Betancourt (2003), González (2003), Guerra (2003), and Trimegistros (2003).

3

Transnational Publics

9

El Rap Cubano: Can't Stop, Won't Stop the Movement!

Roberto Zurbano Translated by Kate Levitt

I

One afternoon, in the spring of 1997, Rodolfo Rensoli came to see me at my office in the Hermanos Saiz Association (AHS) equipped with a modest speech, an unadorned cane and, above all, a challenging idea he had already shown he could realize: the Rap Festival of Havana.[1] It was a strange conversation, during which he filled in the blanks of a world that I had only witnessed a few times out of curiosity and chance during the years I lived in the town of Alamar. There, I used to cross the East Havana *Diente-de-perro* neighborhood every day on my way to Vedado on the M-1, the pink *camello* bus. In transit, I saw graffiti that revealed the existence of a hip-hop universe, and listened to the other passengers improvise ingeniously to the polyrhythmic sounds made by mouths and hands. These were Havana's mobile deejays.

Rensoli formed Grupo Uno (Group One) in 1995, in that same East Havana neighborhood, to energize a growing mass of rappers and promote their work wherever possible; at that time there were very few spaces available to do so. Grupo Uno emerged in response to the increasing organizational and promotional needs of the nascent rap movement. In the beginning it was composed of Rodolfo Rensoli and Balexis Rivero, two young black men from East Havana who were fans of the genre, and to whose ability, determination, and talent we owe the first rap festivals and shows in Cuba. After Rensoli described in detail the new project, he parsimoniously responded to each and every one of my questions. We shared many ideas and talked easily into the night. Then and there we sealed the deal to work toward giving rap music made in Cuba a legitimately visible space. That space was the Hermanos Saiz Association (AHS), the youth wing of the writers and artists organization, of which I was then the vice president. The proposal was that the AHS would take charge of the upcoming annual rap festival. After that, we would discuss how to include rappers in the association, since most of them were not professional musicians, and then how to find an adequate promotional strategy for this new cultural form in a set of difficult, reluctant circumstances. Indeed, rappers had reported institutional resistance and prejudice in the few venues and spaces in which they had worked.

Fernando Rojas, then my superior and president of the AHS, sought the approval of cultural authorities both in Havana and also at the national level with the Provincial Cultural Directorate and the Cuban Music Institute of the Ministry of Culture. Their response was aloof and the effective lack of support convinced us to fully take charge of the rap festival ourselves—after all, we had experience with similar types of events, such as the *Romerias de Mayo* (May Arts Festival) and the *Dias de Musica* (Music Days) festivals,[2] which had succeeded in launching talented young artists with otherwise no access to institutional spaces. These festivals provided incentives for official institutions to support young talent by including young musicians within promotional catalogues compiled by the Ministry of Culture business agencies and record labels. We had achieved this goal with dozens of groups and solo artists; the rappers should be no different, particularly given that at the time the AHS had the steadfast goal to work with sectors, such as rock musicians, often seen as problematic by other official institutions, and to develop a coherent policy that would result in the social acceptance of youth cultures. The AHS's goal was to integrate new cultural forms within enduring frameworks of nation, and national and political culture, opening up utopian possibilities and new forms of expression.

That same year, 1997, on a hot September afternoon, a meeting with more than 100 rappers took place in Central Havana's *La Madriguera*, the space designated for rap music, to define the AHS registration process. As typically the association has been highly selective of its membership, the meeting was marked by polemics, heated discussions, and internal battles. Nonetheless, the seeds of what became a true cultural movement were planted. Distinct aesthetic and ideological viewpoints, as well as professional and commercial aspirations, had to be reconciled on that steamy night of blackouts, from which emerged diverse proposals on rap's place and purpose.

Before the year ended, on December 29, the poet and music producer Pablo Herrera—one of the founders of the rap group *Amenaza*, which would later become the celebrated band *Orishas*, called the AHS to announce Fab Five Freddy's arrival. Herrera suggested that the rap community hold a meeting with the well-known North American hip-hop producer. Indeed, we did meet with Fab Five Freddy and it became clear that the exchange between Cuban and North American rappers could impact sociocultural perspectives on both sides. The Cuban rappers asked many questions to fill in the gaps in their knowledge of hip-hop, and described their own work, conditions, vernacular, and needs, so that Fab Five Freddy could learn about his peers in Cuba. That meeting was particularly illuminating as we realized the kinds of oppression we shared with people supposedly so far-removed from us. Despite comparisons with U.S. hip-hop and the need for the Cuban form to define itself, I consider this shared consciousness key in the formation and configuration of Cuba's rap movement. A poet such as Pablo Herrera was clearly aware of that long before he became the respectable producer he is today, although at the time his impressive ideas were not convincing or acceptable to everyone.

The most significant meeting of this kind, however, took place between Harry Belafonte and a large group of rappers in December of 1999, during Belafonte's appearance at that year's Havana Film Festival. The rappers knew the meeting could lead to important opportunities and they all loudly, clearly, and respectfully described the movement's initial steps, aspirations, and obstacles. Poet and ethnologist Miguel Barnet attended the meeting and was impressed by the hip-hop movement's emancipatory and de-alienating force, something most cultural institutions failed to see, instead dismissing the music as "too Americanizing." But by the end of 1990s, winds of reinvention were blowing through Cuban cultural politics. A narrow-minded, politicized nationalism was fading, allowing for renovation of traditional cultural canons. At that point, the hip-hop movement could make an invaluable contribution to this process, which would cut across complex generational, racial, and international lines.

2

The next step was to begin the institutional process at the AHS—of identifying talented rap artists, legitimizing their activities, improving their social recognition, supporting their initiatives, and incorporating them into more established cultural spaces. Rensoli and an AHS music specialist toured the country with these goals in mind. They confirmed that dozens of rap groups existed outside Havana and throughout the island, registered with the AHS those whose lyrical, musical, and performance skills merited it, and selected the very best for participation in the following year's Rap Festival. These tasks were accomplished with the support of panels and commissions of music critics, academics, and rappers, as well as state record label consultants in the Ministry of Culture provincial employment agencies (with which affiliate professional musicians coordinate for work and wages). The movement was moving along!

That year, 1998, the rap group *Doble Filo* participated in the *Romerias de Mayo*, interacting with other singer-songwriters and performing in

Holguín's main square in front of thousands of fans. Likewise, one year later, the all-female rap group *Instinto* was able to stir up Havana's carnival festival. At the same time, a newly formed committee, the so-called *Juntas de Patrocinio*, emerged. *Juntas* was an institutional structure created at the AHS to lobby state cultural institutions to finance youth projects of experimental, social, and aesthetic quality. The committee met three times per year, and included representatives from the AHS, the Union of Cuban Writers and Artists, UPEC, the Ministry of Culture, and occasionally the Union of Communist Youth. The committee sought to circumvent the bureaucratic roadblocks that often faced emerging, not-yet-professional artists, who were not permitted to perform, or receive financing or any other form of promotion. At each meeting, the committee approved about five projects. Most significantly, they succeeded in securing grants for rappers as well as recording possibilities.

Rappers were not considered professional musicians, and consequently their inclusion in catalogues and databases represented a giant step toward their artistic recognition. Furthermore, the registration allowed them to receive a fixed salary, at least during that first year. Later on, they were offered training courses, in which they were taught various technical music subjects (singing, composition, instrumentation, etc.). In addition, they were also educated on Afro-Cuban history and culture by the renowned specialist Tomasito Fernandez Robaina so that they would be able to recognize their own identity within Cuba's social history and culture. Like their fellow musicians in other genres, rappers were ensured access to continuing education and training, an obligatory practice for all active musicians to maintain the currency of their skills.

Yet departing from the initial view of formal training as elitist gatekeeping, there emerged a new, expanded understanding of training as an operational concept and opportunity for creative exchange among artists. Rap musicians have at times been criticized for their lack of proper music training. At the same time, academic musicians are beginning to concern themselves with a more operational and practical conceptualization of training, which includes strategies for accessing opportunities both in Cuban and abroad, and engaging in hybrid exchange with other music genres and expressions with whom academic musicians may share stage and recording time, TV appearances, international tours, and the like.

By the end of the 1990s, the AHS had in place an alternative training program for musicians with little formal training or education, a strategy that had previously been successful among comedians with continuing education summer courses at the Instituto Superior de Arte. Like comedians, rap artists seldom had formal academic training; nonetheless, they occupied an important space in the culture and their niche audience. Just as previously the AHS created a Center for the Promotion of Comedy to promote and certify comedians, they founded a Cuban Rap Agency in September 2002 in response to the needs of an artistic movement that already had an audience and broad commercialization possibilities.

Another important step toward organizing and institutionalizing this incipient movement was to define its identity, taking the proposals of Grupo-Uno as an initial starting point, and brainstorming about its various musical, sociological, ideological, organizational, promotional, and commercial features. A rap colloquium was held in conjunction with the Rap Festival in 1998, in the eastern Havana neighborhood of Alamar. There, a large number of rap artists were able to interact with audiences, members of the press, radio and television programmers, Cuban and foreign scholars, and authorities from the Ministry of Culture and the government. The colloquium did not receive much public attention beyond these circles and consequently the support of the AHS, the Cuban Institute of Music, and the Rap Agency became more urgent. Nevertheless, even though it would have benefited from an institutional framework, the rap movement showed its organic character, in the Gramscian sense. The movement is characterized by a peculiar way of thinking about itself. Its particular poetics and proposals emerge from the communities in which the rappers live, as well as from exchanges with other artists and spaces they consider legitimate, both within and beyond the island. Over the last 10 years, the AHS was able to help the hip-hop movement acquire more organizational coherence, assist in producing certain projects, and represent rap artists' views in the public sphere. Perhaps the most recognized artists are EPG&B (Executive Plan of the Ghetto), La FabriKa, El Cartel y Omega, but these are not the only groups that have emerged from the movement's ethical-artistic needs and sociocultural goals. Thanks to the work of the movement and AHS, some rappers have also found work in related functions such as promotions, radio programming, music journalism, and so on.

3

In Cuba, people express cultural concepts in a fragmented manner, with supposedly closed codes that do not reveal everything at once. In popular culture, for example, meaning is not closed; rather, many kinds of personal prejudices, stereotypes, and miscomprehensions precede the understandings and relations established through popular culture expressions. The first rappers that I met seemed to be people far-removed from my own cultural milieu. The ways in which they greeted me, spoke, and dressed seemed very foreign, probably similar to the experiences of many *santeros*, whose greetings, speech, and dress are difficult for most people to decipher.

If *santeria* expresses itself through religious rituals, the world of hip-hop uses poetics of the *barrio*, shared by those who live there through their greetings, dress, nicknames, forms of speech, gestures, and the like: languages born of a particular set of urban circumstances. This poetry emerging in the *barrio*, be it on the periphery or not, expresses new changes in urban identity and in the people who reside there. If I have compared rappers with *santeros* it is not because of their differences, but rather because of their commonalities. Both groups reject Eurocentric ethics and aesthetics, and both are accustomed to being associated with low levels of education and sophistication. Further, both groups use informal styles of expression and solidarity. Their codes of expression emerge from popular culture and demonstrate their difference and otherness. This unique self-perception develops in a collective space that corresponds with bloodline or religion, to the *barrio* or to a group of friends with similar expectations and possibilities. Included in this culture is a form of traditional education associated with Afro-religious families in Cuba, as well as other families in many *barrios* on the island.

Rap lyrics reflect all of the characteristics described earlier. Rap artists' preoccupation with the group to which they belong manifests itself in the survival instinct of a community that defines itself by neighborhood, generation, and race, all of which are situated in a tense socioeconomic context. Artists are from communities with limited economic possibilities; they are often disenfranchised from remittances or other forms of access to the dollar, and consequently feel bitter, marginalized, or simply in danger of not making ends meet. Most of the themes that Cuban rappers discuss reveal an anguished solidarity and, along with other problems discussed later in this text, define a new subaltern subject and identity in the Cuban context.

The Cuban rapper, emerging in the Special Period, expresses not only material deprivation but also a deterioration and subversion of the utopian vision of the Cuban Revolution's emancipatory project. The majority of rap artists are young blacks and *mestizos*, and they come from working-class families and neighborhoods with few university graduates or academics among their ranks. Frustrated with their social status, they find a space for expression and organization through hip-hop. Furthermore, the subaltern condition of rappers manifests itself in a culture where the Eurocentric canon continues to be the dominant culture, yet one that is challenged by the rising presence of alternative forms of Cuban popular culture. The Cuban rapper is, then, a subaltern subject with the critical capacity to reject the excessively Eurocentric focus of Cuban culture, which obscures cultural expressions foreign to the Western canon, such as Afro-Cuban religion, popular culture, and informal modes of interaction, such as gesture. The Cuban rapper has therefore both identified and resisted the subtle discrimination founded on Euro-Cuban domination, which while not entirely eliminating alternative cultural expressions does certainly push them to the margins. Rappers are not the only subjects on the island who suffer from and experience this domination—salsa dancers, *timba* players, and *trovadores* have too—but they are the ones whose main artistic content overtly rejects Euro-Cuban domination.

In light of the Special Period's economic adjustments and readjustments, changes in customs and ethics among citizens, as well as the increasing stratification of society, the *barrio*, the community, and the circle of friends and family have also been rearticulated. For instance, the role of the mother has become more significant, perhaps because in the middle of the deterioration of so many traditional and revolutionary values she has been a resistant subject, simultaneously a preserver of old and creator of new attitudes and morality. Notice the number of times that she is mentioned in rap texts, as well as the massive presence of mothers who attend their children's rap shows. The need for social rearticulation also manifests itself in the names many rap groups give themselves. In this case, the act of self-naming explicitly references the local predicament, neighborhood, race, family, and group as spaces for the foundation, defense, and legitimization of hip-hop discourse. Some popular bands have called themselves Familia's Cuba Represent, Hermanos de Causa (Brothers in the Cause), Anonimo Consejo (Anonymous Council), Doble Filo (Double Edge), Instinto (Instinct), Krudas Cubensis, EPG & B (Executive Plan of the Ghetto plus Barbarito), La Fabri-K (The Faktory), Junior Clan, Hermanazos (Big Brothers), Kumar el Menor (Young Kumar), Los Paisanos (The Countrymen), Escuadron Patriotico de Guines (Patriotic Squad of Güines), El Cartel, and other self-affirming names that express collective aspirations and desires to participate in and transform the sociocultural field of which they form a part.

That is to say, rappers construct a decentralized discourse whose space of articulation is not class, but that of an underrepresented social group; this is evidenced in the names of the figures, soloists, groups, and projects that illustrate new identities and subcultures in the cities' changing layouts, and specifically in the marginal neighborhoods that lie on the urban periphery. They are names in search of an alternate identity that is aggressive but nonviolent. Nonetheless, rappers express bitterness and marginality in many other ways than through the defense and articulation of their social group.

The inherently critical character of hip-hop culture makes the Cuban rapper its own revolutionary subject. Here I use revolutionary in the term's strictest philosophical and political sense in Cuba, and not in the rhetoric that often devalues its meaning. I define it, perhaps schematically, as youth capable of describing their sociocultural situation, assuming the emancipatory tradition of the Cuban Revolution, and critically evaluating reality, including an analysis of and emphasis on race in Cuba's historic and cultural discourse. The rap movement comprises young people—female and male—who constantly interrogate society and freely express their approval or rejection of society's values. They articulate their experiences in the Special Period through a generational discourse: in each concert, in each recording we witness their anecdotes and we listen to their complaints, but we also hear their accurate reflections on tourism, prostitution, drugs, hypocrisy, corruption, racial discrimination—of which they are often victims—conformity, political demobilization, mercantilism, the environment, emigration, and other problems of a social reality both within and outside of Cuba. This young revolutionary subject, while speaking about these themes and confronting us with difficult self-reflection, also opens up a transformative path, pushing us to collectively participate in the criticism of and reflection on these issues.

Any rap text is a heterogeneous linguistic expression that, in Cuba, arranges and projects the social expectations of the aforementioned subject. These texts, be they a musical theme, a video clip, a hip-hop poetry performance, a photo exposition, or a graffiti mural irreverently articulate themselves, in a raw and sharp dialogue with reality and more formalized cultural discourses. They are texts hungering for social exchanges with the country's most elite heritage. They are born of an insatiable interrogation where they mix the local, universal, transnational, and marginal with politics and the market, race with ecology, language with community, ideological discourse with sexuality and religion. In sum, we face an aesthetic-ideological phenomenon that recycles everything and suggests a new space for dialogue and integration, both within and outside of Cuban culture and society. Hip-hop presents a new form of articulating the national in relation to other global cultural expressions, in which certain styles (e.g., Rastafarianism), technologies, and identities develop in specific cultural locales, but simultaneously remain open enough to foster international exchanges of culture and identity.

We must analyze Cuban rap through its role in the production of transnational subjects. Cuban rappers work with expressions that are also marginalized in other parts of the planet, incorporating them in the local discourse of the periphery. At the same time, they operate with the same instruments and styles of transnationalized marginal groups, as many foreign academics have analyzed, such as Pacini Hernandez and Garofalo (2000), Alan West-Duran (2004), Sujatha Fernandes (2003), Marc Perry (2004), and others. Cuban rap sounds like a tongue twister but it is not; it sounds like an anguished exchange of influences but it is not. It is a new cultural process, at once local and global.

Consequently, rap places the academy in question, which has refused to offer a nuanced analysis of this new cultural practice. It has also appropriated poetic and political texts, as well as popular and classic lyrics, to create an intertextual dialogue that problematizes their hegemonic, "high culture" propositions. In doing so, rap subverts not only language but also ideological claims, operating in a new imaginary that could be identified as postmodern given the sheer number of texts the music critically and creatively incorporates in its performative body. These rap texts form a cultural matrix that demands an interdisciplinary approach, such as that of cultural studies, despite the fact that this method is hardly accepted in the Cuban academy and other intellectual spaces. This does not justify Cuban cultural criticism's continuing disregard for a new cultural practice rich with ethical and ideological messages. Contrasting the lack of recognition of rap music on the island is the fact that outside of Cuba dozens of researchers—not only from the United States and its well-oiled academic machine, but also from Latin America and Europe—concern themselves with Cuban hip-hop culture and produce a growing number of texts, albums, and films about the cultural form. The Cuban rap movement and its radical discourse obligate a restructuring of Cuban cultural criticism. It is urgent to evaluate cultural criticism's shortcomings, in addition to its contributions and the varied ways in which it appropriates or rejects each new expression of global culture on the island. We need strategies capable of confronting the challenge of globalization, which has rapidly increasing visibility in Cuban daily life, as well as evaluating each of the expressions, phenomena, and cultural dynamics of which we are a part.

Once this is accomplished, I propose to not avoid but rather overcome, in the inevitable comparisons between U.S. and Cuban hip-hop culture, some of the superficialities that pervade the culture's transnational condition. The genre of hip-hop demands a global approach, as all rappers, be they Brazilian, Spanish, Jamaican, Italian, Cuban, or American, participate in a transnational community in which they work to insert local dynamics and exchange aesthetic and ideological messages to legitimize their discourse. In Cuba the constant presence and numerous visits of North American rap artists and hip-hop scholars reveal, among other aspects, an affinity between identities shaped by similar musical, racial, and aesthetic characteristics. Nonetheless, we should be wary of accepting a cultural industry that often promotes the commercialized tragedy of economically and culturally marginalized populations in every corner of the planet. Here we see the challenges of the double topography—local and global—of this culture and its geographic, social, technological, cultural, and discursive contexts.

4

Within social discourse in Cuba, rap places particular importance on the theme of race, from the debate over the term Afro-Cuban to the criticism of neo-racist expressions that have emerged in the twenty-first century. Rap presents a generational approach to its analysis of race problems, one that does not tolerate outdated attitudes that displace public debate on contemporary race matters in Cuba, and instead constructs a transnational intellectual history incorporating the ideas of Mariana Grajales, Antonio Maceo, Fernando Ortíz, Nicolas Guillén, Franz Fanon, Walterio Carbonell, Ernesto Che Guevara, Malcolm X, Fidel Castro, and Nelson Mandela. For example, the discussion of controversial race topics such as "bad hair," hair weaves, dreadlocks, Afros and other hairstyles, and modes of dress of African origin, is informed by an ethical, aesthetic, and ideological affinity for diverse forms of anticolonial, antiracist, and revolutionary thought of the twentieth century, reproduced and rearticulated in numerous rap songs, images, and concerts.[3]

A wide range of rap music concerns itself with critically describing and evaluating problems that one rarely encounters in other areas of Cuban artistic production, and does so with a heartrending authenticity that does not merely inform but testifies within autobiographical narratives of social struggle and confrontation against dominant racist, macho, and neocolonial expressions. The hip-hop movement thus opens spaces for activating imaginaries of struggle shared by many communities in the country and the world.

If the topic of racial discrimination has entered national debate in Cuba over the last several years, it owes much to hip-hop culture's contemplation of the phenomenon. The debate affects a large percentage of the rap community, as the majority is made up of young blacks and *mestizos* proud of their racial identity and its possibilities for new aesthetics and cultural expressions. Still, the Eurocentric influence that survives in Cuba's social conscious largely rejects such alternative displays. For example, police officers frequently demand identification from these young people, given their lack of awareness of the culture and their different geographic origins. Young police officers in Havana generally come from rural areas, and therefore are not familiar with the cultural dynamics of a city expressing itself through myriad fashions, aesthetic affiliations, and other visible marks characteristic of diverse cultural identities, such as rockers, religious groups, homosexuals, and tourists. The police often confuse these differences with marginal or possibly delinquent behaviors. In their lyrics, Cuban rappers relate these situations with a strong reflexive tone and demand that this persistent racist mentality be eradicated. Also of interest are crowd responses at rap performances.

5

Rappers' spoken words express a new kind of poetry in their explicit concern with race. As mentioned earlier, these young people, the majority of which come from marginal neighborhoods and/or families, not only in Havana but also in Santiago de Cuba, Guantanamo, Matanzas, and other cities, express themselves in the language of their respective communities. Their testimonies deal with the world of the *barrio*, the unjust and unequal world that tourism, foreign investment, and the circulation of the U.S. dollar has created. They discuss the police siege on young blacks, prostitution, and drug addiction, and simultaneously criticize the *balseros* who put their lives in danger to abandon the country; they embrace the emancipative ideas of the Revolution, with its proposals for new forms of brotherhood and solidarity.

There are hundreds of rap groups, lacking technology but rich with an approach that responds to and resignifies both Cuban and foreign literary and musical texts: Nicolas Guillén, Benny Moré, Juan Formell, children's and top 40 songs, along with the speeches and letters of Antonio Maceo, José Martí, Che Guevara, Malcolm X, Bob Marley, Nelson Mandela, and many others who fight against racism and colonialism. They adopt a radical and conflicted perspective of the Cuban social project—a rather manipulated paradox outside of Cuba—providing the freshest critical and liberating form of expression of the end of the twenty-first century.

One of the most popular songs from early Cuban hip-hop culture did not have access to traditional modes of distribution but did have such a strong presence in shows, house parties, and unofficial concerts that all of the attendees recited, along with MC Molano: "*Quien tiro la tiza*/Who threw the chalk?" And they did not have to wait for the answer: "*El negro ese*/ That negro." These very lyrics popularized the problem of racism and its presence in schools, the street, and everyday language. "Mambi," a song by the rap group *Obsesion*, links racism to national history in a dialogue with the poetry of Nicolas Guillen and contemporary reality. The song is also dedicated to the black American journalist sentenced to death, Mumia Abu Jamal:

Escucha esto, Nicolas!	*Listen to this, Nicolas!*
Estoy rapeando al compas de mis pasas	*I'm rapping to the rhythm of my steps*
Mi nata, mi bemba, mi arbol genealogico	*My nata, my bemba, my family tree*
Mi religion y mi forma de pensar	*My religion and way of thinking*

In all of the years of the revolutionary process, no discourse has so forcefully addressed the theme of race as the lyrics found in dozens of rap texts. Cuban rappers reject Eurocentric influences in mainstream culture because this bias practically erases any recognition of their own cultural forms, which remain quite separate from the Western canon, and are much closer to Afro-Cuban religious expressions, popular culture, and oral traditions.

6

Havana's rap festivals have become a truly international cultural forum, not simply a platform for exhibitions and public discussions about Cuban hip-hop culture. Undoubtedly, they have been an ideal space for judging production, evaluating talent, and supporting the best products and artists, as well as proposing new initiatives. The festival has also transformed itself into the most popular event in Cuban hip-hop, where the rap community—artists, fans, promoters, and the general public—can meet and interact as part of a sociocultural movement. The MC competitions further validated talent and facilitated product promotion and commercialization of concerts, albums, publications, films, videos, and so on. Now, although EGREM, BIS, and other record labels have included Cuban rap in their catalogues, the majority of rap recordings are still produced alternatively.[4]

The press coverage that has accompanied this movement from its genesis had its moment of apotheosis at the Festival each August. During the Special Period, the press conferences that announced the Festival saw an abundance of international journalists, yet very few Cuban reporters. Consequently, we must work to support the presence of Cuban journalists and include them in the movement. We can convene them in other ways, not only during the Festival, by involving them in projects such as tours, recording, and concerts, and establishing alliances in order to share information, publicity, and criticism. The press represents incredibly varied artistic, cultural, and political opinions, and traffics the majority of all information about the Cuban hip-hop world—information that often bounces back to the island and becomes legitimate as foreign-truth-disguised-as-our-truth. This also occurs in more than a dozen documentaries on Cuban rap, most of which are produced in the United States, and the rest of which are from Europe (France and Germany) or Latin America (Colombia and Brazil), such as Inventos, East of Havana, Cuban Hip Hop: Desde el principio, La Fabri-K, and others.

The international press, as well as underground filmmakers, and also European and North American academics who run around the island all year long inquiring into Cuban rap, have not managed to contribute to the internal debate on this aspect of national culture. Similarly, Cuban media, especially Television Cubana, with the exception of programs like *A Cuerda Viva*, have had a corrosive effect on rap's discourse. In the style of MTV or BET, they discuss the culture in a superficial and distorted way, showing only a partial and exotic image of Cuban rap that is stripped of any political or ideological messages. In addition, the written press in Cuba does not provide opinions on or evaluations of an aesthetic and social phenomenon that offers, at the very least during the Festival, abundant material through its programs, festive environment, and musical and intellectual exchanges. The national press has not asked pertinent questions about the hip-hop phenomenon in Cuba, failing to indicate its commercial significance, aesthetic achievements, prominent influences, and conflicting messages. Given the media's failure, the image of Cuban rap is shallow and fragmented. Yet there is still potential in how the media might learn to discuss a culture such as hip-hop, which never leaves anyone indifferent.

The magazine *Movimiento*, founded three years ago as a project of the Cuban Rap Agency, intended to tackle the challenge that the more mainstream media had avoided. Its goal was to foment new journalistic approaches and dialogue with other publications, and voices without fearing cultural debate. As an editorial project, *Movimiento* filled one of the largest gaps in Cuban media criticism. There are not many texts that are able to elucidate, or even describe, the complicated interstices in which Cuban culture is produced in the twenty-first century. When production is so limited that most texts remain invisible and many voices go unheard, messages often do not reach recipients. Just as rap music's lyrics and sounds attempt to impact the usual auditory journey of daily life, the journal *Movimiento* inaugurates a new type of critical discourse, encouraging and incorporating authors from different perspectives on hip-hop.

7

The precarious environment in which hip-hop artists have worked for more than 10 years can be seen in their expressions. This sense of precariousness becomes incorporated into daily life in the hip-hop scene and leads to creative solutions. For example, the majority of hip-hop concerts are produced with the most minimal resources, often with nothing more than a simple rhythm track in the background. Furthermore, as the visual imaginary of graffiti disappears throughout Havana, including from the very symbolic corner of 19th and 10th streets in the *Vedado* neighborhood, hip-hop artists consequently resort to other modes of expression, such as poster and mural competitions, graphic design, fashion, or editorial projects, in order to convey hip-hop's visual brilliance.

The Cuban Rap Agency, proposed by the AHS, was finally created by the Cuban Institute of Music of the Ministry of Culture in September 2003. It is responsible for promoting all rap music in Cuba, a gigantic task given its small size and insufficient funding. However, their mission does not include ancillary products such as music video production and other material artifacts of hip-hop culture that shape the musical expression. Because organizations registered in the Cuban Institute of Music limit their work to musical expressions, the Cuban Rap Agency does not concern itself with other related artistic forms that have contributed to the expansion of Cuban hip-hop culture. Despite this restriction, the agency made significant achievements in just over two years, including the aforementioned magazine, three albums, various national tours, and a significant number of concerts. Nevertheless, the hip-hop community in Cuba deserves support that exceeds merely including rap in the musical catalogue; there is also a need to address its unique perspectives, as well as its economic and professional needs. The hip-hop community places hope in the Agency, even if only for small advances. It is conscious of the potential of this new cultural form, although aware that the limits of technology, politics, and the market often render it somewhat helpless.

The creation of the Asere Productions record label with the Cuban Rap Agency is an unusual gain in a context where hip-hop culture is constantly losing state support. As described earlier, the Cuban music industry, before the creation of the Agency, recorded several rap albums on its most traditional labels. However, rap music requires a great amount of mobility and flexibility. It often follows new paths, strategies, markets, and alternative networks and business dealings. Asere Productions seeks to fulfill these needs, exploring all possible market opportunities for Cuban rap, both at home and abroad.[5]

The work of institutionalizing rap discourse has only just begun. It is necessary to rethink the fundamental concepts of a business mechanism inserted into a complex web that is simultaneously local and global. Through this we must examine new ideas, incorporate new artists, continue to promote the expansion of spaces, recordings, media presence, market studies, distribution, and nurture public debate, and aggressive international promotion.

8

Hip-hop culture is a musical stew. It is hybrid, yet rooted in Cuban cultural expressions that enrich vocal improvisation. Rap music is inherently open-minded and experimental—it has been described by critic Joaquín Borges-Triana (2001) as "Cuban alternative music." Many established jazz, *trova*, classical, and popular musicians have incorporated rap into their compositions or have collaborated with rap artists. Among these musicians are Jose Luis Cortés, Pablo Menéndez, Edesio Alejandro, Adalberto Alvarez, Gerardo Alfonso, Juan Formell, Maraca, David Calzado, Rafael Lay Jr., and many others, who have worked with rap groups such as *Ogguere*, *Instinto*, *Papo Record*, and others. Rap fusions also configure the musical work of diverse artists such as Athanay, Roberto Carcasses, Equis Alfonso, Telmary Diaz, Omar Sosa, Nilo Castillo, and Descemer Bueno.

Hip-hop constitutes a space of encounter, dialogue, and cultural synthesis that incorporates varied musical and nonmusical forms of expression. Its development unfolds to its own rhythms, relying on its many creative elements and media formats to foster public debate and artistic exchange on a broad level. However, it is likely that parts of hip-hop culture will always remain on the local level, focused on the specific places from which they emerge, the accompanying languages of those locales, and the peripheral identities that are not included in mainstream media. In this sense, hip-hop shares many characteristics with almost any youth subculture, a dynamic artistic and social movement whose expressions are inextricably linked to their places of origin.

9

I must stress an element that marks Cuban rappers' imaginary and differentiates them from other hip-hop artists around the world; that is the legacy of the Revolution. The revolutionary forms of struggle, acts of resistance, anticolonial emphasis, as well as the cultural characteristics of the runaway slave, have shaped Cuban history from the Haitian Revolution to the present day. Cuban rap is an act of racial resistance that rejects the Eurocentric standards still dominant in contemporary Cuban culture. It is located within a Caribbean framework and rearticulates many of its popular expressions, including Afro-Caribbean religions. Hip-hop in Cuba constructs a new discourse based on autochthonous Afro-Caribbean musical forms such as reggae, rumba, samba, jazz, souk, bachata, son, meringue, and others that celebrate the life of the African diaspora in the New World.

Furthermore, Cuban rap contributes to new forms of struggle against a subtle domination that traverses the entire world—the sophisticated views and values of neoliberalism—which circulate through tourism and other forms of commercial culture. Hip-hop constitutes a timeless battle for the emancipation of all subjects, now in a global world; it is also a renewed fight for the defense of youth identities, forces, and strategies that are shaping tomorrow's world. The rap movement puts forth the hope for a better world where identity does not end up alienated, invisible, destroyed, or marginalized by old forms of democracy and dogmatism in disguise. This is a new type of struggle, and I raise my fist to support it; to this end I have visibly and invisibly graffitied my text. Not many Cuban intellectuals are conscious and proud of sharing a cultural process such as this. It will be a long journey and I am a tireless traveling partner.

Notes

1. This essay was written between 2004 and 2006, amidst heat, blackouts, and noise in Callejon de Hammel, in Central Havana. It is dedicated to Victor Gomez for his illuminating conversation, to Inés María Martiatu (Lalita), to my Ceiba tree neighbor, and to Roberto Diago for bringing light. It is partly based on the article "El triángulo invisible del siglo XX cubano: raza, literatura y nación," published in *Temas* 46 (2006).
2. The *Días de la Música* was a biannual competition to recognize the best musical projects of each province, in any genre. We selected the seven best acts from among those showcased throughout one week at various theaters. From those, a panel of judges selected the top best, which were then promoted on radio, television, and to record labels, and sponsored to tour abroad. The *Días de la Música* was organized by the AHS and the Cuban Music Institute. Many well known bands like Aceituna Sin Hueso, Buena Fe, Postrova, and William Vivanco, emerged from this competition.

3. See Alan West Duran (2004) for an analysis of the rap version of a Nicolás Guillén poem, "Tengo lo que tenia que tener."
4. The true history of the sound of rap in Cuba can be found in an immense discography that has been produced in alternative ways for more than a decade. It is composed of recordings produced in home studios and sold at the concerts, showcases, and other presentations for the rap community and also—for higher prices—for the circuit of researchers and foreign fans who have become avid collectors of these types of productions.
5. In 2006, the label Asere Productions received a CUBADISCO award in the rap category for the album *Cabiosile* by Papo Record.

10

Audiovisual Remittances and Transnational Subjectivities

Lisa Maya Knauer

In the summer of 2000 in Havana, Pedro Fariñas, a former member of the acclaimed Cuban folkloric troupe Los Muñequitos de Matanzas, asked me to videotape a rehearsal of a his new rumba group.[1] A few days later, he came to pick up a copy of the tape. Or so I thought. He demanded that I get my video camera out and rolling, and started to sing. He then began a 20-minute monologue addressed to Cuban folkloric performers who had migrated to New York such as Orlando "Puntilla" Rios. He greeted each by name, bragged about the new group, and then admonished them to show they had not forgotten those who remained in Cuba by sending a token or better yet, an invitation to the United States. He finished with stern instructions to show both his diatribe and the rehearsal to everyone named.

In the summer of 2004, at a rumba in the Bronx, René, a Cuban who had migrated to New York in the 1980 Mariel boatlift, smiled approvingly when he saw me taking photographs, remarking, "You're going to show those in Havana, right?" This was less a question than a demand. When I asked whether he wanted me to show the photographs to anyone in particular, he waved his arms dramatically. "To all the *rumberos*![2] To all Havana!" Then, gesturing around, "So they know that there are Cubans in New York who still play rumba."

The deep-rooted tensions between the U.S. and Cuban governments have inevitably impacted Cubans on and off the island, and impeded the kinds of transnational exchanges that many other immigrant communities have with their homelands.[3] Nonetheless, as these two snapshots illustrate, rumba enthusiasts maintain a transnational consciousness in spite or, perhaps because of, the distance. Localized subjects such as René in New York had little contact with Cuba, and no plans to visit, yet not only was the island an essential point of reference but he wanted to ensure that the Afro-Cuban cultural sphere in New York be made visible there.[4] In Cuba, Fariñas had more specific demands, but he, too, needed affirmation by the Cuban *rumberos* in New York. Like Fariñas, most Cubans have little hope of visiting the United States, and many Cuban immigrants/exiles, like René, have never returned. Yet, as I elaborate later, people in both places increasingly see themselves as part of a single, if fractured, interpretive and performative community. This is the case because while transnational linkages between Cuban immigrant/exile communities and the island are not new, they have become more ubiquitous with the increased availability of electronic media, ranging from homemade videos to satellite TV and the Internet. As I elaborate, audiovisual media play a critical role in producing and reproducing a sense of belonging not coterminous with national boundaries.

This essay explores how the production, circulation, and consumption of "audiovisual remittances" enables folkloric performers and audiences in New York and Havana to create new imaginaries and subjectivities that are transnational and transspatial. This circulation is intimately intertwined with the economic and cultural ruptures of the Special Period. Even though these exchanges did not begin in the Special Period, they intensified for several reasons. The emigrants of the 1990s, whether rafters or artists, did not view emigration as a permanent break and maintained contact through phone calls, cash remittances, packages, or messages sent with acquaintances or return visits. As a result and condition of this increased contact between Cubans "*acá*" (here) and "*allá*" (there), islanders and immigrants use these media practices to negotiate legitimacy and authenticity in absentia, both as Cubans and *rumberos*. To return to my opening anecdote, Fariñas's video message to New York *rumberos* not only establishes claims on them, but also tries to parlay those reputed connections to bolster his status in Cuba. Similarly, many try to enhance their prestige among other immigrants by displaying audiovisual evidence of ongoing ties to Cuba. Establishing social capital is thus a transnational process.

This "grassroots transnationalism" has allowed Cubans and Cuban immigrants to establish multilateral exchanges. Many Cuban families have emigrant friends and relatives in multiple locations in the United States, Europe, and elsewhere, and their translocal networks are thus often complex and expansive. I focus here on the linkages between Cubans in the greater New York area and Cuba. New York might seem a counterintuitive choice as Miami hosts a much larger Cuban-origin population. But New York's reputation as a cultural and musical center gives it an important place in the imaginary of many Cubans, especially musicians.

The circulation of people and images between New York and Cuba intensified in the first half of the twentieth century when political and economic turmoil in Cuba, as well as the growth of the "Latin" music industry in

New York, brought a steady stream of Cubans (Glasser 1995; Manuel 2001; Pérez 1999). Rumba was first recorded in New York and then those records were then exported to Cuba.[4] By the mid-1950s, New York housed the largest Cuban community in the United States, with a notable black presence. This gave rise to a flourishing Afro-Cuban culture sphere in New York attracting white Cubans, African-Americans and Puerto Ricans, and others.[5]

Rumba gatherings began in public parks, private homes, restaurants, and clubs. For Cubans, rumba performances were both portable homelands, where they could meet compatriots, and zones of contact with other ethnic groups. As in Cuba, rumba was a racialized cultural practice, and these events acquired a double significance as performances of both national and racial identity. New York's growing reputation as site of Afro-Cuban cultural production, combined with the perceived racial politics of the Miami "enclave," attracted many black Cubans and folkloric performers from postrevolutionary migratory cohorts. According to the 2000 U.S. census, a higher proportion of the Cuban-origin population in New York identifies as "black" or "mixed race" than in Florida. This reinforces the perception of New York as a Mecca for rumba and other Afro-Cuban cultural practices.

Prior to the Revolution Cuban immigrants in New York and their families on the island stayed in close contact. Phone calls, visits, and newspaper articles contributed to a transnational structure of feeling. The mediated links were not only personal: *babalawos* (ritual diviners) in Havana usually called New York to share the spiritual advice of the annual "opening of the year" ritual. The Cuban Revolution and U.S. embargo impeded but did not halt these mediated translocal flows. Starting in the early 1970s, some New Yorkers visited Cuba and brought back records and tapes, as well as homemade audio and later videotapes of rumba and religious music. But musical developments in both cities remained relatively autonomous until the Mariel boatlift when a sizeable number of rumba enthusiasts settled in New York. They not only reshaped the New York Afro-Cuban cultural "scene" but also reignited contact with Cuba, which soon took a mediated form, as seen in the next vignette.

Shortly after his arrival, *Marielito* musician Orlando "Puntilla" Rios recorded a rumba album, *From Havana to New York*, the title capturing the sentiment of many *Marielitos* that they were bringing authentic Afro-Cuban culture to New York.[6] The album featured previously unrecorded works by the Cuban rumba composer Tío Tom. Despite the embargo Puntilla sent one LP to Cuba. The circulation of that single record established Puntilla's influence on the rumba scene in Cuba in absentia, since most Cubans had never heard of Tio Tom, later acknowledged as a major rumba composer. It took Puntilla's departure for New York for Cuban audiences to hear Tio Tom's work recorded. Sending the record to Cuba set the stage for subsequent flows.

A Note on Method

Media practices were not part of my original research project. However, as I videotaped rumba events and religious ceremonies in the United States, participants frequently asked for copies—often, I learned, to send to Cuba. As I started research in Cuba, they asked me to deliver videos or photos on my research trips. Conversely, people in Cuba often asked me to bring recordings of New York rumba events, or to record events in Cuba to take back to New York. Since these often accompanied—or prompted—remittances of goods and cash, I label them "audiovisual remittances."

I first got a clue about how these audiovisual remittances mediated relationships between Cuban immigrants and islanders while preparing for my first research visit to Cuba in 1998. I had met José Alberto, a *balsero*, at an informal rumba in Central Park. Upon learning of my trip, he gave me an assignment (along with gifts and money for his family): of videotaping the all-day rumba his mother held on her birthday. However, once I arrived at the *solar* in Habana Vieja, it was clear that the family in Cuba would shape the audiovisual messages to be seen in New York, although I held the camera and had been sent by the immigrant relative. They also made sure that I left a copy for them, as they lacked the means to record the celebration for themselves.

José Alberto's mother and sister guided me around the courtyard, telling me where to point the camera. They brought over a succession of relatives and friends, and prodded them to send a message to José Alberto in New York. Some, especially the youngsters, were shy and giggly, but others bluntly reminded José Alberto to call his mother and demanded to know when he would visit. Later, Merida and Maritza led me to film huge pots of *congrí* (rice and black beans) and platters of *lechón* (roast pork), as well as people eating, keeping up a running commentary: "Look at how much food there is, it's so rich and tasty, don't you wish you were here?" A few days later, the family asked me to photograph José Alberto's gifts or items purchased with his cash remittances. The video and photos were weighted with multiple meanings. They were proof that the gifts had arrived and the money had been well spent, but were also designed to evoke nostalgia and goad José Alberto's conscience. The family wanted to remind José of his obligations, while asserting their autonomy and independence.

As the examples that follow make clear, since Cuban immigrants and islanders have limited mobility, the exchange of audiovisual remittances often requires intermediaries—either to record the messages, transport them, or both. While there are courier services between the United States and Cuba, many Cuban immigrants prefer to send audiovisual and other remittances with travelers. Islanders have little access to these services and therefore have to be resourceful in finding travelers—visiting Cuban immigrants, foreign tourists, or researchers—to carry their "reverse remittances" (Knauer 2003).

As Zilberg (2002: 190) notes in her study of transnational flows between Salvadorans in Los Angeles and El Salvador:

> ...to the extent that they provide vital alternatives to those immigrants, whose mobility is severely constrained by the cost and danger of passing international borders, the courier is the much celebrated protagonist in the construction of the transnational social field on the ground, and of globalization from below. They, perhaps more than any other figure, effectively suture those formerly distinct hemispheric sites....

An individual who carries remittances becomes a messenger, a mediator, and a surrogate. Both sender and receiver expect that the intermediary will not only deliver the remittance personally, but also visit, and talk. For localized subjects, travelers are a rich source of information about life on the other side Recipients expect the intermediary to provide the kind of eyewitness detail that cannot be easily recorded or photographed. Witnessing and then reporting back is an important part of remittance economies, especially when immigrants use a personal intermediary. Once, a woman in Havana asked me to record the party marking the completion of her sister's initiation as a *santera* (a priestess in *la regla de ocha* or Santeria) to show to relatives in the United States. I arrived in New York to find a message from the relatives begging me to bring the tape to their house the next day. As we watched the tape, they stopped the tape several times to ask me questions, and I was drawn into their speculations about why certain people were absent, and why there was no live music. The intermediary is thus often in an uncomfortable position of deciding how much and what to reveal (see Glick-Schiller and Fouron 2000; Knauer 2003, 2005; Zilberg 2002). These encounters often turn into a form of "reverse ethnography." People in Cuba ask visitors detailed questions about daily life in the United States. This process is often reversed upon returning to the United States; Cuban immigrants pump travelers for information about everyday life in Cuba, from the weather to the prices in the hard-currency stores. This information then circulates throughout the immigrant social networks, along with videos and photos.

Here, I focus on audiovisual remittances for which I was both "recorder" and courier. These are, however, only specific manifestations of a much broader phenomenon. In both Cuba and the United States, people often showed me videos they had received through other means. There are undoubtedly different dynamics when one personally records and transports an audiovisual remittance, and when one simply transports materials produced by others. The video I shot of Havana's Carnival for Leonardo is undoubtedly different from the one he shot when he later visited Cuba himself, although both tapes circulate in the same networks.

Leonardo, a *Marielito*, first returned to Cuba in 2000, and recorded over 15 hours of video footage, and much of it music—hip-hop at Café Cantante, children singing in his native Oriente. Back in New York, he spent weeks editing this material for different audiences. One set of videos was for people in Cuba to see themselves and have promotional materials. But he also made another set for Cuban friends and relatives in the United States who had never returned to Cuba, and whose only source of information was the mainstream U.S. and Spanish language media. His firsthand images would provide a visual counternarrative, and hopefully offset their fears. He performed a double surrogacy, both for people in Cuba who lacked recording equipment, and for fellow immigrants who did not travel to Cuba. He continues to visit Cuba, and record both family and musical events, but now with a heightened consciousness of how and where and by whom the images will be seen. He has learned to see, he told me, through the eyes of these various audiences as he is filming.[7]

Who the courier and the recorder are, and whether they are the same or different people, and how each is positioned in relationship to the people who are sending and receiving the audiovisual remittances, certainly shapes the mediation.

Homemade Media and the Transnational Politics of Recognition

In general, the emergence of low-cost audiovisual equipment has allowed groups that formerly had little access to media technologies to become active producers of their own images, not simply consumers and subjects of images produced by others (Aufderheide 1995; Turner 1995). Cuban immigrants and islanders can now exchange visual narratives, bypassing state and commercial media and circumventing obstacles erected by both the U.S. and Cuban governments. They surmount or get around (to a degree) their relative immobility by exchanging sounds and images to construct a "third space," to use Bhabha's term (1994). The translocal subjectification, however, occurs in home media environments "saturated" with many different sounds and images, as Cuban households on and off the island often have television, radio, and CDs playing simultaneously. In this case, however, the saturation is relative. U.S. broadcasters provide little information on Cuba and Cuba only had two national TV channels during most of the Special Period, and broadcast hours shrank due to shortages and blackouts.[8]

While I focus on media not produced for commercial distribution, in everyday media practices it is hard to distinguish between homemade and state-produced or commercial media, as pirated copies of the latter circulate through the same informal networks as the former, and are consumed in a similar manner. They function in a "small media" framework, creating or reinforcing structures of feeling that join dispersed individuals into communities. The media worlds constructed and inhabited by islanders and emigrés are thus permeated by "establishment"—both Cuban and U.S.—media. What I am calling translocal subjectification, or the politics of identity "from below," is also shaped more directly by the politics of identity from above, as both the Cuban government and the Cuban-American elite try to mold specific forms of belonging on the island and among the immigrant/exile population. However, homemade media, along with satellite and other pirated forms, help islanders and immigrants resist both the territorially based constructions of *cubanidad* (Cubanness) articulated by Cuban nationalists before and after the 1959 Revolution, and the equally insular politically charged definitions promoted by the "exile" leadership.

For exile and diaspora communities that exist in a state of dislocation and flux, representations of the homeland offer "discursive and symbolic order" and serve as visual or sonic "anchors" (Naficy 1993: 118). But representations of the immigrant/diaspora communities also provide alternative renditions of national identity to people in the "home country," and for others in the diaspora. The bidirectional traffic of homemade videos expands and redraws community boundaries, as Schein (2002) notes in regard to the Hmong diaspora, remapping both the nation and the exiles/immigrants vis-à-vis each other. Similarly, "Chineseness" on the mainland is increasingly produced through popular consumption of videos and music from Hong Kong and Taiwan or images of Chinese-American visitors disseminated through state-run media (Louie 2000; Yang 2002).

If we agree with Hall (1990) and Ginsburg (1991), among others, that identities are made *through* representation, then we have to conclude that the exchange of audiovisual materials is not simply a way of staying in touch, but rather an integral part of how Cubans on and off the island produce and negotiate their respective subjectivities. In the case of immigrants and their homelands or among multisited diasporic communities those representational processes are not complete unless they engage those at the other end, or at another node, of the transnational circuit. Each needs affirmation by the other to be authenticated.[9] Hence dispersed communities often engage in a multisided as well as multisited "cultural politics of recognition" to affirm their existence among themselves and in relationship to the home country.[10] In the Cuban case, the mutual construction of subjectivities is translocal as well as transnational. That is, the imaginaries and geographies connected through these mediated exchanges are often very local, Cayo Hueso and the Bronx, in addition to or instead of Cuba/USA, or Havana/New York. The new subjectivities are also very contextual and relational: they are informed by how subjects seek to position themselves within their respective local and national contexts.

The politics of mutual recognition are essential to self-identification both in Cuba and abroad. They are also shaped by larger debates over national identity—in particular how race and Afro-Cuban culture (i.e., black people and the cultural practices historically defined as "black" or "Afro-Cuban") figure into discourses of *cubanidad* on both sides of the Florida Straits. In Cuba, rumba and Santeria are still marked by a legacy of prerevolutionary racial ambivalence when they were frequently criminalized and marginalized, and thus while official discourse in the Special Period celebrated them (at least in their folkloricized renditions) as icons of Cuban national identity, many Cubans still view them as uncouth, low-class and *cosas de negros* ("black people's stuff"). The persistence of racialized thinking and discourse means that how these practices are represented, both in and outside of Cuba, is of more than passing interest to their participants. *Rumberos* and *santeros* in both Cuba and the United States often describe themselves as carving out a space for these cultural practices, and "defending" them from commercialization on the one hand, and marginalization or discrimination on the other.[11]

These racial dynamics are both carried over and reshaped in the context of the United States. Black Cubans are relatively invisible within the broader Cuban-American community, which most U.S. residents, regardless of race, view as white. In New York, they suffer from the additional burden of being nearly invisible in the city's variegated ethnoscape. Like other Afro-Latino groups, they fall outside the conventional definitions of "Latino" and "African-American." Their demands for recognition are thus directed both at these latter communities—whose lives are intertwined with those of Cuban immigrants through coresidence in multiethnic neighborhoods, participation in cultural and religious events, and intimate relationships—and at their counterparts on the island.

I use the plural, subjectiv*ities*, deliberately: as the following discussion illustrates, audiovisual remittances are produced and consumed in varied ways. There are imbalances, even inequalities between islanders and immigrants in terms of access to the means of audiovisual production and consumption (cameras and VCRs), and the claims immigrants make upon islanders do not carry the same weight as those claims in the other direction. The media products themselves are subject to multiple, sometimes divergent encodings and decodings. A single video may be "read" in several different ways, even in the same household. There is not a homogenous or unitary transnational Cubanness that all Cubans profess; perhaps the discussion of national (and diasporic) identity needs to embrace multiple *cubanidades* (see chapter 5, this volume). For one thing, rumba is highly gendered and so this interpretive and performative community is shaped by homosocial bonding. Some of the messages read as the kind of male posturing that characterizes rumba, hip-hop, and other Afrodiasporic musical forms transposed into a transnational media space, but those are not the only messages—as the pleas, reminders, and self-justifying statements make clear.

To contextualize my discussion of how the politics of mutual recognition are enacted, and new subjectivities negotiated, through the production and reception of audiovisual remittances, I sketch the contours of the Cuban mediascape. I then look at how the economic, political, and discursive shifts of the Special Period shaped and were shaped by the intensified translocal exchanges between islanders and immigrants.

Mediations: New Technologies and Transnational Afro-Cuban Culture

As noted earlier, audiovisual remittances are produced and consumed in media environments shaped by both state and commercial actors. In Cuba, the revolutionary government early on realized the potential of electronic media to solidify citizens' attachment to the revolutionary project, extending electrification and the broadcasting signals, while providing televisions and radios at low or no cost, often through workplaces or mass organizations to reward exemplary work and loyalty. Consequently, most households, especially in urban centers, have at least one television set. Television occupies a central place in many homes and the set is often kept on as audiovisual wallpaper. However, the state-run channels offer a fairly limited diet—at least compared to the United States and other countries where Cuban immigrants have settled. While there are occasionally new programs and new formats, Cubans frequently complain about how boring and repetitive the programming is. This Revolution *has* been televised—ad nauseum, for some Cubans.

The explosion of consumer electronics and increased contact with Cuban immigrants has changed the Cuban mediascape. The legality and availability of VCRs and DVD players has fluctuated, but many electronic items are (in 2007) available at state-owned stores at inflated prices, along with blank media, as well as DVD and VHS movies ranging from Hollywood blockbusters to Cuban film classics. There is a flourishing media black market, ranging from sales of "burned" CDs to semi-clandestine video rental services (colloquially called *bancos de videos* or video banks) to illegal satellite dishes.[12] Meanwhile, as Cuban emigrants stepped up material and cash remittances (and visits) in the 1990s, they also started to send or bring videos, including popular programs from Spanish-language television in the United States, and homemade recordings of significant family events, cultural performances, and religious ceremonies.[13] Often, they left video and still cameras so those on the island could reciprocate. The production and reception of audiovisual remittances became commonplace particularly among Cubans who resettled in the 1990s as a result of the 1994 balsero crisis, the U.S. lottery, or other opportunities in Europe and Latin America, and who saw themselves as immigrants, remaining closely connected to their families on the island. For these, particularly the young, emigration was no longer seen as a permanent rupture but a reasonable alternative to achieve professional goals or help one's family.

Furthermore, tens of thousands took advantage of new policies that allowed exiles and expatriates to return, increasing the traffic that brought the new media back and forth. The restoration of direct phone communication and the legalization of electronic money transfers facilitated transnational sentiments. By the late 1990s, visits by Cuban immigrants had become fairly routine. On Cuba-bound flights I have met Cuban immigrants who claim to have visited 50 times or more. Increasingly, these immigrants and their families live almost fully transnational lives.[14] The numerous photographs of émigré relatives that are prominently displayed in Cuban living rooms, or kept in albums that are proudly handed around when visitors arrive, evidence the normalization of emigration and the reality of transnational families. Having relatives abroad is no longer a liability but an asset.

Folkloric Negotiations: Mediating Claims among Musicians

In Havana, musicians would frequently ask me to record rehearsals and performances. But, as my encounter with Pedro Fariñas, described earlier, illustrates, they sought both promotional materials, and my complicity in their efforts. What I saw as an ethnographic interview would be turned into an audition tape, or an opportunity to register claims on *los cubanos de allá* (the Cubans from "over there," meaning in this case the United States). By turning the tables, the musicians were exercising agency and subverting the inequalities in their relationships with both me, the foreigner with a camera, and the intended viewers of the videos: their relatives or colleagues in the United States.

Their agendas often focused on increased professional opportunities. The tourist economy, and its promotion of Cuba as a musical paradise suggested more jobs for Cuban performers. In the 1990s, old cabarets were reopened and new ones built due to market reforms and tourism development, many included rumba or Afro-Cuban sacred music and dance. State-sponsored and foreign tourist industries active promoted "folklore."[15] Rumba and Afro-Cuban religion were revalorized, at least to a degree, as social capital (although still viewed with suspicion or worse by many white Cubans), and many black Cubans sought to parlay this into economic and social benefits (see chapter 4, this volume). This heightened international interest in Cuban music along with a relaxation of the U.S. embargo on cultural exchanges during the Clinton years also created new opportunities for Cuban performers to travel abroad. Touring helped increase the cultural traffic between the Afro-Cuban cultural spheres in New York and Cuba. During the 1990s several Cuban folkloric groups performed at major venues in New York, but also at lesser-known locales frequented by Cuban immigrants. Invariably, some performers stayed behind. This small number of "folkloric migrants" had a disproportionate impact as they propelled more direct and sustained engagement between the United States and Cuba.

For the Cuban government, the export of Cuban folkloric musicians provided hard currency; for performers, tours promised prestige as well as cash. For older musicians touring validated their life's work. Who gets invited to tour outside of Cuba was (and still is) a highly politicized process. State officials determined who traveled abroad, often influenced as much by favoritism, friendship, repayment of past professional debts, and good connections as rewarding political loyalty. The gap between musicians' desires and available opportunities heightened competition. Recording opportunities were also scarce. Electronic media offered one way to get a leg up on others, either through self-produced videos and CDs, or mediated appeals to Cuban musicians overseas, as the following vignette illustrates.

On a hot August day, I climbed the dusty streets of the Havana neighborhood of Atares on a battered bicycle to interview the elderly *rumbero* Mario Dreke ("Chavalonga") about how the genre had evolved during his lifetime. But he also pumped me for details about the New York rumba scene—who the musicians were and what songs were they playing. Another musician, Luis Fernández, was passing by the door, propped open to break up the heat, and joined in. Back in New York, Luis told me, I had to find a Cuban musician named Puntilla "and tell him that you talked to Chavalonga. And you have to show him this interview along with our greeting."[16] For the next several minutes, Chavalonga and Fernández spoke directly to the camera, sending good wishes to Puntilla and other compatriots in New York. But embedded in the pleasantries was a subtext that recurred throughout my fieldwork: that Cubans like Puntilla who had migrated to the United States should not forget those who nurtured them, and that they needed to return the favor by helping those who had stayed behind. Chavalonga's and Fariñas's video "letters" were significant not because they were unique but precisely because those appeals became commonplace.[17] Likewise, Cubans often converse among themselves about friends or relatives who have emigrated, critically evaluating their level of communication, remittances, visits, and whether or not they have improved their own—and their families'—situations.

Émigrés, for their part, are keenly aware of this critical scrutiny, and often seek to justify their decision to settle in the United States to people in Cuba who might feel abandoned, or distrust the migrant's motive. To this end, they sometimes send audiovisual remittances going the other way, as the following episode makes clear. A (non-Cuban) professional colleague hired me to videotape the encounter between a Nigerian cultural organization from the Cross River region, and Cuban immigrants in New York. The Cubans performed music and dance from that same region of Africa, brought to Cuba hundreds of years ago by slaves and preserved or remade through a secret society called the *Abakuá*. The Nigerians surged forward into a tight circle around the Cuban performers, recognizing dance gestures and songs.

While women ululated, both sexes danced up to the Cubans and plastered crisp banknotes onto their foreheads.[18] As I headed out, two of the Cubans beseeched me to take copies of the tape to their relatives and colleagues in Cuba.

One of them, Román, later discussed why it was important that his family and *Abakuá* "brethren" in Cuba see that tape. As he saw it, the meeting with the Nigerians could only have happened in the United States. It was a turning point in his decision to stay in the United States. "And for me, it was like a justification for why I am here." The video needed to be sent to Cuba "in order to say to them, 'Look, listen, I'm here...and this thing that we are doing is in the name of all of us." He had to send the video to Cuba so people would understand why he was in the United States and so he could be at peace regarding that decision.[19]

Sometimes the requests came from the Cuban side; while in Havana, people would ask for videos of performances, ceremonies, or dance classes with their loved ones on my next trip. Some loved ones had not maintained contact with their families and thus the request for a recording was itself an encoded message. However, the Cuban immigrants seized the chance to encode messages of their own—even if the request came from someone else's family. Stanley, a Cuban friend, asked me to videotape his father, a folkloric performer in New York, whom I tracked down at a rehearsal. As the rehearsal ended, another performer seized the moment. After ensuring that I had enough tape, he took charge and introduced everyone to the camera. He noted the many non-Cubans as a sign that Afro-Cuban culture was thriving in New York, and spreading to other communities. He then called upon the others to "say something to your people." As in the earlier case of José Alberto's family in Havana, some had to be prodded to speak, and many messages were formulaic, "I'm doing well, don't worry about me." But others had a self-justificatory tone, echoing Román's sentiments earlier. "We're here in New York but we are keeping the rumba tradition alive." Not all dispersed families maintain consistent transnational connections, and some Cuban immigrants (particularly those who have not achieved economic success) send few audiovisual or other remittances. Nonetheless, those eager for contact have learned to mobilize the resources of more mobile persons—whether tourists or researchers—to obtain photographs, audio, and video recordings for their own purposes.[20]

Meanwhile, video and audio recordings from Cuba—brought back by travelers—formed a kind of cultural currency among New York rumba enthusiasts; even localized subjects who would not or could not travel to Cuba could participate in the transnational structure of feeling. Videos of folkloric performances and rituals began to crop up at venues frequented by Cuban immigrants and Cuban music enthusiasts. Scenes of rumba performances in Havana or Matanzas formed a video wallpaper, and patrons and performers often watched and discussed the images as they went about their business. They reinforced the sense that a nightclub in Union City, New Jersey and the Gran Palenque in Havana shared a social and cultural, if not territorial, geography. Music and image sutured the fragmented geography and created a performative and interpretive universe where race, class, culture, and marginality were experienced similarly vis-à-vis the larger society.

To sum up, sometimes the requests for filming came from the Cuban side, sometimes from the United States. As in the episode with José Alberto and his family in Cuba, there are often multiple agendas at work, and the mediated encounter reflects a negotiation between the person (immigrant or islander) who requests images from *"allá"* (over there), and the person(s) *"allá"* with their own messages to send. The circulation of audiovisual materials thus highlights, and is shaped by, some of the larger dynamics that shape the relationships between Cuba and Cubans "in the exterior."

Multiple Agendas: Decoding from the Other Side

As the foregoing discussion demonstrates, there are varied agendas and both the images and their intended meanings are actively—even literally—negotiated between people on the island and in the United States. José Alberto, transplanted to New York, wanted a visual record of what he had left behind, and to vicariously participate in a family event. But the family in Cuba ensured that the video would carry other messages. Stanley, in Havana, wanted to see his father, but the other musicians present used the chance to communicate with the musical community in Cuba. The negotiation continues as the audiovisual remittances are interpreted by those who requested them, or to whom they have been sent.

Media reception needs to be understood in its social context. In Cuba, as noted earlier, the few households that had VCRs were popular gathering places, and many who received videos had to view them at someone else's house, so even watching home movies became a social event. Interpretation is thus a social act. In both Cuba and among Cubans in the United States, interpretation of the audiovisual remittances is a communal endeavor. A single video is often only a starting point for judgment, evaluation, and reflection. In the United States, videos are often watched by heterogeneous groups of Cubans who came to the United States under different circumstances, including some with few ties to the island, and others who have visited themselves. So the images of dilapidated buildings that permeated movies, photos, and home videos during the Special Period might convince some immigrants of their wisdom in coming to the United States. For others, these same images might evoke nostalgia that inspires a return visit, or a desire to help out. As I discuss later, screenings allow Cubans to collectively decode the multiple layers of meanings from these videos.[21]

When I arrived in Havana with the video that Stanley requested, he seized it and popped it in the VCR. He watched it several times, inviting relatives and friends to watch, discuss, and dissect. For several days, nearly every time someone walked up the stairs, he played the video. As someone from "*allá*," I was asked to provide contextualizing information. Word spread, and more people came just to see the video. The video, in effect, produced its audience, just as the audience collectively made meaning of the video. Viewers pored over minute aspects of the immigrants' physical appearance. They paid especial attention to clothing, critically evaluating their compatriots' sense of style and even choice of brands. They also evaluated the songs, the arrangements, and the musicianship. The performances on this video were compared with other videos sent from the United States, or the viewers' memories of how those musicians had played before emigrating. The "messages" at the end were scrutinized, with as much attention to what was not said, as to what was said. Viewers sometimes articulated a desire to see their loved ones—but at least as often, they expressed a desire to be in New York. Such tapes were watched repeatedly, and circulated to other Cubans eager for a glimpse of their loved ones or a hint of life "*allá*." Since there are more limited opportunities to duplicate tapes in Havana than in the United States I learned to make multiple copies before traveling, so that viewers might enjoy their own copies, both for prestige, repeated viewing, and to circulate through *their* networks.

For Cuban islanders and immigrants, watching videos of their friends and family is not a passive activity. As described earlier, Cubans actively engage the sounds and images on the screen, to decode them. A similar process takes place in New York. José Alberto, the *balsero* who sent me to his mother's birthday rumba, came over almost as soon as I returned to New York, and was so eager to see Cuba, and his family, that he insisted on watching the tape immediately. It was as though he were in that solar in Old Havana and not in front of a television set in the East Village. He sang along, beat out rhythms on my chairs, noted aloud who had gained weight or gotten pregnant, and responded to their appeals or admonitions. He would not allow me to be a passive spectator but drew me in as both an audience to his reception and a co-participant in his "decoding," pressing me for more details. It was a dialogic, or even a three-way process—involving not only the senders and receivers but also the intermediary. When people in one place view videos from "the other side," they begin to establish a conversation—sometimes quite literally—with the people on screen. Even with recordings of public performances or edited documentaries, viewers often behave as though the words and actions are aimed directly at them. As Román in New York commented while we watched a video of his former colleagues in Havana, "... at the moment that they are performing, you feel as though they are talking to you.... You say to yourself, 'Shit, they're talking to me.' And so that relationship exists. That they know where they are sending the message." The message can be a particular set of song lyrics—for example, in the video Román and I watched, one of the songs repeatedly addressed *"los rumberos en Nueva York,"* and that is enough to foster a sort of translocal intimacy and longing. In both places the longing was not only for the copresence of friends and relatives but also for a physical universe that could only be experienced vicariously.

News programs on Spanish-language television in the United States regularly report on Cuba, but many Cuban immigrants want more than short news items. Ethnic media entrepreneurs cater to this growing market for alternative sounds and images of Cuba, peddling everything from 1950s Cuban TV programs to film classics and independent videos of religious ceremonies. Most Cuban immigrants I met had substantial personal collections of videos and CDs from varied sources.[22] When I first met Leonardo, a few years before his first trip back to Cuba, his West Harlem apartment was filled with visual references to Cuba and an entire wall of his bedroom was devoted to shelves holding over 1,000 meticulously organized VHS cassettes. These included tapes he had recorded at rumba performances in New York, but most of them were from Cuba: both the commercial cassettes mentioned earlier and home videos from recent visitors to Cuba. Watching these videos, he told me, allowed him to imagine himself in Cuba, to erase the physical and temporal distance.

For Cuban expatriates, watching videos of folkloric music or religious ceremonies in Cuba evoked reactions on several levels, as I witnessed in Román, a "folkloric migrant" who came to New York in 1999. One afternoon in 2003, he played and discussed several videos from Cuba from his impressive collection, inviting me "inside" his personal reveries. He told me how he had obtained each video, why he would watch it, and what it meant to himself and other viewers. He spent a long time dissecting a Cuban television program featuring a new folkloric company that included many former colleagues. Watching one young performer evoked memories of older performers he had known, allowing him to time-travel.

> So, the image sometimes... brings to mind someone else who isn't there but had to do with his life. And so, when you come to look at it, as you are seeing the image, you enter into the image, and you begin to walk along with the image and at the same time that the film is running through your head, you begin to make another movie.

The videos allowed him not only to "visit" with old friends, but also to take stock of the current state of rumba performance. As Román watched another dancer, he explained how he scrutinized the composition of the group on screen to understand how the "constellation" of the various folkloric groups in Cuba had changed since he left: "So when you see it, you say, 'Hmm, who's that dancing Elegguá? Oh, Dionisio.' Dionisio is a proof that time has passed. So, you say, 'Well, he was dancing in the [Conjunto] Folklórico but now he's not there, so what happened? And who are the people that are playing?'"

As the camera moved closer, he continued, "and then you begin to recognize the faces... and so you are gaining information to use in your environment." As a Cuban musician in New York, he needed to hear the current repertoire and arrangements. Seeing who was playing with which groups made him feel part of the family. This information could be traded with, or displayed in front of, other musicians in New York. Knowing the latest songs, or musical gossip from Havana, underscores a New York musician's claims to authenticity.

In watching videos from Cuba, Cuban immigrants also insert themselves to see whether they still fit into the picture. Their sense of self is only partly based on adaptation to their new surroundings. While Cuban immigrants frequently proclaim they are the same as when living in Cuba, several privately expressed concern that the United States had changed them. As we watched his former colleagues, Román called my attention to the men's shirts. "You see, those are the shirts from here, right now. And so that is another type of emotion. When you see your people, and they're dressed in the current mode.... the video also... advises you whether or not you are still part of the inner circle."

Rumba is not merely a musical genre but also a bodily practice: verbal and physical posturing are an integral part of rumba performance. Rumba enthusiasts in both Cuba and New York identify themselves with a distinctive "look"; and photographs and videos help transmit hair and clothing styles. Román pointed out that one of the musicians' shirts was nearly identical to one in his closet and he held it next to the TV to show me.

> So that means this spiritual unity continues. It's a conversation that you establish when you see the video. When you make a comparison, you say, "I'm far away but I will continue being from there... [I say to myself] 'Shit, if I were there,' but I'm here, I like those shirts, will I be changing how I am, have I changed?" I haven't changed, because look what I left behind, and look at how they are. There you have it.

Conclusion

These representations self-consciously produced for circulation allow Cubans and Cuban immigrants to construct their own narratives about "the other side" and their relationship to it. They can insert themselves into the video (as Román suggests) or separate themselves from what they see. This communication, in some cases, transcends or at least circumvents politics. While some collaborators were strongly pro- or anti-Castro, or strongly pro- or anti Revolution, most said they were not involved in politics (either in Cuban or in the United States). Their interest in maintaining contact with Cuba, or Cubans in the United States—either directly, or through the medium of music, religion, and performance—was in a separate realm. As Román commented, "They [people in Cuba] know that we're here, that there's a lot of tension between one side and the other, but that at the end of the day, neither we nor they have anything to do with those politics."

Media is, thus, an arena in which Cubans attempt to renegotiate their relationship to the state. By creating an alternative realm of media consumption, they challenge, subtly and privately, state use of media to create disciplined—or at least complacent—citizen-subjects. Homemade videos provide less "mediated" access to distant compatriots and allow Cubans to imagine themselves "*allá*." Pertierra (2005) argues that videos provide a broader range of narratives than state-run TV and also permit viewers to control time. This is also true for Cuban immigrants in the United States, who can enter private media worlds whenever and as often as they want. By selecting segments for repeated viewing, fast forwarding, and rewinding, Cubans become producers and not just consumers. Leonardo's story illustrates how some embrace the exercise, recording, and editing images for themselves and others.

Cuban immigrants resist the disciplinary technologies of both the U.S. society and the most vocal "Cuban-American" leaders, which collaborate to produce a specific subordinated subjectivity and ensure invisibility of those diverging from dominant normalizations of assimilation and/or exile (Lowe 1996). The Cuban immigrants in the "Afro-Cuban cultural community" I studied want to claim a specific niche within New York's variegated ethnoscape, distinguishing themselves from other Latino and African-descent communities. Documenting culturally specific traditions provides audiovisual testimony that they have not assimilated, or become generic Latinos or black Americans. Meanwhile, these Cuban immigrants resist interpellation into the hegemonic "exile" community by consuming contemporary Cuba audiovisually.

From another angle, these recordings—and the varied settings of production and consumption—are part of a continuous renegotiation of authority and identity between families and communities separated by emigration. These videos are structured by, and themselves structure, an ongoing—if sporadic—dialogue. Román's insistence that a video of his encounter with Nigerians will explain to Cubans why he stayed in New York responds to the kinds of claims and challenges in videos from Cuba, whether directly articulated—as by Fariñas and Chavalonga—or merely implied. New York *rumberos* want islanders to know that there are Cubans in New York who are not fully Americanized and maintain the vitality of cultural practices threatened by discrimination, exoticization, and commercialization. René's request that I show people in Havana photos of rumbas in the Bronx forcefully articulates these desires. Islanders need to remind immigrants about their obligations to those left behind, while asserting their own agency, to resist being positioned solely as needy or dependent upon their relatives' largesse. By demonstrating that Cuba is where these traditions not only were born but continue to develop they imply that immigrants will need to "return to the source."

Cubans produce themselves as Cubans by producing audiovisual media for relatives and friends overseas—and by consuming audiovisual remittances from *el extranjero* (abroad). Cuban immigrants in the United States produce themselves as both diasporic and Cuban by reversing those exchanges. These new subjectivities dissolve the fixity of the nation-state to constitute a new form of long-distance nationalism, or even replace nationalism with some other form of identification. From both sides, they help produce new horizontal forms of solidarity and belonging, reformulate dominant constructions of Cubanness, and suggest alternatives.

Notes

1. Rumba is a percussion-driven music and dance form that originated in the black and poor neighborhoods of nineteenth-century Havana and Matanzas.
2. This term refers to a rumba musician or enthusiast.
3. Both countries make it hard for Cuban immigrants to see their families. The United States grants few nonimmigrant visas to Cubans, and the Cuban government grants few passports. In 2004, the Bush administration limited Cuban immigrants to one visit every three years. For more details on these policies see Sublette (2004) and Human Rights Watch (2005).
4. Jorge "Pepe" Reyes, personal communication (2006).
5. Boggs (1992) and Flores (2000) among others discuss multiethnic exchanges between Cubans, Puerto Ricans, and others. Fania Records was a microcosm of that.
6. "*Marielito*" was originally a pejorative term but was reclaimed as a term of endearment. This is the same Puntilla discussed earlier.
7. He has purchased a few inexpensive video cameras and left them behind so friends and family on the island will not be dependent upon him to be their documentarian.
8. The Cuban state established some local channels that did not broadcast full-time. Havana has had a municipal channel since the late 1990s. In 2005 the government established two new national channels targeting younger viewers.
9. Brian Axel (2002) suggests, provocatively, that the diaspora creates the homeland.
10. In her study of Polish immigrant radio in Germany, Morawska defines cultural politics of recognition as "performative acts...or practices aimed at the establishment and confirmation of the [immigrant or minority] group's collective existence, identity and interests...." However, she locates the objects of these recognition politics as group members, and "the surrounding, host society" (Morawska 2006: 1–2), not the home country.

11. See Fernandez (2006) and Knauer (2005) on the racialization of urban space in Cuba.
12. The ban had been sporadically enforced, but, in early August 2006, the Cuban government announced harsh new sanctions against citizens with illegal satellite dishes, and especially those who "rented" their signal to others for a fee. See Navarro (2006).
13. Videos sent by relatives are often used to start *bancos de videos*. See Pertierra (2005).
14. The transnationalization of the Cuban immigrant experience has been the subject of recent scholarship, including Duany (2001), Eckstein and Barberia (2003), and Fernandez (2004).
15. For a discussion of the renewed attention to "folklore" in the 1990s, see, among others, Hagedorn (2001) and Hernandez-Reguant (this volume and 2006b).
16. This is the same Puntilla discussed earlier.
17. They are so commonplace to have produced a deft parody in the 2001 Cuban feature film, *Video de Familia*.
18. Showering performers with money is a common gesture of appreciation in West Africa and has been carried over into some new world African cultures.
19. All comments are from an interview conducted in January 2003.
20. My informants report that in the 1980s drummers were wary of visitors with cameras.
21. I use the generic term "video" to refer to videocassettes, VCDs, and DVDs, both professionally produced movies and homemade recordings.
22. The Cuban music "boom" of the late 1990s produced several recordings of rumba and Afro-Cuban sacred music. Two in particular—*En el Solar de la Cueva del Humo* (1997) and *Rapsodia Rumbera* (2000)—were avidly consumed by New York-area rumba enthusiasts.

11

Ending the Century with *Memories*...: Paper Money, Videos, and an *X-Acto* Knife for Cuban Art

Antonio Eligio Fernández, "Tonel"
Translated by Kate Levitt

I maintain lucidity. An unpleasant lucidity, an emptiness...

—*Sergio Carmona, in* Memorias del Subdesarrollo *(1968)*

The last decade of the twentieth century was a time of transition and readjustment for visual artists in Cuba. A considerable number of artists emigrated from the country, among them central figures from the generation responsible for an artistic renewal in the 1980s. That movement, called "New Cuban Art," was later reinterpreted in the first half of the 1990s by a group of very young artists, who explored art's communicative and cultural possibilities to better fit the country's changing social and economic circumstances in the aftermath of the fall of the Berlin Wall and the dismantling of the Soviet Union. The shock of that time period, baptized from the beginning as the Special Period, had profound consequences on national consciousness, culture, and ideology. The damages range from more overt racism to increasing class differences and inequality among diverse groups of the Cuban population. Each in their own way, the artists whose works I examine in this essay have confronted some of these issues and have tried to respond to the complex questions posed by the Special Period at the end of the twentieth century.

A Brief Background: Cultural Policy and "New Cuban Art"

The late 1970s saw the genesis of what was later labeled by many critics as the "new Cuban art." The visual arts had been central to the new literary and artistic culture of the Cuban Revolution, and by the end of the 1970s they thrived in a fertile and open space, clearly connected to contemporary art trends in Latin America, Europe, and the United States. From the rise of photorealism midway through the decade to the groundbreaking exhibition *Volumen Uno* in 1981, the visual arts experienced a reinvigoration that would extend well into the beginning of the 1990s. During this period, artistic changes took place within a sweeping readjustment of cultural policy, including the creation of new cultural institutions in 1976, such as the Ministry of Culture and the Instituto Superior de Arte (ISA). These institutions were essential in advancing a new policy that featured the foundation of a network of cultural sites, from theaters to bookstores to art galleries throughout the island. The increasing support for local art schools led to a rise in the number of students who enrolled, thereby planting the seeds for a thriving art scene. Furthermore, cultural policies sought to counterbalance the Soviet influence on the country at the time, instead reaffirming Cuba's unequivocal place in Western culture at domestic and international forums. This strategic position was very well illustrated by the newly appointed Minister of Culture Armando Hart (1983: 34–36):

> Within her own tradition, which to a great extent was born in Europe, Cuba's ideological, political and cultural discussions add to the West.... We, geographically and culturally, are part of the West, but we do not enclose ourselves within boundaries that separate us from the rest of the world.... We do not isolate ourselves but rather open ourselves to the world; not to limit ourselves, but to enrich ourselves.

The winds of change blowing through the cultural sector in the late 1970s have been at times interpreted as pragmatic responses from a revolutionary regime confronted with unfavorable social and political circumstances—the same ones that would lead to the Mariel exodus of 1980. Indeed, for the Cuban government, the images of tens of thousands of citizens competing for space in the boats leaving for the United States from the port of Mariel must have delivered a serious shock that sent tremors through Cuba's national consciousness, as well as a reason for concern and an opportunity for reflection. While it is true that the artistic boom of the 1980s could not have taken place without the fervent support of the new Ministry of Culture, headed by Hart, it should be emphasized that this process of renewal had begun earlier, in the mid-1970s, and was therefore not a direct result of the traumatic spectacle of the Mariel boatlift.

Ending the Century with Memories   181

As the 1980s progressed, the auspicious relationship between artists and institutions began deteriorating and by the end of the decade it was fraught with friction and infighting. Tomas Esson's 1988 show "A Tarro Partido II" at the *12 y 23* Art center, which was shut down less than seventy-two hours after it opened, was one of the most well-known events demonstrating this rising tension. At Armando Hart's suggestion, Esson later unveiled another very different exhibition in the gallery of ISA, a space officially considered "experimental" and therefore more tolerant of unconventional displays. Another controversial project was the *Castillo de la Fuerza* (1989), a series of exhibitions featuring a number of polemic presentations. One of these, by Eduardo Ponjuán and René Francisco Rodríguez stands out since it was closed and later reopened. Notably, it included a number of works that played with the image of Fidel Castro which were immediately removed from the show. Another controversial exhibition in the series, *Homenaje a Hans Haacke*, was also ultimately censured; its creators were artists Tanya Angulo, Juan P. Ballester, Ileana Villazón, and José Toirac. In response, a few months later a number of artists protested through the collective performance of a baseball game. The following year yet another show, *El Objeto Esculturado* (The Sculptural Object), was also shut down. The show took place in Havana's Center for the Development of Visual Arts and resulted in a six-month prison sentence for the artist Angel Delgado whose impromptu performance during the opening involved shitting on a newspaper. Due to these multiple incidents and the increasing difficulties exhibiting and promoting their work, many well-known artists left Cuba in the early 1990s, most often to establish themselves in Mexico and Miami.[1] This wave of migration was concurrent with the emergence of the Special Period and its associated economic crisis, which further forced artists to seek alternative livelihoods.

The emigration of key Cuban art figures broke the movement's continuity, creating a sudden vacuum that greatly affected the art scene in the following years. This emptiness actually became a cohesive factor for a younger generation just entering the arts in the beginning of the 1990s. For this generation, the absence of many teachers and colleagues, accompanied by a shortage of opportunities for professional exchange and dialogue, was very unfavorable. However, the massive absence of established figures allowed for a unique generational identity that developed in a much less competitive environment, in which many of their immediate predecessors were distant memories; at most a canon to emulate, but almost never an actual presence.

The years 1993 and 1994 were important in solidifying what would be recognized from then on as the "generation of the nineties." In 1993, *Las metaforas del templo* (The Metaphors of the Temple), the first of two decisive exhibitions, was organized by artists and participants Carlos Garaicoa and Esterio Segura.[2] It opened at Havana's Center for the Development of Visual Arts and immediately generated great interest. Partly because of this attention, many of the participants of *Las metaforas* were invited to the Fifth

Havana Art Biennial in 1994 (Molina 1997). *Las metaforas* thus constituted a platform that launched some of these young artists into the international art scene thus opening another chapter in the narrative that began at the end of the 1970s. Indeed, *Las metaforas* displayed continuities between the art of the 1980s and 1990s, although all the artists were from the latter generation—many of them graduates of ISA who had been participating in Havana's art gallery circuit since their student days. In some cases they were disciples of the few members of the previous generation who had remained in Cuba, artists such as Lázaro Saavedra, René Francisco, Eduardo Ponjuán, and José Toirac, and theory and aesthetics professors such as Lupe Alvarez and Magaly Espinosa.

The works of this group of "new" youth reflected many strategies of the preceding generation. Like their immediate predecessors, these younger artists were concerned with historical and political themes, as well as social commentary and critical reflections on art itself. Some installations and objects used conceptual and minimalist approaches to suggest links with the recent local past. Others, in a very different tone, reclaimed popular art traditions. The young group also demonstrated an appreciation for artisanship and technical mastery, with some producing highly polished, often ostentatious objects which would be attractive in the international art market (Montes de Oca 2006: 157). The turn toward a more conventional packaging of their work, as well as a related emphasis on form, were some of the new generation's defining attributes.

Although critics Kevin Power (1999) and Lupe Alvarez (1999) both note the similarities between the generation of the 1990s and their 1980s predecessors, the two periods cannot be seen as merely different stages within one coherent process. For some critics, a key distinction between the generations is the younger artists' cynicism and opportunism. Art from the 1990s is often recognized by its "postmodern investitures" that create a path for, among other things, a "culture of cynicism" (Espinosa 2006: 58). Likewise, poet and art critic Orlando Hernández (2005: 19) has described the 1990s artistic scene as "becoming increasingly more negligent and hedonistic, preoccupied with its own appearance, and possible successes and rewards." Hernández is not alone in contrasting the artists' cynicism and eagerness to enter the international art market with the profound critical and social commitment of artists in the 1980s. For the most part, the critical diagnosis concerning the Special Period's artists paints them as cynical and faithless characters, imbued with a distant intellectual attitude whereby the creative subject is only superficially involved in his or her environment. According to Lupe Alvarez (1999: 116), "[C]reation hid itself in artistic autonomy, it protected itself in an aesthetic distance, preserving a space undisturbed from what is outside." In response, Magaly Espinosa (2006) argued that for these artists it did not make sense to consider themselves agents of transformation. The loss of utopia and the demands of the market asked for and generated new approaches.

These types of debates actually recalled earlier moments in the art and culture of revolutionary Cuba. What comes to mind, in particular, is the work that has best expressed cynicism, that scathing distance of an intellectual summoned by the Revolution, trying to make sense of a world transformed before his eyes while struggling to avoid being dragged down by these very transformations. That work is the film *Memorias del Subdesarrollo* (*Memories of Underdevelopment*) by Tomás Gutiérrez Alea.

Memorias: So Much to Remember

Tomás Gutiérrez Alea directed *Memorias* in 1968. The film was based on a homonymous novel by Edmundo Desnoes (1965). As film historian Michael Chanan (1990) later remarked, the film reproduces the "fragmentation and dissociation" caused by revolutionary change "as the prerevolutionary world is dismembered [and] new cultural forms have yet to emerge." The action takes place in 1961, during the days preceding the Bay of Pigs invasion and the events leading up to the missile crisis. Sergio, the protagonist, is an observant character, full of doubt and cynical skepticism. His individualism is frequently highlighted in the film through the contrast between his physical presence and a crowd that never manages to dissolve him. It is not an accident that the film frequently uses a telephoto lens to convey Sergio's image; the character retreats into the distance, where his silhouette slides like liquid mercury before the background of a markedly gray city. That city is the dramatic setting of Havana, and the cinematography of Ramón F. Suárez displays images that went on to become prototypes—repeated ad nauseam—for the cinematic and photographic portrait of Havana's landscape: the *malecon* (sea wall) with its crashing waves, the rooftops and buildings emerging through a curtain of smog, and the shady streets framed by doorways and columns. To emphasize distance, Sergio's telescopic gaze—toward the urban setting that surrounds him, toward his fellow citizens, toward history—projects from the heights of a balcony in one of those tall buildings that in the 1950s announced a never-delivered promise of a city that would be defined by a forest of elegant skyscrapers. The film, designed like a collage, pieces together fragments of pornographic movies from the United States and quotes—taken from the Cuban press—from Mao Tse Tung. We also see and hear a panel of Cuban and foreign intellectuals discussing "the fundamental contradiction of our time," the voiceover of John F. Kennedy announcing the Cuban missile crisis to the United States and the world, and Fidel Castro's television appearance in 1962, denouncing the possibility of a U.S. nuclear attack on the island.

The paradigmatic quality of *Memorias* comes from its poignant representation of the inner crisis experienced by the intellectual who has decided to bear witness to the triumphant Revolution, contemplating it as a bricolage of images. The film is also a self-portrait of its authors, who seek a critical distance from both themselves and their works. Both writer Edmundo Desnoes and director Gutiérrez Alea appear in the film as themselves, thereby becoming characters and distancing themselves from their own authorship.

Another suggestive detail is that the main character, Sergio Carmona, is played by another Sergio (Corrieri). *Memorias* is an exemplary work of synthesis; in just over one hour and thirty minutes Gutiérrez Alea compresses a partial but intense version of Cuba's history by means of stringing together both documentary and fiction. The film's structure, the importance it gives to Havana, the city's architecture as the setting for historical drama, the reiteration of fragments, the effect of collage, the appeal of the documentary, the resourceful use of music and popular dance as essential embodiments of tragedy, race, and class tensions—all of these elements are part of the film's profound aesthetic mark on Cuban contemporary art.

Memorias truly establishes a continuous relationship and inaugurates a dialogue with later Cuban art. In the 1990s, the interlocutors will be artists working in painting, video, experimental film, and installation, all of whom engage the reflexive, critical, and self-critical tone that *Memorias* embodies. More than a cinematic creation, Gutiérrez Alea's work was the creative synthesis of a broad historical moment. During the years of the Special Period, artists constructed new works as well as sketched new artistic genealogies in a similar landscape characterized by unexhausted aesthetic potential. Knowingly or unknowingly, the film has influenced many artists during the 1990s, including Pedro Alvarez, Juan Carlos Alom, Manuel Piña, and Felipe Dulzaides. Along with many of their contemporaries, who could be considered as part of the Revolution's organic intellectuals, these artists use the uncontainable ambivalence and sarcasm that had paralyzed *Memoria*'s Sergio as a creative tool. Sergio's lucidity continues to be unpleasant nearly three decades later; however, for the new artists I discuss, this inherited lucidity is not a precursor of emptiness, but rather expresses what is commonly called "inspiration"—an intense, complex, and occasionally bitter strength upon which great art works are built.

Pedro Alvarez: Painting with an *X-Acto* Knife

Pedro Alvarez was part of that group of young artists invited to the Fifth Havana Art Biennial in 1994, his first opportunity to show work on an international level. At the core of Alvarez's creative method one finds a voluminous and varied accumulation and recycling of images, constituting an archive that questions the possible, but never obligatory, relationship between the artist and Cuba's history, institutions, and characters. This relationship to Cuba is sometimes very slight, simply suggested through montages and juxtapositions created by an artist who once defined himself as a "curator assisted by an Exacto [sic] knife"[3] (P. Alvarez 1999: 75). His curatorial procedure is a true surgery of culture, assisted by an X-acto knife that allows for editing, cutting, and attaching material in a repetitive and almost obsessive way. Through this, Alvarez links himself with a style that Michael Chanan (1995: 236) had long before defined as essential in *Memorias*, with its "exercise in the fragmentation and dissociation of imagery and representation." Indeed, at the end of the 1990s collage became both literally and materially the foundation upon which Alvarez would apply paint. With this method he expanded his interest in (neo)colonialism and the cultural and economic relations established between Western capitalist powers and the dependent nations of Africa, Latin America, and Asia. To convey these messages, Alvarez favored cutting and editing images to reveal correspondences with regard to design, typology, and color. Given this practice, it is not surprising that he has described his work as an exercise in "selecting works, artists, styles, nationalities, and epochs, but the fundamental criteria are eminently formal" (P. Alvarez 1999: 75).

Kevin Power (1999: 108) has pointed out the theatrical power of Alvarez's painting, defining his work as "a dramatically lit new theater of nothing... an ideological debate playing itself out in terms of sheer theater." In this theatrical space, the historical image expands in a diorama without beginning or end, and representations refuse to conform to a linear chronology. The constant anachronistic juxtapositions indicate an ambiguous time referent, made out of circular moments that escape the fixity of before and after, and whose "now" eludes any clear and specific date. When some detail in the work, such as a slogan, a placard, or perhaps a building refers to the present time, other images in the same scene remind the viewer of the impossibility of defining either the moment or the place with any kind of precision. In his paintings, Alvarez inserts a multitude of symbols as familiar as they are errant. In fact, they are often raw stereotypes that sarcastically refer to Cuban, Spanish, American, and Soviet identities. When these images are juxtaposed, however, they impede an understanding of history as a linear or progressive process. His paintings also negate any kind of spatial certainty: from the José Marti monument in Havana's Central Park, to the abundance of cars and the variety of brand-name products—Coca Cola, Disney, Benetton—that speak of consumerism and colonization, to a representation of the Republic of Cuba as a white and Rubenesque woman, all these images inhabit his canvasses to produce a theatrical, Brechtian estrangement. It seems that his intention is to produce uncertainty for the spectator, therefore reinforcing the distance between the work and the public critically observing it.

Havana Dollarscape and *The Romantic Dollarscape Series* (see fig. 11.1) are the titles of two groups of paintings that Alvarez made between the mid-1990s and the beginning of the following decade. In these canvases, and particularly in the *Havana* series, Alvarez directly confronts the problematic of the art market, and most significantly the implications—for art and for Cuban society in general—of what has been called the "decriminalization" of the U.S. dollar, which took place in 1993. The works combine images from both sides of U.S. paper currency, from the portrait of the historical figure that appears on one side (George Washington, Andrew Jackson, Ulysses S. Grant, etc.) to the different buildings reproduced on the reverse side (Monticello, the Treasury, the White House, etc.). The idea of recreating and reproducing paper money using traditional artistic media, such as paint, drawing, and prints, in order to critique or comment on social, political, and economic conditions, is part of the contemporary art experience—Andy Warhol, Robert Watts, Cildo Meireles, J.S.G. Boggs, and Joseph Beuys, among others have all used the same strategy. In *Imaginary Economics*, Olav Velthuis (2005: 10) aptly comments, "[I]t is striking to see just how many artists are concerned...with ordinary economic phenomena such as markets, money, consumption or the possession of property." In Cuba in the 1990s, Alvarez's *Dollarscapes* brought his particular approach to this crowded tradition, a perspective inspired by the specific circumstances of the Special Period.

All of Alvarez's ideas regarding collage, montage, and the manipulation of texts and images converge on the *Havana Dollarscapes* canvases. The importance Alvarez places on language and words is evident in the title itself. That title is notably in English, the language of the enemy in revolutionary Cuba, and draws on a neologism formed by the inextricable combination of "dollar" and "landscape." The English word Havana (*La Habana* in Spanish) connotes an external linguistic reality, that of the West and its power to name. Hence the city is presented as perceived from the outside, conceptualized in English, inseparable from and codependent on a foreign reality. It is an exotic Havana for tourists; a territory whose independence is and was placed in doubt: a city imagined and possessed by the United States, or at least by Anglophone tourists. The landscape and the people of that "Havana" combine, in paintings made of oil and collage, with the iconography of American money to transparently express the kinship between art and money, between art and the market; a relationship that the circumstances of the Special Period made more pronounced than ever before in Cuba.

Pedro Alvarez indicates how a Cuban artist's access to the market during the 1990s depended in good measure on his or her relationship with a special type of tourist and their foreign money. Specifically, he refers to the frequent presence of curators, private collectors, and representatives of U.S. institutions on the island during those years. These tourists exerted a considerable power over art on the island, as they became the most assiduous and prodigious clients of the local scene. As Kevin Power (1999: 101) commented, "[T]o be an artist is to occupy a privileged position in Cuba, in the sense that if an artist is successful they directly enter into the omnipotent and omnipresent American market."

The dominant symbols of capitalist financial power in Alvarez's paintings are always accompanied by people and landscape fragments that form part of the colonial iconography of the nineteenth century. In the canvasses we find caricatures of the lascivious black chauffeur and the happy-go-lucky mulatta, of the *Abakuá iremes*, and of other figures that were fixtures in the *costumbrismo* of painter and printmaker Federico Mialhe and in the pictorial work of Victor Patricio de Landaluze, a nineteenth-century Basque-Cuban caricaturist and painter, and a fervent defender of pro-Spanish colonialist ideology. In the *Dollarscapes*, the transformation of money into a form of stage design creates an environment defined by images that are inseparable from the colonial imagination (see figure 11.1). In *Fifty*, one of the *Havana Dollarscape* paintings, Alvarez places Ulysses S. Grant in a setting with characters that belong to the tradition of *costumbrismo* and to Landaluze's satirical pictures: the mulatta, and people in costumes who look like participants in an *Abakuá* ceremony. This particular scene, like almost all that comprise the series, has been painted over a dramatic, neo-romantic landscape background. In this landscape of stormy skies and palm trees battered by the wind, in front of the Capitol Building in Washington, D.C., the blending colors become a monochromatic palette dominated by green.

Time and again, by combining symbols of U.S. power with those that evoke the colonial past, Pedro Alvarez delineates a nightmarish "Havana," a site where neither foreign domination nor racist humiliation ends, and where the fixity of who plays master and slave is irremediable. The *Dollarscape* series represents the frustration of all Cuban nationalism, conveying sarcasm but not bitterness; the theatrical component lends a farcical nuance, like *bufo* theater or *pachanga* dancing and drunkenness. That drunkenness is further represented in the work *Ron y Coca Cola* (Rum and Coca Cola) (see figure 11.2), with the image of two drunken black characters, like those one finds on cigar box labels, at the foot of the José Martí monument in Havana's Central Park. The two drunken characters are observed by a smiling couple, a well-dressed white woman and man recreated from a well-known 1950s Coca Cola advertisement, who drink the soda of the title and establish the scene's framework. Again, North American and Spanish iconographies complement each other to round out a commentary on race and class, this time branded from the perspective of the white middle class, whose point of view dominates and defines the composition.

Figure 11.1   *Fifty* from The Romantic *Dollarscape* Series, 2003, oil on linen. Estate of the artist.

188 Antonio Eligio Fernández, "Tonel"

Figure 11.2 *Ron y Coca Cola*, 1995, oil on canvas, Private Collection.

Havana Dollarscape's overarching style introduces objects whose function is to reinforce the U.S. presence in Cuba's cultural and physical environment. So, President Grant—who seems to be making himself comfortable beneath the shade of a banana tree—looks entrenched, protected behind one of those magnificent automobiles made in Detroit factories in the 1940s and 1950s. For anyone with access to a few recent coffee table books, the unique design of those old cars is easily identifiable with the tourist's image of a Havana frozen in time, effectively recreated by Wim Wenders and embellished by Ry Cooder's guitar strings.

The representation of money articulates itself in a coherent landscape, a unified setting with recognizable characters and historical, cultural, and economic factors. The concentration of all these elements provides an understanding of how important "hard" currency became in the Cuba of the Special Period. At the same time, these pictorial collages scoff at the "new" reality of the 1990s, constructed around the dollar as a sum of both past and present times. Painted money thus becomes a narrative tapestry recasting circumstances and people according to the central, intimidating iconography of the dollar: the racism that permeates everything, as symbolized by Landaluze's *costumbrista* paintings; the tourist economy, dependent on an insular and exoticized image as projected by the Studebaker, Bel Air, or Edsel cars still running and being photographed in Havana; the mulatta, perhaps enticed to turn herself into a *jinetera*, or street hustler, riding in dilapidated American cars; and the practitioners of Afro-Cuban religions, reduced in this setting to the role of quaint and always subordinate figures.

The concern with inequality and racial identity is not unique to Alvarez. It was central to many Cuban artists during the 1990s. It is worth briefly noting the pictorial and installation work of Alexis Esquivel, who occasionally shares Alvarez's sarcastic tone and use of montage and collage to form the painting's base. Several of Esquivel's most significant works investigate the role of memory in Afro-Cuban culture and allude to the importance of Afro-Cuban intellectuals such as Martín Morúa Delgado and Evaristo Estenoz, who are seldom recognized in mainstream versions of national history. Other artists, in contrast, focus on the black body, either parodying racist assumptions of black hypersexuality (as in the work of Elio Rodríguez) or by way of detailed explorations of a racialized, eroticized, and performative black male body, as in René Peña's photographs, which deliberately play with an ambivalent tone in their criticism and reflection of racial stereotypes (see figure 5.1).

René Peña's work exemplifies the central role of photography in the panorama of Cuban art during the 1990s. In the next section, I discuss photography and the medium's transformation as it evolved toward audio-visual work.

Camera in Hand; from the Photograph to the Moving Image

In the early 1980s, Cuban photography began to gradually distance itself from its association with propaganda and journalism. Since 1959 and well into the 1970s, an epical and documentary tone had dominated the medium, providing emblematic images of the Revolution. During the 1980s, artists from diverse generations, such as Raúl Martínez, María Eugenia Haya, Rogelio López Marín, José M. Fors, Arturo Cuenca, and Marta María Pérez revitalized photography, some through the reinvention of procedures like photomontage, manually lit impressions, and color manipulation in the laboratory, and others through intimate and autobiographical images, or by means of exploring the relationship between photography and literature.

The work of these photographers created a bridge between the Conceptual art scene of the 1980s and the changing cultural and social climate of the 1990s. In the mid-1990s, new photographers like René Peña, Eduardo Muñoz Ordoqui, Abigaíl González, Kattia García Fayat, and Cirenaica Moreira were able to make a name for themselves. Of interest here, however, are a few individuals who also started out as photographers but later moved on to video and film. It should be mentioned that video arrived comparatively late to the Cuban art scene, given the fact that in the Americas, Europe, and Asia it had become commonplace by the end of the 1970s. On the island, however, video only gained popularity in the second half of the 1990s during the Special Period. In this section I will focus on Juan Carlos Alom, Felipe Dulzaides, and Manuel Piña, three artists who were central, each in his own unique way, to the incorporation of film and video into Cuban art.

Like the paintings of Pedro Alvarez, the video works of Juan Carlos Alom, Felipe Dulzaides, and Manuel Piña include sharp, piercing commentaries on contradictions between real-life conditions and Cuban socialist ideology. Juan Carlos Alom's achievement in film stands out as early as 1997, when he completed his 16 mm film *Una Harley recorre La Habana* (A Harley Travels around Havana), a group portrait of Harley motorcycle lovers. In the film he introduces a wide array of Cuban individuals and families united by their love for Harley-Davidson motorcycles. Using interview footage, Alom shows a proud community whose identity developed around this hobby. The film covers the bike's history on the island, a testament to the fervor and dedication these men and women have had for their machines. Even though these artifacts were doomed for extinction due to the U.S. embargo, the creativity and experimentation of the Caribbean "bricoleur" guaranteed their survival, as the motorcycles experienced a second life of polished chrome and shiny rivets.

Perhaps it is because *Una Harley* explores so many multiple perspectives (anthropological, sociological, aesthetic) that the story line feels at times to be full of digressions. Concomitantly, the music—some of the most experimental work of *timba* composer José Luis Cortés—is at times poorly synchronized. Made with minimal resources in precarious material circumstances, this film reflects the insecurity of an "opera prima." Despite Alom's novice errors and his lack of resources, the main idea comes across clearly, thanks in part to the film's disarming crudeness. Alom's camerawork, especially when the lens scrolls over the city, has moments of absolute brilliance, which takes his cinematography to the same high level as his most well-known photography. The use of 16 mm film—a practice Alom reproduced in later films—recalls, perhaps unwittingly, an earlier period in Cuban film history, when filmmakers such as Manuel Octavio Gómez and Sara Gómez also used 16 mm to take advantage of the camera's portability and create a more intimate result, closer to the authenticity of documentary images (Chanan 1990: 280).

One of Alom's most significant works is *Habana Solo* (2000), a short film in which the city of Havana along with Cuban music and musicians are the protagonists. The underlying idea is simple. Alom asked a number of Cuban musicians, including stars like Frank Emilio Flynn, Tata Güines, Enrique Lázaga, and José Luis Cortés, to compose an instrumental solo—thus the title—of no more than two minutes. He then took to the streets of Havana with his 16 mm camera and composed a portrait with images of rundown neighborhoods and gesturing city dwellers. To these visuals, Alom added the musician's recordings, turned now into soundtracks as well as images of the performers playing. The ending includes a solo dance, performed on a rooftop without music, which displays the unparalleled exuberance of the human body. Dancing is here an individual act. The dancer, a slim black man, dances for the city, with and before her, and the whole sequence unfolds from a perspective that takes the audience back to Memorias…, to Sergio's balcony and his telescopic view of Havana's rooftops. A backdrop of ruined buildings, sky, and clouds transforms this choreography into a ceremonial offering that explodes into a brilliant crescendo at the end of the movie. The piece is a heart-rending tribute that Alom offers to Havana as well as to the individuals inhabiting this urban landscape.

In San Francisco, California, on a sunny day in 1999, Felipe Dulzaides pauses at a fruit-stand, buys, and then drops an orange, which starts to roll down a slope. First slowly, then at increasing speed, Dulzaides follows and films the rolling orange. *Following an Orange* was Dulzaides's first video work. In a little over one minute the orange becomes the protagonist of a perilous journey, managing to circumvent all types of obstacles, including a heavily trafficked intersection, before getting lost on the other side of the street. That the fruit's vertiginous adventure could serve as a metaphor did not escape Dulzaides, as it resonated with his own biography. In 1991 Dulzaides crossed the straits, more dangerous than any congested street, separating Cuba from the United States, and like the orange, he arrived in one piece.

A few weeks after that downhill run in San Francisco, Dulzaides undertook the trip in reverse, returning to a Havana he had not seen for eight years. There he filmed *Deicing*, a work about absence that explores the experience of rekindling relationships with family and friends after a distance created by emigration. In *Deicing*, all of the action occurs at a goodbye party in his mother's apartment, organized by Dulzaides's family and friends at the end of his visit. The gathering is captured by an immobile camera, focused on a block of ice resting on a table. In front of this camera, moving around or interacting with the ice, the film's characters ceremoniously repeat rituals of friendship and intimacy.

Felipe Dulzaides's video work is frequently based on the recording of his performances. It is equally a reflection of his theater experience in Cuba during the 1980s as it is a result of his artistic training in the United States, and in particular at the San Francisco Art Institute, where he studied with professors such as the Cuban-American artist Tony Labat. Both Labat's and Dulzaides's video practices are informed by European and American art developments since the mid-1960s: specifically, the dematerialization of the artistic object, the use of time as a medium for art, the introduction of everyday objects as part of the art work, and the combination of diverse disciplines such as painting, sculpture, music, theater, and video (Rush 2003). Thus in works such as *On the Ball* (2000), *Time on My Hand* (2000), *Killing My Thirst* (2001), and *Blowing Things Away* (2001), Dulzaides effectively uses all those principles, further referring to an early tradition in video art—that of Bruce Nauman, Vitto Acconci, Carolee Schneemann, Charlotte Moorman, among others— that situates the acting, performative body of the artist at the center of the work; in this case, in front of the camera.

On the Ball is one fundamental contribution to this performative tradition. In one single take of less than three minutes, Dulzaides's performance unfolds, featuring him singing the chorus of a popular Cuban song from the middle of the 1990s, "La Bola," by Manolín, aka "The Salsa Doctor," whose version of *timba*—a high-energy form of dance music popular in the 1990s— dominated Havana's dance halls and radio and television music programming until the Doctor emigrated to Miami. In the piece, Dulzaides sings, or rather murmurs, Manolin's famous chorus line and a popular expression: "Because you have to be on the ball, on the ball, on the ball," which means that you always have to be alert, prepared, staying at maximum attention all the time. Dulzaides's a cappella interpretation highlights the drama of that common expression, removing text and melody from the association with fun and cheer, as well as from the song's undercurrent of bragging machismo. While the original "La Bola" presents dance, song, and spoken words as a collective experience shared by social groups reaffirming the internalization of a common cultural repertoire, Dulzaides finds a pretext for the solitary lament of the emigrant, and assembles a confessional discourse, which is filmed in a minimal, claustrophobic space. What stands out in Dulzaides's performance is the theme of absence, as the song's original version is stripped from its chorus lines, from laugher and clapping, from its contagious percussion beat, and the sharp accents of the wind section. In his voice and body, and above all in his face, the repetition of the popular chorus line—as the person in front of the camera gradually moves toward the lens, reaches to touch it with his mouth, and steams it up with his breath—becomes an obsessive act, charged with erotic reverberations, and yet always pathetic.

Dulzaides exemplifies the quasi-nomadic predicament of many Cuban artists today. The making of art has become for him an increasingly itinerant practice taking place between San Francisco and Havana. This transitory character confirms the expansion of the Cuban art scene outside of the geopolitical contours of the island, as well as the influence of the market and international institutions within Cuba. His mobility, and that of others, interrogates what it means to be a Cuban artist today, all the more so when the work is inseparable from the author's emigrant condition and sustained attachment to his homeland.

In one of his more recent works, the 2004 video-installation *Proyecto Invitación*, presented at Cuba's Fototeca, Dulzaides explores the work of Italian architect Roberto Gottardi, who at the beginning of the 1960s, along with the Cuban Ricardo Porro and the Italian Vittorio Garatti, designed Havana's National Art Schools in Cubanacán—undoubtedly the most successful architectural work undertaken during the revolutionary period. Dulzaides is interested in the utopian impulse of the constructive and pedagogical school project, and with his camera in hand establishes a direct dialogue with one of the transformed protagonists, to give a face and voice to the realizations and frustrations born of this utopian chapter.

Like Dulzaides, Manuel Piña intertwines personal and social issues in his works. In *The Hope and the Rope* (2003), Piña presents a story combining intimate autobiographical fragments with testimonies on the development of Cuban photography, all taking place on the gray and monotonous landscape of a cheap, modern apartment building built by *microbrigadas*.[4] In a sober style combining image and text, Piña explains the *microbrigadas'* tradition and weaves their history with his own. A work rich with humorous anecdotes, *The Hope* juxtaposes moving text over images in the style of Cuban documentary film in the 1960s and 1970s, particularly recalling the work of the officially little-acknowledged filmmaker Nicolás Guillén Landrián. Central to *The Hope and the Rope* are the photographs from Piña's previous photography series *Of (De)Contructions and Utopias (Hommage to Eduardo Muñoz)* (1996), which included images that Piña printed from original negatives discarded by photographer Eduardo Muñoz Ordoqui. Both Muñoz, with his abandoned project, and Piña, by reclaiming his colleague's negatives, use the Revolution's building construction ambitions—and particularly the *microbrigada* concept—as metaphors for a society in flux. In so doing they also reflect on the role of utopia in historical change. The question of the failure, or at least of the stagnation, of utopian aspirations for positive transformation, underlies both the earlier photography series and the video *The Hope and the Rope*.

Piña's works clearly refer to filmmaker Sara Gómez's productions from the 1960s and 1970s. Gómez drew a parallel between the construction of new housing and the construction of new lives. Urban renewal, hence, was a starting point for analyzing the Revolution's repercussions on individuals and families. Her film *One Way or Another* (1974) combined documentary and fiction, voiceover and written text, information and commentary, and amateur and professional actors, to reinforce the story's credibility. Yet a key difference between Gómez and Piña lies in their views and hopes for a better world. *One Way or Another* presented social conflicts, like machismo and social hypocrisy (what in Cuban Spanish is referred to as "double moral"), which, according to the message in the film, could eventually be overcome outside the screen as a result of the Revolution's education and progress. That optimism, which to some extent applies to a majority of literary and artistic production in Cuba during the 1960s and 1970s, distances Gómez's work from that of Piña's, as much as it separates cultural production of that era from that of the 1990s. *The Hope and the Rope*, in contrast, is a work defined by its skepticism and irony, leaving little or no space for hopeful optimism; one could say the same about *Dreams* and *Heaven*, two other works by Piña.

Dreams and *Heaven* have been exhibited as part of multimedia installations. In both videos, superimposed lines of text quickly move across the screen. These are transcriptions, fragments of conversations surreptitiously recorded by Piña in Havana, which can be heard on the soundtrack. These dialogues show the existence of an underground, marginal world of dog fights, poverty, black-market transactions involving large sums of cash, and violence. Most importantly, the fragmented dialogues evidence the thoughts of those located at the bottom of the social pyramid and their vision of the lives of the powerful as dreamworlds filled with pleasure.

As mentioned earlier, both Manuel Piña and Juan Carlos Alom were trained in photography. While Alom stays closer to the narrative conventions of genre and uses techniques historically associated with film, Piña conceives his work in a space that identifies with both well-established cinematographic traditions and more recent forms of multimedia, as well as with installation as a site-specific work with room for the moving image and for sound.

Apart from some tactical differences, all of the artists considered here share what I would call a "genealogical conscience"; one inspired by the Cuban documentary film tradition of the 1960s and 1970s, and exemplified by the aforementioned Sara Gómez (*One Way or Another* 1974) and Tomás Gutiérrez Alea (*Memories of Underdevelopment* 1968), as well as by Santiago Alvarez (*Ciclón* 1963), Sabá Cabrera Infante and Orlando Jiménez Leal (*PM* 1961), Nicolás Guillén Landrián (*Coffea Arábiga* 1968), and Manuel Octavio Gómez (*La primera carga al machete* 1969). It was a tradition of experimental and innovative cinema, carefree in form and eclectic in influences. This was a cinema that took risks, while maintaining a critical perspective from which to observe what was happening at that time, shedding light on marginal characters and problems, on phenomena that the more complacent versions of history had placed on the outer edges of dominant accounts.

The nonconformist sensibility, the will to experiment, and the critical concerns shared by Alvarez, Alom, Dulzaides, and Piña extend to other artists, and to a considerable part of visual arts, film, music, and literature works created in the tremendous circumstances of the Special Period, and its aftermath. Similar characters, issues, and scenes are deeply explored from different perspectives by artists such as Luis Gómez, Lázaro Saavedra, Sandra Ceballos, and Ezequiel Suárez, by filmmakers such as Fernando Pérez (*Madagascar* 1994, *Suite Habana* 2003), Humberto Padrón (*Video de familia* 2002), and Arturo Infante (*Utopia* 2005), by the poet Carlos Augusto Alfonso (*Cabeza abajo* 1998 and *Cerval* 2004), and by the musician José Luis Cortés, "El Tosco," whose repertoire of dance songs contributes a harsh and challenging tone as compared to what became the more accepted, "mainstream" version of *timba*.

For all of these artists, and for so many others who are not mentioned here, an unpleasant lucidity, inaugurated by *Memorias*, belongs to them all.

Notes

1. For more on these artists, see Camnítzer (2003). Among those who migrated to Mexico are Alejandro Aguilera, José Bedia, Adriano Buergo, María Magdalena Campos, Consuelo Castañeda, Arturo Cuenca, Ana Albertina Delgado, Tomás Esson, Flavio Garciandía, Florencio Gelabert, Rogelio López Marín, Gustavo Pérez Monzón, Martha María Pérez, Glexis Novoa, Segundo Planes, Ciro Quintana, Angel Ricardo Ríos, Carlos Rodriguez Cárdenas, Leandro Soto, Rubén Torres Llorca, Pedro Vizcaíno.
2. Participating artists were Alexander Arrechea, Abel Barroso, Alberto Casado, Marcos Castillo, Carlos Garaicoa, Ernesto García, Jorge Luis Marrero, Douglas Pérez, Fernando Rodríguez, Dagoberto Rodríguez, Esterio Segura, and Osvaldo Yero.
3. Translator's note: *X-acto* is a brand of utility knives used for cutting and trimming pieces of paper.
4. Translator's note: *Microbrigadas* were small teams of workers released from their regular jobs to construct housing, in which they could typically claim an apartment for themselves.

Bibliography

Abreu, Juan. 2004. "Deuda." Paper delivered at Kosmopolis (Café Europa-La Habana, September 18). Barcelona, Spain: Centro de Cultura Contemporánea.
Abu-Lughod, Lila. 2002. "Egyptian Melodrama: Technology of the Modern Subject?" In *Media Worlds: Anthropology on New Terrain*. Faye Ginsburg, Lila Abu-Lughod, and Brian Larkin, eds. Berkeley: University of California Press.
Alonso, Alpidio. 2004. "El objetivo último de todo este esfuerzo es transformar, mejorar al hombre." *Juventud Rebelde* (Havana) (December 5): 6–7.
Alvarado Ramos, Juan Antonio. 2000. "Atlas Etnográfico de Cuba: Cultura Popular Tradicional." CD-ROM. Havana: Centro de Investigación y Desarrollo de la Cultura Cubana "Juan Marinello."
Alvaray, Luisela. 2005. "Settling a New Fad: Latin American Pictures Go Global." Paper presented at the *Cinematic Dislocations and Relocations Conference* (April 8–9). Milwaukee, Wisconsin.
Alvarez, Enrique, dir. 2001. *Miradas*. VHS. 90 min. Cuba: ICAIC.
Alvarez. José B. 2002. *Contestatory Short Story of the Cuban Revolution*. Lanham: University Press of America.
Alvarez, Lupe. 1999. "Contar en Cuba. El relato y la sospecha." In *While Cuba Waits: Art from the Nineties*. Kevin Power, ed. Santa Mónica: Smart Art Press.
Alvarez, Pedro. 1999. "On Vacation." In *While Cuba Waits: Art from the Nineties*. Kevin Power, ed. Santa Mónica: Smart Art Press.
Alvarez García, Alberto F. and Gerardo González Núñez. 2001. *¿Intelectuales vs. Revolución? El Caso del Centro de Estudios Sobre América*. Montreal: Eds. Arte D.T.
Alvarez Gil, Antonio. 2002. *Naufragios*. Sevilla: Algaida.
Appadurai, Arjun. 1990. "Disjuncture and Difference in the Global Cultural Economy." *Public Culture* 2 (2): 1–24.
Argüelles, Aníbal. 2003. "La Letra del Año." *Revista de la Universidad de La Habana* (Havana) 258: 208–213.
Aufderheide, Pat. 1995. "The Video in the Villages Project: Videomaking with and by Brazilian Indians." *Visual Anthropology Review* 11 (2): 83–93.
Axel, Brian Keith. 2002. "The Diasporic Imaginary." *Public Culture* 14 (2): 411–428.
Apter, Andrew. 1992. *Black Critics and Kings: The Hermeneutics of Power in Yoruba Society*. Chicago: University of Chicago Press.

Ayorinde, Christine. 2000. "Regla de Ocha-Ifá and the Construction of Cuban Identity." In *Identity in the Shadow of Slavery*. Paul E. Lovejoy, ed. London: Continuum.

———. 2004. *Afro-Cuban Religiosity, Revolution, and National Identity*. Gainesville: University Press of Florida.

Badiou, Alain. 2007. *The Century*. London: Polity Press.

Bain, Mervyn. 2006. "Gorbachev and Cuba: His Legacy for Russian-Cuban Relations in the 1990s." In *Redefining Cuban Foreign Policy*. John. M. Kirk and H. Michael Erisman, eds. Gainesville: University Press of Florida.

Baquero, Gastón. 1996. "La Cultura Nacional es un lugar de encuentro." *Encuentro* (Madrid) 1. http://www.cubaencuentro.com/es/encuentro-en-la-red/cultura/encuentro-una-decada/la-cultura-nacional-es-un-lugar-de-encuentro/(gnews)/1150430400 (accessed July 3, 2006).

Barash, Zoia. 2006. "Notas acerca de los dibujos animados en Rusia." *Miradas: Revista del audiovisual (Havana)*. http://www.eictv.co.cu/miradas/index.php?option=com_content&task=view&id=457&Itemid=99999999 (accessed May 5, 2007).

Barber, Karin. 1981. "How Man Makes God in West Africa: Yoruba Attitudes towards the Orisha." *Africa* 51 (3): 724–745.

Barnet, Miguel. 1994. "Miosvatis." In *Anuario 1994/ Narrativa*. Havana: Ediciones Unión.

Barrera, Olegario, dir. 1988. *Un domingo felíz*. Film. 90 min. Spain: International Network Group S.A. and Televisión Española.

Barroso, Mariano, dir. 2006 [2005]. *Hormigas en la Boca*. DVD. 96 min. U.S.A.: Warner Home Video.

Bascom, William, R. 1951. "The Yoruba in Cuba." *Nigeria* 37:14–20.

Bauman, Zygmunt. 1994. "A Revolution in the Theory of Revolutions?" *International Political Science Journal* 15 (1): 15–24.

Beasley-Murray, Jon. 2003. "On Posthegemony." *Bulletin of Latin American Research* 22 (1): 117–125.

Behar, Ruth. 1994. "Introduction." *Michigan Quarterly Review* 33 (3): 399–414.

———, dir. 2002. *Adió Kerida*. VHS. 82 min. U.S.A.: Women Make Movies.

Behar, Ruth and Lucia Suárez. 1994. "Two Conversations with Nancy Morejón." *Michigan Quarterly Review* 33 (3): 625–635.

Bejel, Emilio. 2001. *Gay Cuban Nation*. Chicago: University of Chicago Press.

Bell, Daniel. 1960. *The End of Ideology*. London: Collier-Macmillan.

Benjamin, Walter. 1969. *Illuminations*. New York: Schocken Books, 1969.

Benkomo, Juan. 2000. "Crafting the Sacred Batá Drums." In *Afro-Cuban Voices: On Race and Identity in Contemporary Cuba*. Pedro Pérez Sarduy and Jean Stubbs, eds. Gainesville: University of Florida Press.

Bernaza, Luis Felipe and Margaret Gilpin, dirs. 1998 [1996]. *Mariposas en el Andamio*. VHS. 74 min. U.S.A.: Water Bearer Films.

Betancourt, Victor. 2003. "Las incomprendidas letras de un año." *Revista de la Universidad de La Habana* (Havana) 258: 221–227.

Bettelheim, Judith. 1998. "Women in Masquerade and Performance." *African Arts* 31 (2): 68.

Bhabha, Homi K. 1994. *The Location of Culture*. London: Verso.

Birkenmaier, Anke. 2004. "El realismo sucio en América Latina: Reflexiones a partir de Pedro Juan Gutiérrez." *Miradas* (Havana) 6. http://www.miradas.eictv.co.cu (accessed January 15, 2006).

Birri, Fernando, dir. 1988. *Un señor muy viejo con unas alas enormes*. Film. 90 min. Cuba: ICAIC, and Spain: Televisión Española.
Black, George. 1988. "Cuba: The Revolution; toward Victory Always, but When?" *The Nation* 247 (October 24): 373–386.
Boal, Augusto. 1975. *Tecnicas Latinoamericanas de Teatro Popular: Una revolución copernicana al revés*. Buenos Aires: Corregidor.
———. 1985. *The Theater of the Oppressed*. New York: Theatre Communications Group.
Bobes, Marilyn. 1996. "Pregúntaselo a Dios." In *Estatuas de sal: Cuentistas cubanas contemporáneas*. Mirta Yáñez and Marilyn Bobes, eds. Havana: Ediciones Unión.
Boggs, Vernon. 1992. *Salsiology: Afrocuban Music and the Evolution of Salsa in New York City*. New York: Excelsior Music.
Bollain, Iciar, dir. 2005 [1999]. *Flores de otro mundo*. DVD. 100 min. U.S.A.: Image Entertainment.
Borges-Triana, Joaquín. 2001. "Música Cubana Alternativa: Del Margen al Epicentro." *Dédalo* (Havana) 0: 23–27.
Borland, Isabel Alvarez: 2004. " 'A Reminiscent Memory': Lezama, Zoé Valdés, and Rilke's Island." *MLN* 119 (2): 344–362.
Bosch, Carlos and Doménech, Jose Maria, dirs. 2003 [2005]. *Balseros*. DVD. 120 min. U.S.A.: New Video.
Boudet, Rosa Ileana. 1983. *Teatro Nuevo: Una Respuesta*. Havana: Editorial Letras Cubanas.
Bourdieu, Pierre. 1984. *Distinction: A Social Critique of the Judgment of Taste*. Cambridge: Harvard University Press.
———. 1993. *The Field of Cultural Production*. New York: Columbia University Press.
Boym, Svetlana. 2001. *The Future of Nostalgia*. New York: Basic Books.
Brezinski, Horst. 1993. "Cuba/Europa del este. Consecuencias para Cuba del derrumbe del socialismo en el Este de Europa." *Desarrollo y Cooperación* 2: 23–25.
Bronfman, Alejandra. 2004. *Measures of Equality: Social Science, Citizenship, and Race in Cuba 1902–1940*. Chapel Hill: University of North Carolina Press.
Brown, David H. 2003a. *Santería Enthroned: Art, Ritual, and Innovation in an Afro-Cuban Religion*. Chicago: University of Chicago Press.
———. 2003b. *The Light Inside: Abakuá Society Arts and Cuban Cultural History*. Washington DC: Smithsonian Institution Press.
Brown, Francisco, Ariel Dacal, Julio A. Díaz Vázquez, et al. 2004. "¿Por qué cayó el socialismo en Europa oriental?" *Temas* (Havana) 39–40: 92–111.
———. 2006. *Rusia: del Socialismo Real al Capitalismo Real*. Havana: Editorial de Ciencias Sociales.
Buck-Morss, Susan. 2000. *Dreamworld and Catastrophe: The Passing of Mass Utopia in East and West*. Cambridge: MIT Press.
Bueno, Salvador. 1995. "Significance of Cuban Culture Day." *Granma International* 30 (October 18) (41): 13.
Bunck, Julie Marie. 1994. *Fidel Castro and the Quest for a Revolutionary Culture in Cuba*. University Park: Pennsylvania State University Press.
Cabrera, Carlos. 1990. "National Assembly Session. Two Main Challenges for 1990: Solve Shortage of Hard Currency and Meet People's Needs." *Granma International* 7 (January 1990): 3.

Cabrera, Carlos. 1991. "Revolution Square." *Granma International* 14 (April 1991): 4–5.
Cabrera, Lydia. 1980 [1974]. *Yemayá y Ochún*. New York: C.R. Publishers.
Cabrera Infante, Guillermo. 2000. "Santeros Link Castro's Future to Elian." *The Miami Herald* (April 17) http://www.cubanet.org/CNews/y00/apr00/17e15.htm (accessed May 17, 2007).
Camnitzer, Luis. 2003. *New Art from Cuba*. Austin: University of Texas Press.
Campa, Homero. 2002. "Libros sin capital." *Hoja por hoja (book supplement)*. Mural (Guadalajara, Mexico) (November 30): 8–9.
Cancio Isla, Wilfredo. 2000. "Alicia en el pueblo de Maravillas: cinta maldita." *El Nuevo Herald* (March 9): 16D.
Canizares, Raul. 1993. *Walking with the Night: The Afro-Cuban World of Santeria*. Rochester: Destiny Books.
Cantor, Judy. 1999. "Welcome to the Bureaucracy: Why Cubans Call the Ministry of Culture the 'Mystery of Culture.'" *Miami New Times* (June 24). http://www.miaminewtimes.com/Issues/1999-06-24/news/feature2_full.html (accessed July 5, 1999).
Carbonell, Walterio. 2005 [1961]. *Como Surgió la Cultura Nacional*. Havana: Biblioteca Nacional Jose Martí.
———. 1993. "Birth of a National Culture." In *Afrocuba: An Anthology of Cuban Writing on Race, Politics, and Culture*. Pedro P. Sarduy and Jean Stubbs, eds. New York: Ocean Books.
Carneado, José Felipe. 1986. "Acerca de la Educación Patriótica e Internacionalista de Nuestro Pueblo." *Cuba Socialista* (Havana) 19 (1): 1–12.
Carpentier, Alejo. 2001 [1966]. "Publicaciones y libros cubanos después del triunfo de la revolución." *La Jiribilla* (Cuba) 26. http://www.lajiribilla.cu/2001/n26_noviembre/762_26.html (accessed February 3, 2002).
Carranza Valdés, Julio, Luis Gutiérrez Urdaneta, and Pedro Monreal González. 1995. *Cuba. La Restucturación de la Economía. Una propuesta para el debate*. Havana: Ed. Ciencias Sociales.
Carroll, Lewis. 1991 [1865]. *Alice in Wonderland*. Electronic document, Project Gutenberg E-text. http://www.gutenberg.org/etext/11 (accessed May 20, 2007).
Castilla, Amelia and Mauricio Vicent. 1997. "La explosión literaria de La Habana." *El País* (Madrid) (December 29): 27.
Castro Ruz, Fidel. 1977. "Palabras a los intelectuales." In *Política cultural de la Revolución Cubana*. Havana: Editorial de Ciencias Sociales.
———. 1989. "Discurso pronunciado en el acto de despedida de duelo a nuestros internacionalistas caidos durante el cumplimiento de honrosas misiones militares y civiles." December 7, 1989. http://www.cuba.cu/gobierno/discursos/1989/esp/f071289e.html (accessed March 3, 2006).
———. 1990a. "Discurso por la clausura del V Congreso de la Federacion de Mujeres Cubanas." March 7, 1990. http://www.cuba.cu/gobierno/discursos/1990/esp/f070390e.html (accessed March 3, 2006).
———. 1990b. "Discurso por el XXXVII aniversario del asalto al cuartel de Moncada." *La Habana*, July 26, 1990. http://www.cuba.cu/gobierno/discursos/1990/esp/f260790e.html (accessed March 3, 2006).
———. 1990c. "Discurso pronunciado en la tercerda graduacion del contingente del Instituto de Ciencias Médicas de La Habana." August 27, 1990. http://www.cuba.cu/gobierno/discursos/1990/esp/f270890e.html (accessed March 3, 2006).

———. 1990d. "Discurso por el XXX aniversario de los Comités de Defensa de la Revolución." September 28, 1990. http://www.cuba.cu/gobierno/discursos/1990/esp/f280990e.html (accessed March 3, 2006).
———. 1990e. "Speech Delivered at the 5th National Forum on Spare Parts." *Granma International* (December 30): 2.
———. 2000. "Discurso pronunciado en el Consejo Nacional de la UNEAC." *Granma* (Havana) (June 10): 14.
———. 2001. "Discurso pronunciado por Fidel Castro Ruz, Presidente de los Consejos de Estado y de Ministros de la República de Cuba, en el acto en conmemoración del aniversario 40 de la proclamación del carácter socialista de la Revolución, efectuado en 12 y 23, el 16 de abril del 2001." http://www.cuba.cu/gobierno/discursos/2001/esp/f160401e.html (accessed March 3, 2006).
———. 2005. "Discurso pronunciado en el acto central por el Aniversario 52 del asalto a los cuarteles Moncada y Carlos Manuel de Céspedes, en el teatro "Carlos Marx", el 26 de julio de 2005." http://www.cuba.cu/gobierno/discursos/2005/esp/f260705e.html (accessed August 2, 2005).
Cervera, Elvira. 2004. *El arte para mi fue un reto.* Havana: Eds. Unión.
Chanan, Michael. 1990. "Lessons of Experience." In *Memories of Underdevelopment and Inconsolable Memories.* Tomás Gutiérrez Alea and Edmundo Desnoes. New Brunswick: Rutgers University Press.
———. 2001. "Cuba and Civil Society, or Why Cuban Intellectuals Are Talking about Gramsci." *Nepantla* 2 (2): 387–406.
———. 2004. *Cuban Cinema.* Minneapolis: University of Minnesota Press.
Chávarri, Jaime, dir. 1988. *Yo soy el que tú buscas.* Film. 90 min. Spain: Televisión Española and Austria: Österreichischer Rundfunk.
Chijona, Gerardo, dir. 1991 *Adorables Mentiras.* VHS. 100 min. Cuba: ICAIC.
———. 2004. *Perfecto Amor Equivocado.* Film. 94 min. Cuba: ICAIC.
———. 2005 [1998]. *A Paradise under the Stars.* DVD. 90 min. U.S.A.: Vanguard Cinema.
Clarke III, Irvine, Kathleen S. Micken, and H. Stanley Hart. 2002. "Symbols for Sale…at Least for Now: Symbolic Consumption in Transition Economies." *Advances in Consumer Research* 29 (1): 25–30.
Clifford, James and George E. Marcus, eds. 1986. *Writing Culture: The Poetics and Politics of Ethnography.* Berkeley: University of California Press.
Cohen, Erik. 1988. "Authenticity and Commoditization in Tourism." *Annals of Tourism Research* 15: 371–386.
Colomo, Fernando. dir. 1999. *Cuarteto de la Habana.* DVD. 103 min. Spain: Lider Films.
Comisión Económica para América Latina y el Caribe (CEPAL). 2000. *La economía cubana: Reformas estructurales y desempeño en los noventa.* México: CEPAL/Fondo de Cultura Económica.
Commission for Assistance to a Free Cuba. 2004. *2004 Report to the President: Commission for Assistance to a Free Cuba.* http://www.state.gov/p/wha/rt/cuba/ (accessed August 13, 2006).
Cooper, Carolyn. 1993. *Noises in the Blood: Orality, Gender and the "Vulgar" Body of Jamaican Popular Culture.* London: Macmillan Caribbean.
Correa, Armando. 1997. "Discordia divide a santeros." *El Nuevo Herald* (January 15). www.cubanet.org/CNews/y97/Jan97/16sante.html (accessed September 16, 2008).

Cortés, Rubén. 1998. "La buena salud de las letras cubanas." *La Crónica de Hoy* (Mexico). (February 21).
Corrales, Javier. 2004. "The Gatekeeper State: Limited Economic Reforms and Regime Survival in Cuba, 1989–2002." *Latin American Research Review* 39 (2): 35–65.
Cosentino, Donald J. 1995. "Imagine Heaven." In *The Sacred Arts of Haitian Vodou.* Donald. J. Cosentino, ed. Los Angeles: UCLA Fowler Museum of Cultural History.
Cremades, Raúl and Esteban, Angel. 2000. "El nuevo *boom* de la narrativa cubana en España." *Leer* (Madrid) XVI (113): 48–51.
Cremata Malberti, Juan Carlos, dir. 2001. *Nada +.* DVD. U.S.A.: Global Lens Collection.
———. 2005. *Viva Cuba.* DVD. 80 min. U.S.A.: Film Movement.
Cuenca, Manuel Martin, dir. 2001. *El Juego de Cuba.* Film. 93 min. Spain: Avidea Producciones.
———. 2005. *Malas Temporadas.* DVD. 115 min. Spain: Cameo.
De Aguila, Rafael. 1998. "¿Pathos o Marketing?. *El Caimán Barbudo.* (Havana) 31 (292): 2–3.
De Costa, Elena. 1992. *Collaborative Latin American Popular Theatre: From Theory to Form, from Text to Stage.* New York: P. Lang.
De la Campa, Román. 1994. "The Latino Diaspora in the United States: Sojourns from a Cuban Past." *Public Culture* 6: 293–317.
De la Fuente, Alejandro. 2001. *A Nation for All: Race, Inequality and Politics in Twentieth Century Cuba.* Chapel Hill: University of North Carolina Press.
De la Nuez, Iván. 1998. *La Balsa Perpetua. Soledad y Conexiones de la Cultura Cubana.* Barcelona: Casiopea.
———. 2008. "Cuba regresa al presente." *El Periódico de Catalunya.* http://www.elperiodico.com/default.asp?idpublicacio_PK=46&idioma=CAS&idnoticia_PK=485597&idseccio_PK=1006 (accessed February 23, 2008).
De la Nuez, Iván and Juan Pablo Ballester. 1994. "El Post Exilio y las Post Guerra." *Memorias de la Postguerra* (Cuba) 1 (2): 1.
De la Torre, Carolina. 1995. "Conciencia de Mismidad: Identidad y Cultura Cubana." *Temas* (Havana) 2: 111–115.
De la Torre, Miguel A. 2003. *La Lucha for Cuba: Religion and Politics on the Streets of Miami.* Berkeley: University of California Press.
———. 2004. *Santería: The Beliefs and Rituals of a Growing Religion in America.* Grand Rapids: William B. Eerdmans.
De Sica, Vittorio, dir. 2004 [1952]. *Umberto D.* DVD. 91 min. Criterion Collection.
Del Rey Roa, Annet Aracelia. 2002. "(Re)-construccion de un discurso africanista entre babalawos y santeros cubanos." In *America Latina y el Caribe: Realidades sociopoliticos e identidad cultural.* Silke Helfrich and Marina Sandoval, eds. San Salvador: Ediciones Heinrich Böll.
Delgado, Frank. 1995. "Konchalovski hace rato que no monta en Lada." In CD *Trova-tur.* Argentina: Mutis.
Dell'Amico Ciruta, Souleen. 1999. "Contradicciones." In *El ojo de la noche: Nuevas cuentistas cubanas.* Amir Valle, ed. Havana: Letras Cubanas.
Díaz, Jesús. 1998. "*Encuentro*, entre la isla y el exilio. Interview with François Maspéro." *Encuentro de la Cultura Cubana* (Madrid) 10 (Fall): 101–103.

———. 2002. "Interview." *El Mundo* (Spain) February 21, 2002. http://www.elmundo.es/encuentros/invitados/2002/02/381/ (accessed June 7, 2002).
Díaz, Rolando, dir. 1995. *Melodrama*. Film. 56 min. Cuba: ICAIC.
———.1998. *Si me comprendieras*. VHS. 87 min. First Run/Icarus Films, USA.
Díaz Fabelo, Teodoro. 1974. *Diccionario de la lengua Congo residual en Cuba*. Santiago de Cuba: Casa del Caribe.
Díaz Torres, Daniel, dir. 1990. *Alicia en el pueblo de Maravillas*. Film. 94 min. Cuba: ICAIC.
———. 1992. "Sobre el riesgo del arte." *Cine Cubano* 135 (April-June): 23–25.
———, dir. 2001. *Hacerse el sueco*. Film. 105 min. Germany: Arthaus Filmverleich, and Spain: Impala.
Dilla, Haroldo and Philip Oxhorn. 2002. "The Virtues and Misfortunes of Civil Society in Cuba." *Latin American Perspectives* 125, 9 (4): 10–30.
Domínguez, Jorge I. 2004. "The Cuban Economy at the Start of the Twenty-First Century: An Introductory Analysis." In *The Cuban Economy at the Start of the Twenty-First Century*. Jorge I. Domínguez, Omar Everleny Pérez Villanueva, and Lorena Barberia, eds. Cambridge: Harvard University David Rockefeller Center.
Dopico, Ana Maria. 2002. "Picturing Havana: History, Vision and the Scramble for Cuba." *Nepantla* 3 (3): 451–493.
Duany, Jorge. 2000. "Reconstructing Cubanness: Changing Discourses of National Identity on the Island and in the Diaspora during the Twentieth Century." In *Cuba: The Elusive Nation*. Damián Fernández and Madeline Cámara, eds. Gainesville: University Press of Florida.
———. 2001. "Redes, remesas y paladares: La diáspora cubana desde una perspectiva transnacional." *Nueva Sociedad* (Venezuela) 174: 40–51.
Dubocq, José de la Tejera. 1990. *Por Qué la Enseñanza de la Historia en el Nivel Primario*. Havana: Pueblo y Educación.
Duque, Lisandro, dir. 1989. *Milagro en Roma*. Film. 90 min. Colombia: Elisa Cinematográfica, and Spain: Televisión Española.
Eckstein, Susan and Lorena Barbería. 2003. "Grounding Immigrant Generations in History: Cuban-Americans and Their Transnational Ties." *International Migration Review* 36 (3): 799–837.
EFE. 2006. "La Habana prepara un carnaval muy austero." *El Nuevo Herald* (July 24). www.elnuevoherald.com/news/world/americans/15107160.htm (accessed August 7, 2006).
Erisman, H. Michael. 2000. *Cuba's Foreign Relations in a Post-Soviet World*. Gainesville: University Press of Florida Press.
Erjavec, Ales. 2003. "Introduction." In *Postmodernism and the Postsocialist Condition*. Ales Erjavec, ed. Berkeley: University of California Press.
Espinosa, Magaly. 2003. *El Nuevo Arte Cubano y su Estética*. Pinar del Río: Cauce.
———. 2006. "Las narraciones del nuevo arte cubano." In *Antología de textos críticos: el nuevo arte cubano*. Magaly Espinosa and Kevin Power, eds. Torrevieja (España): Perceval Press and Ayuntamiento de Torrevieja.
Estévez, Abilio. 1999. "Méditations sur la littérature cubaine d'aujourd'hui." *Cahiers des Amériques Latines* (Paris) 31–32: 211–221.
Fagen, Richard R. 1979. *The Transformation of Political Culture in Cuba*. Stanford: Stanford University Press.

Fagin, Steve, dir. 1997. *Tropicola*. DVD. 96 min. U.S.A.: Steve Fagin Productions.
Fairley, Jan. 2006. "Dancing Back to Front: Reggaeton, Sexuality, Gender and Transnationalism in Cuba." *Popular Music* 25 (3): 471–488.
Fernandes, Sujatha. 2003. "Island Paradise, Revolutionary Utopia or Hustler's Haven? Consumerism and Socialism in Contemporary Cuban Rap." *Journal of Latin American Cultural Studies* 12 (3): 359–375.
———. 2004. "Fear of Black Nation: Local Rappers, Transnational Crossings, and State Power in Contemporary Cuba." *Anthropological Quarterly* 76 (4): 575–608.
———. 2006. *Cuba Represent! Cuban Arts, State Power, and the Making of New Revolutionary Cultures*. Durham: Duke University Press.
Fernandez, James W. 1986. *Persuasions and Performances*. Bloomington: Indiana University Press.
Fernández, Nadine. 1999. "Back to the Future? Women, Race and Tourism in Cuba." In *Sun, Sex and Gold: Tourism and Sex Work in the Caribbean*. Kemala Kempadoo, ed. Lanham: Rowman & Littlefield.
———. 2001. "The Changing Discourse on Race in Contemporary Cuba." *International Journal of Qualitative Studies in Education* 14 (2): 117–132.
Fernández Pintado, Milene. 1999. "El día que no fui a Nueva York." In *Anhedonia*. Havana: Unión.
Fernández Retamar, Roberto. 1971. "Calibán." CASA (Havana: Casa de Las Américas) 68: 124–151.
———. 2001. "Palabras a los intelectuales: Cuarenta años después." *La Gaceta de Cuba* (Havana), (July/August): 47–53.
Fernández Robaina, Tomas. 1990. *El Negro en Cuba, 1902–1958*. Havana: Ed. Ciencias Sociales.
———. 2001. *Hablen Paleros y Santeros*. Havana: Ed. Ciencias Sociales.
Ferraz, Vicente, dir. 2007 [2004]. *Soy Cuba, O Mamute Siberiano*. VHS. 90 min. U.S.A.: New Yorker Video.
Ferrer, Jorge. 2000. "Regresos de Mañach." *Encuentro de la Cultura Cubana* (Madrid) 16 (17): 241–243.
Festival Internacional de Cine Pobre. 2004. "Memorias." www.cubacine.cu/cinepobre/memorias (accessed May 14, 2006).
Fitzgerald, Nora. 2003. "Artifacts of Uberkitsch Evoke Old East Germany; High and Low Culture Offer Powerful Reminders." *The New York Times* (September 30): E1.
Flores, Juan. 2000. *From Bomba to Hip Hop: Puerto Rican Culture and Latino Identity*. New York: Columbia University Press.
Fornet, Ambrosio. 1997. "Soñar en Cubano, Escribir en Inglés." *Temas* (Havana) 10: 4–12.
———. 2002. "The Cuban Literary Diaspora and Its Contexts: A Glossary." *Boundary 2* 29 (3): 91–103.
Fowler Calzada, Victor. 1996. "Miradas a la identidad en la literatura de la diaspora." *Temas* (Havana) 6: 122–132.
———. 1998. "Cubanidades Liminares." *La Gaceta de Cuba* (Havana) 36 (5): 15–18.
———. 2001a. "The Day After." In *Cuba y el día después: doce ensayistas nacidos con la revolución imaginan el futuro*. Iván de la Nuez, ed. Barcelona: Mondadori.

———. 2001b. "Lo que se perdió: Crítica del presente." *Dédalo* (Havana) 0 (February): 12–13.
Frederik, Laurie Aleen. 2000. "Una mirada al trabajo colectivo del Teatro de los Elementos." *Conjunto* (Havana) 117: 58–73.
———. 2005. "Cuba's National Characters: Setting the Stage for the Hombre Novísimo." *Journal of Latin American Anthropology* 10 (2): 401–436.
Freire, Paulo. 1970. *The Pedagogy of the Oppressed.* New York: Seabury Press.
Frow, John. 1991. "Tourism and the Semiotics of Nostalgia." *October* 57: 123–151.
Furé Davis, Samuel. 2005. "Lyrical Subversion in Cuban Reggae." *Image & Narrative* 11 (2). www.imageandnarrative.be/worldmusicb_advertising/samuelfuredavis.htm (accessed May 14,2007).
Fusco, Coco. 1994. "El Diario de Miranda/Miranda's Diary." *Michigan Quarterly Review* 33 (3): 477–496.
———. 1998. "Hustling for Dollars: *Jineterismo* in Cuba." In *Global Sex Workers: Rights, Resistance and Redefinition.* Kemala Kempadoo, ed. New York and London: Routledge.
García, Daniel, ed. 1995. *Cuba. Cultura e Identidad Nacional.* Havana: Unión.
García Canclini, Nestor. 1989. *Culturas Híbridas. Estrategias para entrar y salir de la modernidad.* Mexico DF: Grijalbo.
———. 1995. *Hybrid Cultures: Strategies for Entering and Leaving Modernity.* Minneapolis: University of Minnesota Press.
———. 1999. *La Globalización Imaginada.* Buenos Aires: Paidós.
García Espinosa, Julio, dir. 1993. *El Plano.* Film. 94 min. Cuba: ICAIC and EICTV.
———, dir. 1994. *Reina y Rey.* Film. Cuba: ICAIC.
———. 1997 [1969]. "For an Imperfect Cinema." In *New Latin American Cinema: Theory, Practice and Transcontinental Articulations.* Michael T. Martin, ed. Vol. 1. Detroit: Wayne State University Press.
García-Zarza, I. 2000. "Cuba aún guarda huellas de la era soviética." *El Nuevo Herald* (December 10): 21A (3).
Gaulke, Uli, dir. 1999. *Havanna mi amor.* DVD. 82 min. Germany: Salzgeber & Company Medien.
Gilroy, Paul. 1992. "It's a Family Affair." In *Black Popular Culture.* Gina Dent, ed. Seattle: Bay Press.
———. 1993. *The Black Atlantic: Modernity and Double Consciousness.* London: Verso.
———. 2000. *Against Race: Imagining Political Culture beyond the Color Line.* Cambridge: Harvard University Press.
Ginsburg, Faye. 1991. "Indigenous Media: Faustian Contract or Global Village?" *Cultural Anthropology* 6 (1): 92–112.
Ginsburg, Faye, Lila Abu-Lughod, and Brian Larkin, eds. 2002. *Media Worlds: Anthropology on New Terrain.* Berkeley: University of California Press.
Gleijeses, Piero. 2002. *Conflicting Missions: Havana, Washington, and Africa, 1959–1976.* Chapel Hill: University of North Carolina Press.
Glick-Schiller, Nina and Georges Fouron. 2000. *When Georges Woke Up Laughing: Long Distance Nationalism and the Search for Home.* Durham: Duke University Press.
Glasser, Ruth. 1995. *My Music Is My Flag: Puerto Rican Musicians and Their New York Communities, 1917–1940.* Berkeley: University of California Press.

Goldberg, Alan. 1983. "Identity and Experience in Haitian Voodoo Shows." *Annals of Tourism Research* 10 (4): 479–495.
González Echevarría, Roberto. 1999. *The Pride of Havana: A History of Cuban Baseball*. New York: Oxford University Press.
———. 1999b. "Cuba está de moda." *El País* (Madrid) March 15, p. 16.
González, Flavia. 2003. "El legado de los ancestros." *Revista de la Universidad de La Habana* (Havana) 258: 176–181.
Gonzalez-Wippler, Migene. 1994 [1989]. *Santería: The Religion*. St. Paul: Llewellyn.
Goux, Jean-Joseph. 1999. "Cash, Check or Charge?" In *The New Economic Criticism: Studies at the Intersection of Literature and Economics*. Martha Woodmansee and Mark Osteen, eds. London and New York: Routledge.
Granda, Julio O. 1995. "A Materialist View of Santería and the Expenses Associated with the Initiation." Unpublished master's thesis. Department of Anthropology, Florida State University at Tallahassee.
Greenwood, Davyd J. 1989. "Culture by the Pound: An Anthropological Perspective on Tourism as Cultural Commoditization." In *Hosts and Guests: The Anthropology of Tourism*. V.L. Smith, ed. Philadelphia: University of Pennsylvania Press.
Gregory, Steven. 1999. *Santería in New York City: A Study in Cultural Resistance*. New York: Garland.
Guanche, Jesús. 1996a. *Componentes Etnicos de la Nación Cubana*. Havana: Unión.
———. 1996b. "Etnicidad y Racialidad en la Cuba Actual." *Temas* (Havana) 7: 51–69.
Guerra, Rosa María de Lahaye. 2003. "Del oráculo y la profecía: La letra del año." *Revista de la Universidad de La Habana* (Havana) 258: 206–207.
Guerra, Rosa María de Lahaye and Zardoya Loureda. 1999. "Las letras del año: Entre el azar y destino." *Catauro* (Havana) 1 (0): 118–138.
Guerra, Ruy, dir. 1988. *La fábula de la bella palomera*. Film. 78 min. Spain: International Network Group S.A. and Televisión Española.
Guevara, Alfredo. 2003. *Tiempo de Fundación*. Madrid: Iberautor Promociones Culturales.
Guevara, Ernesto "Ché." 1968. *Socialism and Man in Cuba, and Other Works*. London: Stage 1.
Gutiérrez, Pedro Juan. 1998. *Trilogía sucia de La Habana*. Barcelona: Anagrama. Natasha Wimmer, trans. *Dirty Havana Trilogy*. New York: HarperCollins: 2002.
———. 1999. *El Rey de La Habana*. Barcelona: Anagrama.
———. 2000. *Animal Tropical*. Barcelona: Anagrama.
———. 2002. *El insaciable hombre araña*. Barcelona: Anagrama.
———. 2003. *Carne de perro*. Barcelona: Anagrama,
Gutiérrez Alea, Tomás, dir. 1998 [1966]. *Muerte de un burócrata*. VHS. 87 min. New Yorker Video.
———. 1989 *Cartas del parque*. Film. 87 min. Cuba: ICAIC and Spain: Televisión U.S.A.: Española.
———. 2004 [1993]. *Fresa y Chocolate*. DVD. 110 min. Walt Disney Video.
Gutiérrez Aragón, Manuel, dir. 2001 [1997]. *Cosas que dejé en La Habana*. DVD. 110 min. U.S.A.: Vanguard Cinema.
Habermas, Jürgen. 1989. *The New Conservatism*. Cambridge: MIT Press.
Hagedorn, Katherine J. 2001. *Divine Utterances: The Performance of Afro-Cuban Santería*. Washington DC: Smithsonian Institution Press.

Hall, Stuart. 1977. "Culture, Media and the Ideological Effect." In *Mass Communication and Society*. James Curran, Michael Gurevitch, and Janet Woollacott, eds. London: Edward Arnold.

———. 1980. "Encoding/Decoding." In *Culture, Media and Language*. Stuart Hall, Dorothy Hobson, Andrew Lowe, and Paul Willis, eds. London: Hutchinson.

———. 1990. "Cultural Identity and Diaspora." In *Identity: Community, Culture, Difference*. Jonathan Rutherford, ed. London: Laurance and Wishart.

Hamilton, Annette. 2002. "The National Picture: Thai Media and Cultural Identity." In *Media Worlds: Anthropology on New Terrain*. Faye Ginsburg, Lila Abu-Lughod, and Brian Larkin, eds. Berkeley: University of California Press.

Hanly, Elizabeth. 1995. "Santería: An Alternative Pulse." *Aperture* 141: 30–37.

Haraszti, Miklos. 1987. *The Velvet Prison: Artists under State Socialism*. New York: Basic Books.

Hart, Celia. 2003. "La bandera de Coyoacán." Asociación Cultura y Paz y Solidaridad. http://www.nodo50.org/haydeesantamaria/docs_ajenos/bandera_coyoacan.htm. (accessed May 14, 2007).

Hart Dávalos, Armando. 1960. *Mensaje Educacional al Pueblo de Cuba*. Havana: MinEd.

———. 1983. *Cambiar las Reglas del Juego*. Havana: Letras Cubanas.

Hardt, Michael and Antonio Negri. 2000. *Empire*. Cambridge: Harvard University Press.

Harvey, David. 1989. *The Condition of Postmodernity*. Oxford: Blackwell.

Hennesy, C.A.M. 1963. "The Roots of Cuban Nationalism." *International Affairs* 39 (3): 345–359.

Herman Dolz, Sonia, dir. 2004 [1997]. *Lágrima negras*. DVD. 73 min. Venezuela: Venevision.

Hermosillo, Jaime Humberto, dir. 1988. *El Verano de la Señora Forbes*. Film. 89 min. Spain: International Networking Groups, S.A. and Televisión Española.

Hernández, Orlando. 2005. "La importancia de ser local." In *Alberto Casado. Todo clandestino, todo popular*. New York: Art in General.

Hernández, Rafael. 1993. "Mirar a Cuba. Notas para una discusion." *La Gaceta de Cuba* (Havana) (September–October): 37.

———. 1994. "La Otra Muerte del Dogma." *La Gaceta de Cuba* (Havana) (May): 12–18.

Hernández Busto, Ernesto. 2006. "La lección de Demonia." *Cuadernos Hispanoamericanos* (Madrid) 673–674: 47–50.

Hernandez-Reguant, Ariana. 1999. "Kwanzaa and the U.S. Ethnic Mosaic." In *Representations of Blackness and the Performance of Identities*. Jean Rahier, ed. Westport, CT: Greenwood Press.

———. 2000. "The Nostalgia of Buena Vista Social Club: Cuban Music and 'World' Marketing." Paper Presented at "Exporting the Local, Importing the Global. Cuban Music at the Crossroads." Toronto (November) Panel of the International Association for the Study of Popular Music Meetings.

———. 2002. *Radio Taino and the Globalization of the Cuban Culture Industries*. Ph.D. Dissertation. Department of Anthropology. University of Chicago.

———. 2004a. "Copyrighting Che: Art and Authorship under Cuban Late Socialism." *Public Culture* 16 (1): 1–29.

———. 2004b. "Return to Havana: Adió Kerida and the Films of the One-and-a-Half Generation." *Journal of Latin American Anthropology* 9 (2): 495–498.

Hernandez-Reguant, Ariana. 2005. "Cuba's Alternative Geographies." *Journal of Latin American Anthropology* 10 (2): 275–313.

———. 2005b. Interview with BBC. *The World: Global Hit*. January 19. http://www.theworld.org/globalhits/2005/01/19.shtml (accessed February 7, 2006).

———. 2006a. "Radio Taíno and the Cuban Quest for Identi...qué?" In *Cultural Agency in the Americas*. Doris Sommer, ed. Durham: Duke University Press.

———. 2006b. "Havana's Timba: A Macho Sound for Black Sex." In *Globalization and Race: Transformations in the Cultural Production of Blackness*. Kamari Clarke and Deborah A. Thomas, eds. Durham: Duke University Press.

Hernández-Valdés, Emilo. 1997. "Pase de Revistas." *Temas* (Havana) 10: 117–126.

Herrero, Ramiro, ed. 1983. *Teatro de relaciones*. Havana: Editorial Letras Cubanas.

Himpele, Jeffrey D. 1996. "Film Distribution as Media: Mapping Difference in the Bolivian Cinemascape." *Visual Anthropology Review* 12 (1): 47–66.

———. 2002. "Arrival Scenes: Complicity and Media Ethnography in the Bolivian Public Sphere." In *Media Worlds*. Faye D. Ginsburg, Lila Abu-Lughod, and Brian Larkin, eds. Berkeley: University of California Press.

Huggan, Graham. 2001. *The Postcolonial Exotic: Marketing the Margins*. London and New York: Routledge.

Human Rights Watch, 2005. "Families Torn Apart: The High Cost of U.S. and Cuban Travel Restrictions." http://hrw.org/reports/2005/cuba1005/ (accessed August 13, 2006).

Humphrey, Caroline. 1995. "Introduction." *Cambridge Anthropology* 18 (2): 1–12.

Hutchinson, John. 1992. "Moral Innovators and the Politics of Regeneration: The Distinctive Role of Cultural Nationalism in Nation-Building." In *Ethnicity and Nationalism*. Anthony Smith, ed. New York: Brill.

Ichaso, Leon, dir. 2001 [1996]. *Bitter Sugar*. DVD. 75 min. U.S.A.: New Yorker Video.

Instituto de Cinematografía y las Artes Audiovisuales (ICAA). N.d. "Cine Español, Tendencias 1996–2003." http://www.mcu.es/publicaciones/docs/EvolucCineEsp 1996–2003.pdf (accessed May 14, 2007).

Jameson, Fredric. 1984. "Postmodernism, or the Cultural Logic of Late Capitalism." *New Left Review* 146: 53–92.

Jara, Rebeca and Caridad Suárez. 1999. *Reporte del estudio de identidad en Radio Taíno*. (internal document). Havana: ICRT.

Jatar-Hausmann, Ana Julia. 1999. *The Cuban Way: Capitalism, Communism and Confrontation*. West Hartford: Kumarian Press.

Kalatozov, Mikhail, dir. 2000 [1964]. *Soy Cuba*. DVD. 141 min. Image Entertainment.

Kapcia, Antoni. 2000. *Cuba: Island of Dreams*. Oxford: Berg.

———. 2005. "Educational Revolution and Revolutionary Morality in Cuba: The 'New Man,' Youth and the New 'Battle of Ideas.'" *Journal of Moral Education* 34 (4): 399–412.

Knauer, Lisa Maya. 1997. "Las Culturas de la Diáspora. Rumba, Comunidad e Identidad en Nueva York." *Temas* (Havana) 10: 13–21.

———. 2003. "Remesas Multidireccionales y Etnografía Viajera." *Sociedade e Cultura* (Brasil) 6 (1): 13–24.

———. 2005. "Translocal Counterpublics: Rumba and Santeria in New Cork and La Habana." Unpublished doctoral dissertation. Department of American Studies, New York University.

Kracauer, Siegfried. 1995 [1927]. "The Mass Ornament." In *The Mass Ornament: Weimar Essays*. Cambridge: Harvard University Press.
Kruger, Loren. 1992. *The National Stage: Theatre and Cultural Legitimation in England, France, and America*. Chicago: University of Chicago Press.
Kumar, Krishan. 1992. "Understanding Political Change in Eastern Europe: A Sociological Perspective." *Sociology* 27 (3): 451–470.
Lachatañeré, Rómulo. 2001 [1942]. *El sistema religioso de los afrocubanos*. Havana: Ed. Ciencias Sociales.
———. 2001. *Manual de Santería*. Havana: Ed. Ciencias Sociales.
Lampland, Martha. 1995. *The Object of Labor: Commodification in Socialist Hungary*. Chicago: University of Chicago Press.
Lantigua, John. 1998. "Holy Wars, Inc." *Miami New Times* (April 9). http://www.miaminewtimes.com/Issues/1998-04-09/news/feature.html (accessed July 23, 2007).
Lauten, Flora. 1981. *Teatro La Yaya*. Havana: Editorial Letras Cubanas.
Lecchi, Alberto, dir. 1993. *Operación Fangio*. Film. 105 min. Spain: Alta Films and United Internacional Pictures.
Lee, Susana and Joaquin Oramas. 1990. "Cuba Has Entered the Special Period; the Situation Is Not Yet Very Acute." *Granma International* (December 30): 1–2.
Lee, Tong Soon. 1999. "Technology and the Production of Islamic Space: The Call the Prayer in Singapore." *Ethnomusicology* 43 (1): 86–100.
Leitch, Christopher, dir. 2000. *A Family in Crisis: The Elian Gonzalez Story*. 90 min. U.S.A.: TV Fox Family Channel.
Lewis, Oscar, Ruth M. Lewis, and Susan M. Rigdon. 1977. *Four Men. Living the Revolution: An Oral History of Contemporary Cuba*. Urbana: University of Illinois Press.
Lightfoot, Claudia. 1998. "Publishing in Cuba." *Bellagio Publishing Newsletter* 22 (July): 10.
Liss, Sheldon B. 1987. *Roots of Revolution: Radical Thought in Cuba*. Lincoln: University of Nebraska Press.
Loomis, John A. 1999. *Cuba's Forgotten Art Schools: Revolution of Forms*. New York: Princeton Architectural Press.
Louie, Andrea. 2000. "Reterritorializing Transnationalism: Chinese Americans and the Chinese'Motherland,'" *American Ethnologist* 27 (3): 645–669.
López, Ana M., dir. 1996. "Greater Cuba." In *The Ethnic Eye: Latino Media Arts*. Chon A. Noriega and Ana M. López, eds. Minneapolis: University of Minnesota Press.
López, Rigoberto. 1996. *Yo Soy del Son a la Salsa*. Film. 100 min. RMM Productions.
Loss, Jacqueline. 2003. "Global Arenas: Narrative and Filmic Translation of Identity." *Nepantla* 4 (2): 317–344.
———. 2004. "Vintage Soviets in Post-Cold War Cuba." In *Mandorla: Nueva Escritura de las Américas* 7: 79–84.
Lowe, Lisa. 1996. *Immigrant Acts*. Berkeley: University of California Press.
Louie, Andrea. 2000. "Reterritorializing Transnationalism: Chinese Americans and the Chinese'Motherland,'" *American Ethnologist* 27 (3): 645–669.
Lynn, Stoner K. 2003. "Militant Heroines and the Consecration of the Patriarchal State: The Glorification of Loyalty, Combat, and National Suicide in the Making of Cuban National Identity." *Cuban Studies* 23: 71–96.
MacCannell, Dean. 1999. [1976] *The Tourist: A New Theory of the Leisure Class*. Berkeley: University of California Press.

Manuel, Peter, ed. 1991. *Essays on Cuban Music: Cuban and North American Perspectives.* Lanham: University Press of America.
Manzor-Coats, Lillian and Inés María Martiatu Terry. 1995. "VI Festival Internacional de Teatro de La Habana. A Festival against All Odds." *The Drama Review* 39 (2): 39–70.
Marcovich, Carlos, dir. 2000 [1997]. *Who the Hell Is Juliette.* DVD. 91 min. U.S.A.: Kino Video.
Marcus, George E. and Michael M.J. Fischer. 1986. *Anthropology as Cultural Critique: An Experimental Moment in the Human Sciences.* Chicago: University of Chicago Press.
Martín, Jose Luis. 1995. "Tendencias Temáticas de las Ciencias Sociales en Cuba." In *Cuba Cultura e Identidad Nacional.* Daniel Garcia, ed. Havana: Unión.
Martin, Randy. 1994. *Socialist Ensembles: Theater and State in Nicaragua and Cuba.* Minneapolis: University of Minnesota Press.
Martín Cuenca, Manuel, dir. 2005. *Malas Temporadas.* Film. 115 min. Spain: Golem.
Martin de Holan, Pablo and Phillips, Nelson. 1997. "Sun, Sand and Hard Currency: Tourism in Cuba." *Annals of Tourism Research* 24 (4): 777–795.
Martínez Furé, Rogelio. 2000. "A National Cultural Identity? Homogenizing Monomania and the Plural Heritage." In *Afro-Cuban Voices: On Race and Identity in Contemporary Cuba.* Pedro Pérez Sarduy and Jean Stubbs, eds. Gainesville: University of Florida Press.
Martínez Heredia, Fernando. 1995. "Izquierda y Marxismo en Cuba." *Temas* (Havana) 3: 23.
———. 2002. "In the Furnace of the Nineties: Identity and Society in Cuba Today." *boundary 2* 29 (3): 137–147.
Martínez Shvietsova, Polina. 2004. "¿Koniec?2004 - Asere , -Nu pogogy." Paper presented at Koniec, First Encounter of Cuban-Euro-Asian Youth Conference (March 11). Sancti Spiritus, Cuba.
Martínez Shvietsova, Polina and Dmitri Prieto Samsonov. 2003. "RecUrSO al Ser en CUBA." Paper Presented at Nuestra, Romerías de Mayo Conference (May). Santa Cruz del Norte, Holguín, Cuba.
Mason, Michael Atwood. 2002. *Living Santeria: Rituals and Experiences in an Afro-Cuban Religion.* Washington, DC: Smithsonian Institution Press.
Maspéro, François. 1998. "*Encuentro*, entre la isla y el exilio." *Encuentro de la Cultura Cubana* (Madrid) 10: 101–103.
Mateo Palmer, Margarita. 2007. "Postmodernismo y Criterios: Prólogo para una antologia y para un aniversario." In Desiderio Navarro, ed. *El Postmoderno, el Postmodernismo y su Crítica.* Havana: Criterios.
McClintock, Anne. 1993. "Family Feuds: Gender, Nationalism and the Family." *Feminist Review* 44: 61–80.
Medin, Tzvi. 1990. *Cuba: The Shaping of Revolutionary Consciousness.* Boulder: Lynne Rienner.
Mejides, Miguel. 1994. "Trópico." In *Anuario 1994/ Narrativa.* Havana: Ediciones Unión.
Melgar, Ricardo. 1993. "Los orishas y la ciudad de La Habana en tiempos de crisis." *Cuadernos Americanos* (Mexico DF) 5: 165–184.
Menéndez Plasencia, Ronaldo. 1995. "El pez que se alimenta de su sombra: De novísimos y crítica, hipótesis y tipologías." *La Gaceta de Cuba* (Havana) 3: 53–55.

———. 1997. *El derecho al pataleo de los ahorcados.* Havana: Casa de las Américas.
Mijalkov-Konchalovsky, Andrei. 2004. "Interview by Alexander Lipkov." *Miradas: Revista del audiovisual.* (Havana) (May). http://www.eictv.co.cu/miradas/index.php?option= com_content&task=view&id=247&Itemid=99999999 (accessed May 15, 2007).
Miller, Ivor. 2000. "Religious Symbolism in Cuban Political Performance." *The Drama Review* 44 (2): 30–55.
Ministerio de Cultura de España. 2002. "Películas realizadas en coproducción con otros paises." http://www.mcu.es/cine/MC/BIC/Produccion2002.html (accessed May 14, 2007).
Mitrani, Rhonda L. dir. 2004 [2002]. *Cuba mía.* 49 min. U.S.A.: LAVA, Latin American Video Archives.
Molina, Juan Antonio. 1997. "Cuban Art: The Desire to Go On Playing." *Utopian Territories. New Art from Cuba.* Eugenio Váldes Figueroa et al., eds. Vancouver: Contemporary Art Gallery, Morris and Helen Belkin Art Gallery, and Ludwig Foundation.
Montes de Oca, Dannys. 1995. "Afro-Cubans and the Communist Revolution." In *African Presence in the Americas.* T.R. Saunders and S. Moore, eds. Trenton: Africa World Press.
———. 2006. "El oficio del arte." In *Antología de textos críticos: el nuevo arte cubano.* Magaly Espinosa and Kevin Power, eds. Torrevieja (España): Perceval Press and Ayuntamiento de Torrevieja.
Monroe, Alexei. 2005. *Interrogation Machine: Laibach and NSK.* Cambridge: MIT Press.
Moore, Robin D. 1997. *Nationalizing Blackness: Afrocubanismo and Artistic Revolution in Havana, 1920–1940.* Pittsburgh: University of Pittsburgh Press.
———. 2006. *Music and Revolution: Cultural Change in Socialist Cuba.* Berkeley: University of California Press.
Morawska, Eva. 2006. "The Recognition Politics of the Polish Radio MultiKulti in Berlin." Paper presented at the IMISCOE B-6 Workshop on Immigrant Cultural Productions and Political Expression (June 29), Oxford, England.
Morejón Almagro, Leonel. 1999. "Carnaval en La Habana." Cubanet. www.cubanet.org/CNews/99/ago00/02a3.htm (accessed May 19, 2007).
Moreno Fraginals, Manuel. 1997. "Transition to What?" In *Toward a New Cuba? Legacies of a Revolution*, Miguel Angel Centeno and Mauricio Font, eds. London: Lynne Rienner Publishers.
Mosquera, Gerardo. 1988. "Identidad y cultura popular en el Nuevo arte cubano." *Made in Havana.* Sydney: Art Gallery of New South Wales.
———. 1989. *El diseño se definió en octubre.* Havana: Arte y Literatura.
———. 1994. "Se Acabó el Querer, Prosiguen las Metáforas." *Memorias de la Postguerra* 1 (2): 11–12.
———. 2003. "The New Cuban Art." In *Postmodernism and the Postsocialist Condition.* Ales Erjavec, ed. Berkeley: University of California Press.
Muestra de Cine Joven. 2001. *Nuevos Realizadores.* Havana: ICAIC. www.cubacine.cu/muestrajoven (accessed May 14, 2007).
Muguercia, Mabaly. 1981. *Teatro: En Busca de una Expresión Socialista.* Havana: Editorial Letras Cubanas.

Murphy, Joseph. 1981. *Ritual Systems in Cuban Santería.* Ph.D. Dissertation. Department of Religion. Temple University.
———. 1998 [1988]. *Santería: African Spirits in America.* Boston: Beacon Press.
Naficy, Hamid. 1993. *The Making of Exilic Cultures: Iranian Television in Los Angeles.* Minneapolis: University of Minnesota Press.
Navarro, Desiderio. 2001. "In Medias Res Publicas: On Intellectuals and Social Criticism in the Cuban Public Sphere." *Nepantla: Views from South* 2 (2): 355–371.
Navarro, Lourdes Pérez. 2006. "Piratería de señales satelitales." *Granma* (Havana), (August 9): 3.
Newport, Cynthia, Barbara Koppel, and Boris Ivan Crespo, dirs. 2004. *Dance Cuba.* Film. 103 min. U.S.A.: Ilume Productions.
Nooter, Mary H. 1993. "Secrecy: African Art That Conceals and Reveals." *African Arts* 26 (2): 55–69, 102.
Olasagasti, Eneko and Carlos Zabala, dirs. 1994. *Maité.* Film. 92 min. Spain: Alta Films.
Oliva Alicea, Felipe. 1998. "El Cepo del Silencio. Presencia y ausencia del héroe negro en la narrative infantil cubana." *El Caimán Barbudo* (Havana) 31 (288): 8–9.
Ong, Aihwa. 2000. *Flexible Citizenship: The Cultural Politics of Transnationality.* Durham: Duke University Press.
Oppenheimer, Andres. 1992. *Castro's Final Hour.* New York: Simon & Schuster.
Orishas. 2002. "¿Qué Pasa?" In CD *Emigrante.* Emi Music.
Orovio, Helio. 2004 [1992]. *Cuban Music from A to Z.* Durham: Duke University Press.
Oroza Ernesto, Maja Asaa et al. (n.d.) "Arquitectura de la Necesidad." http://www.architectureofnecessity.com/teoria%20oroza.htm (accessed May 16, 2006).
Orozco, Román and Natalia Bolívar. 1998. *Cuba Santa: Comunistas, santeros y cristianos en la isla de Fidel Castro.* Madrid: El Páis Aguilar.
Ortíz, Fernando. 1996 [1936]. "Los Factores Humanos de la Cubanidad." In *Fernando Ortíz y la Cubanidad.* Norma Suárez, ed. Havana: Unión.
Otero, Lisandro. 1971. "Notas sobre la funcionalidad de la cultura. " *CASA* (Havana) 68: 94–109.
Pacini Hernandez, Deborah and Reebee Garofalo. 1999–2000. "Hiphop in Havana: Rap, Race, and National Identity in Contemporary Cuba." *Journal of Popular Music Studies* 11–12: 18–47.
Padrón, Humberto, dir. 2001. *Video de familia.* VHS. 47 min. Cuba: ICAIC, Producciones AcHePé, and Distribución Bay Vista.
———. 2005. *Frutas en el café.* Film. 95 min. Spain: Lente Abierto.
Padura Fuentes, Leonardo. 1994. "Cachao: Mi Idioma es el Contrabajo." *La Gaceta de Cuba* (Havana) (May): 42–45.
———. 2001. "Epilogue: Living and Creating in Cuba: Risks and Challenges." In *Culture and the Cuban Revolution: Conversations in Havana.* John M. Kirk and Leonardo Padura Fuentes, eds. Gainesville: University Press of Florida.
Palmié, Stephan. 2004. "*Fascinans* or *Tremendum*? Permutations of the State, the Body, and the Divine in Late-Twentieth-Century Havana." *New West Indian Guide* 78 (3–4): 229–268.
Paull, Laura, dir. 1995. *Havana Nagila.* VHS. 57 min. U.S.A.: Ergo Media Incorporated.
Pedroso, Luis Alberto. 2002. "Las exposiciones de 'cultos afrocubanos' y la necesidad de su reconceptualización." *Catauro. Revista Cubana de Antropología* (Havana) 3 (5): 126–141.

Perdomo, Ismael, dir. 2006. *Mata que Dios perdona*. DVD. 86 min. Cuba: Ismael Perdomo Producciones.
Perdomo, Omar. 1999. "Cuban Novel Boom." *Granma International* (February 3). http://www.granma.cu/1999/ingles/febrero3/6feb11i.html (accessed February 4, 1999).
Pérez, Fernando, dir. 1994. *Madagascar*. VHS. 48 min. Cuba: ICAIC.
Pérez, Louis A. Jr. 1999. *On Becoming Cuban: Identity, Nationality, and Culture*. Chapel Hill: University of North Carolina Press.
Perez-Firmat, Gustavo. 1994. *Life in the Hyphen. The Cuban American Way*. Austin: University of Texas Press.
Pérez Rivero, Pedro. 1998. "Otro Carnaval de La Habana." *La Gaceta de Cuba* (Havana) 36 (6): 59.
Pérez Rosado, Pedro, dir. 2005. *Agua con sal*. Film. 93 min. Spain: Wanda Vision.
Pérez Sarduy, Pedro and Jean Stubbs eds. 1993. *Afrocuba: An Anthology of Cuban Writing on Race, Politics and Culture*. Melbourne: Ocean Press.
———. 2000. "Introduction: Race and the Politics of Memory in Contemporary Black Cuban Consciousness." In *Afro-Cuba Voices: On Race and Identity in Contemporary Cuba*. P. Pérez Sarduy and J. Stubbs, eds. Gainesville: University Press of Florida.
Pérez-Stable, Marifeli. 1993. *The Cuban Revolution: Origins, Course, and Legacy*. New York: Oxford University Press.
———, ed. 2006. *Cuba en el siglo XXI. Ensayos sobre la transición*. Madrid: Ed. Colibrí.
Perna, Vincenzo. 2005. *Timba: The Sound of the Cuban Crisis*. Burlington: Ashgate.
Perry, Marc. 2004. *Los Raperos: Rap, Race, and Social Transformation in Contemporary Cuba*. Ph.D. dissertation. Department of Anthropology. University of Texas, Austin.
Pertierra, Anna Cristina. 2005. "Private Pleasures: How to Rent a Video in Santiago de Cuba." Paper presented at the American Anthropological Association meetings (November 29–December 4), Washington, DC.
Pessoa, Carlos, 2003. "On Hegemony, Post-Ideology and Subalternity." *Bulletins of Latin American Research* 22 (4):484–490.
Pogolotti, Graziella, Rine Leal, and Rosa Illeana Boudet, eds. 1980. *Teatro y Revolución*. Havana: Editorial Letras Cubanas.
Pollo, Roxana. 1990. "El Siglo de Humberto Solás." *Granma* (Havana) (September 12): 5.
Ponte, Antonio José. 2001. "La fiesta vigilada." In *Cuba y el día después*. Iván de la Nuez, ed. Barcelona: Mondadori.
Power, Kevin. 1999. "Cuba: una historia tras otra." *While Cuba Waits: Art from the Nineties*. Kevin Power, ed. Santa Mónica: Smart Art Press.
Pratt, Mary Louise. 1986. "Fieldwork in Common Places." In *Writing Culture*. James Clifford and George E. Marcus, eds. Berkeley: University of California Press.
Prensa Latina, 2005. "Cuba to Produce More Films in 2006" (December 28). www.plenglish.com (accessed December 29, 2005).
Prieto, Abel. 1994. "Cultura, Cubanidad y Cubanía." In *Conferencia La Nación y la Emigración. Ponencias*. Havana: n.p. (publisher not specified).
———. 2000. "Nación, identidad y cultura en Cuba." Speech delivered at Cuba's Union of Writers and Artists (UNEAC), November 22–23.

Prieto Samsonov, Dimitri. 2004. "Jurel en Pesos." In *Ternura entre milenios*. Polina Martínez Shvietsova and Dimitri Prieto Samsonov, eds. Havana: Unicornio.
Programa Ibermedia. 1997. http://www.programaibermedia.com (accessed May 14, 2007).
Przeworski, Adam. 1993. "Economic Reforms, Public Opinion, and Political Institutions. Poland in the Eastern European Perspective." In *Economic Reforms in New Democracies: A Social-Democratic Approach*. Luis Carlos Bresseir Pereira, José María Maravall, and Adam Przeworski, eds. New York: Cambridge University Press.
Quinto, Pacho. 1999 [1997]. *En El Solar de la Cueva del Humo*. CD. Round World Music.
Quiroa, Leonel Menéndez. 1977. *Hacia una Nuevo Teatro Latinoamericano: Teoría y Metología del Arte Escénico*. San Salvador: UCA/Editores.
Quiroga, José. 2005. *Cuban Palimpsests*. Minneapolis: University of Minnesota Press.
Rama, Angel, ed. 1981. *Más allá del boom: Literatura y Mercado*. Mexico DF: Marcha.
Ramos, Miguel W. n.d. "Diplo Santería and Pseudo-Orishas." From eleda.org http://ilarioba.tripod.com/articlesmine/diplorishas.htm (accessed July 3, 2007).
———. 2000. "The Empire Beats On: Oyo, Batá Drums and Hegemony in Nineteenth-Century Cuba." Unpublished Master's Thesis. Department of History, Florida International University.
———. 2003. "La División de La Habana: Territorial Conflicts and Cultural Hegemony in the Followers of Oyo Lukumí Religion, 1850s-1920s." *Cuban Studies* 34 (1): 38–70.
Rasmussen, Susan J. 2003. "When the Field Space Comes to the Home Space: New Constructions of Ethnographic Knowledge in a New African Diaspora." *Anthropological Quarterly* 76 (1): 7–32.
Ravsberg, Fernando. 2005. "El cine asiste a su cita annual con Cuba." *BBC Mundo*, (December 12). http://news.bbc.co.uk/hi/spanish/misc/newsid_4508000/4508596.stm (accessed May 14, 2007).
Redaccion. 2006. "Reseñas de cortos de animación soviética de la selección Masters of Russian Animation." *Miradas: Revista del audiovisual*. (January). http://www.eictv.co.cu/miradas/index.php?option=com_content&task=view&id=458&Itemid=99999999 (accessed May 15, 2007).
Redonet, Salvador, ed. 1993. *Los últimos serán los primeros*. Havana: Letras Cubanas.
Reed, Roger. 1991. *The Cultural Revolution in Cuba*. Geneva: Latin American Round Table.
René, Ernesto, dir. 2002. "Los músicos de Bremen" VHS. 3 min. Havana: Unreleased music video.
Risk, Beatriz. 1987. *El Nuevo Teatro Latinoamericano: Una lectura histórica*. Minneapolis: Institute for the Study of Ideologies and Literature, Prisma Institute.
Ritter, Archibald R.M and Rowe, Nicholas. 2003. "Cuba: 'Dedollarization' and 'Dollarization.'" In *The Dollarization Debate*. Dominick Salvatore, James W. Dean, and Thomas D. Willett, eds. Oxford: Oxford University Press.
Rivero-Valdés, Sonia. 1997. *Las historias perdidas de Marta Veneranda*. Havana: Casa de las Americas.
Rocha, Glauber. 1997 [1965]. "An Aesthetics of Hunger." In *New Latin American Cinema: Theory, Practice and Transcontinental Articulations*. Michael T. Martin, ed. Vol. 1. Detroit: Wayne State University Press.

Rojas, Fernando. 2002. "De lo efímero, lo temporal y lo permanente." In *Vivir y pensar en Cuba*. Enrique Ubieta, ed. Havana: Centro de Estudios Martianos.
———. 2004. "El triunfo de Stalin." *El Caimán Barbudo* (Havana) 321 (April). http://www.caimanbarbudo.cu/caiman321/especial1.htm (accessed July 6, 2005).
Rojas, Rafael. 2008. "Souvenirs de un Caribe soviético." *Encuentro de la Cultura Cubana* (Madrid) 48/49: 18–33.
Rolando, Gloria, dir. 1996. *My Footsteps to Baraguá*. VHS. 53 min. Afrocubaweb.
Romberg, Raquel. 2003. *Witchcraft and Welfare: Spiritual Capital and the Business of Magic in Modern Puerto Rico*. Austin: University of Texas Press.
Rubio Cuevas, Iván. 2000. "Lo marginal en los novísimos narradores cubanos: estrategia, subversión y moda." In *Todas las islas la isla*. Janett Reinstädler and Ottmar Ette, eds. Madrid and Frankfurt: Iberoamericana & Vervuert.
Ruf, Elizabeth. 1997. "¡Que Linda es Cuba!: Issues of Gender, Color, and Nationalism in Cuba's Tropicana Nightclub Performance." *The Drama Review* 41 (1): 86–105.
Ruiz, Ana Maria. 1987. "El Rey Yorubá en Cuba." *Prisma Latinoamericano* (Havana) 8 (180): 22–23.
Rush, Michael. 2003. *Video Art*. London: Thames and Hudson.
Saludes, Miguel. 2005. *Libros e ideología en la Feria de La Habana*. Cubanet. February 14, 2005. http://www.cubanet.org/CNews/y05/feb05/14a6.htm (accessed May 14, 2007).
Sánchez, Juan. 2000. "La Cultura y sus filos." *Bohemia* (Havana) 92 (October 20) 22: 24.
Sargeant, Joseph, dir. 2000. *For Love or Country: The Arturo Sandoval Story*. DVD. 120 min. HBO Films, USA.
Schnabel, Julian, dir. 2000. *Before Night Falls*. DVD. 133 min. U.S.A.: AOL/Fine Line/ Time Warner.
Schein, Louisa. 2002. "Mapping Hmong Media in Diasporic Space." In *Media Worlds: Anthropology on New Terrain*. Faye Ginsburg, Lila Abu-Lughod, and Brian Larkin, eds. Berkeley: University of California Press.
Schwartz, Rosalie. 1997. *Pleasure Island: Tourism and Temptation in Cuba*. Lincoln: University of Nebraska Press.
Selier, Yesenia and Penélope Hernández. 2004. "Identidad Racial de 'Gente Sin Historia.'" *Caminos* (Havana: Centro Memorial Martin Luther King, Jr.), 24–25: 84–90.
Sequera, Vivian. 2000. "Los rusos llevan apacible vida en Cuba." *El Nuevo Herald*, (December 10) http://www.cubanet.org/CNews/y00/dec00/11o1.htm (accessed May 14, 2007).
Sheriff, Robin. 2000. "Exposing Silence as Cultural Censorship: A Brazilian Case." *American Anthropologist* 102 (1): 114–132.
Sigler, Bret. 2005. "God, Babalawos, and Castro." In *Capitalism, God, and a Good Cigar: Cuba Enters the Twenty-First Century*. Lydia Chávez and Mimi Chakarova, eds. Durham: Duke University Press.
Smith, Martin Cruz. 1999. *Havana Bay*. New York: Random House.
Smith, Valene L. 1989. *Hosts and Guests: The Anthropology of Tourism*. Philadelphia: University of Pennsylvania Press.
Smorkaloff, Pamela. 1997. *Readers and Writers in Cuba: A Social History of Print Culture, 1830s-1990s*. New York: Garland.
Sociedad General de Autores y Editores. 2005. "La Fundación Autor participa de manera destacada en el 27 Festival del Nuevo Cine Latinoamericano"

(December 7). http://www.sgae.es/tipology/notice/list/es/2005_12_1559.html (accessed December 12, 2005).

Solanas, Fernando and Octavio Getino. 1997 [1969]. "Towards a Third Cinema: Notes and Experiences for the Development of a Cinema of Liberation in the Third World." In *New Latin American Cinema: Theory, Practice and Transcontinental Articulations*, vol. 1. Michael T. Martin, ed. Detroit: Wayne State University Press.

Solás, Humberto. n.d. "Manifiesto de Cine Pobre." www.cubacine.cu/cinepobre (accessed May 18, 2006).

———, dir. 1968. *Lucía*. Film. 160 min. Cuba: ICAIC.

———. 1992. *El siglo de las luces*. Film. 247 min. Cuba: ICAIC, and Spain: Televisión Española.

———. 2004 [2001]. *Miel para Oshun*. DVD. 125 min. U.S.A.: Maverick Latino.

———. 2005. *Barrio Cuba*. Film. 105 min. Cuba: ICAIC.

———. 2007 [1981]. *Cecilia*. DVD. 168 min. Cuban Masterworks Collection, U.S.A.: First Run Films.

Spitulnik, Debra. 2002. "Mobile Machines and Fluid Audiences: Rethinking Reception and Zambian Radio Culture." In *Media Worlds: Anthropology on New Terrain*. Faye Ginsburg, Lila Abu-Lughod, and Brian Larkin, eds. Berkeley: University of California Press.

Sreberny-Mohammadi, Annabelle and Ali Mohammadi. 1994. *Small Media, Big Revolution: Communication, Culture and the Iranian Revolution*. Minneapolis: University of Minnesota Press.

Stanton, Kimberly. 2006. *Retreat from Reason: U.S. Academic Relations and the Bush Administration*. Latin American Working Group Education Fund.

Stolcke, Verena. 1995. "Talking Culture. New Boundaries, New Rhetorics of Exclusion in Europe." *Current Anthropology* 36 (1): 1–23.

Strausfeld, Michi. 2000. "Isla-Diáspora-Exilio: anotaciones acerca de la publicación y distribución de la narrativa cubana en los años noventa." In *Todas las islas la isla: Nuevas y novísimas tendencias en la literatura y cultura de Cuba*. Janett Reinstädler and Ottmar Ette, eds. Madrid: Iberoamericana.

Suárez, Karla. 1999. "Aniversario." In *Espuma*. Havana: Ed Letras Cubanas.

Suárez, Luis. 1991. "Anyone Who Wants Can Leave the Country." *Granma International* (July 21): 2–3.

Suárez, Norma, ed. 1996. *Fernando Ortiz y la Cubanidad*. Havana: Ed. Ciencias Sociales.

Sublette, Ned. 2004. "The Missing Cuban Musicians." Albuquerque: Cuba Research and Analysis Group.

Tabío, Juan Carlos, dir. 1988. *Plaff*. VHS. 90 min. Cuba: ICAIC.

———. 2004 [2000]. *Lista de espera*. DVD. 102 min. Fox Lorber.

Tamayo, Juan O. 1998. "In Cuba, a Clash between Religions." *The Miami Herald*, (January 12): A1.

Taylor, Diana. 1991. *Theatre of Crisis: Drama and Politics in Latin America*. Lexington: University Press of Kentucky.

Temas. 2000. "Controversia: Buena Vista Social Club y la cultura musical cubana." *Temas* (Havana) 22–23: 163–179.

Torres, Maria de los Angeles. 1995. "Encuentros y Encontronazos: Homeland in the Politics and Identity of the Cuban Diaspora." *Diaspora* 4 (2): 211–238.

———. 2001. *In the Land of Mirrors: Cuban Exile Politics in the United States.* Ann Arbor: University of Michigan Press.
Trimegistros, Hermes. 2003. "Concepto 'Letra del Año.'" *Revista de la Universidad de La Habana* (Havana) 258: 214–215.
Turner, Terence. 1995. "Representation, Collaboration, and Mediation in Contemporary Ethnographic and Indigenous Media." *Visual Anthropology Review* 11 (2): 102–106.
Turnley, David. 2006 [2002]. *La Tropical.* DVD. 93 min. Hart Sharp Video.
Ubieta Gómez, Enrique. 1993. *Ensayos de Identidad.* Havana: Letras Cubanas.
——— 2002. *Vivir y pensar en Cuba.* Enrique Ubieta, ed. Havana: Centro de Estudios Martianos.
UNEAC. 1994. *Anuario 1994/ Narrativa.* Havana: Ediciones Unión.
Valdés, Nelson. 2001. "Fidel Castro, Charisma and Santería: Max Weber Revisited." In *Caribbean Charisma: Reflections on Leadership, Legitimacy and Populist Politics.* Anton Allahar, ed. Boulder: Lynne Rienner Publishers.
Valdés, Zoé. 1995. *La nada cotidiana.* Barcelona: Emecé.
———. 1996. *Te dí la vida entera.* Barcelona: Planeta. (Trans. Nadia Benabid. *I Gave You All I Had.* New York: Arcade, 1999.)
———. 1997. *Yocandra in the Paradise of Nada.* New York: Arcade.
Valdés Bernal, Sergio. 1998. *Lengua nacional e identidad cultural del cubano.* Havana: Ciencias Sociales.
Valdés Figueroa, Eugenio. 2001. "Trajectories of a Rumor. Cuban Art in the Postwar Period." In *Art Cuba: The New Generation.* Holly Block, ed. New York: Harry N. Abrams.
Valiño, Omar. 1997. "La Cruzada Teatral: Otra Ventana al Universo." *Revolución y Cultura* (Havana) 36 (5/97): 18–21.
Van de Port, Mattijs. 2005. "Circling around the Really Real: Spirit Possession Ceremonies and the Search for Authenticity in Bahian Candomblé." *Ethos* 33 (2): 149–179.
Various artists. 2000. *Rapsodia Rumbera.* CD Egrem, Cuba.
Vega Serova, Anna Lidia. 1998. "Erre con erre." In *Catálogo de Mascotas.* Havana: Letras Cubanas.
Vélez Bichkov, Antón. 2004. "¿Son rusos los muñequitos? Koniec." Paper delivered at the First Encounter of Cuban-Euro-Asian Youth Conference (March 11). Sancti Spiritus, Cuba.
Velthuis, Olav. 2005. *Imaginary Economics: Contemporary Artists and the World of Big Money.* Rotterdam: NAi Publishers.
Verdery, Katherine. 1991. *National Ideology under Socialism.* Berkeley: University of California Press.
———. 1991. "Theorizing Socialism: A Prologue to the 'Transition.'" *American Ethnologist* 18 (3): 419–439.
Verdery, Katherine. 1993. "Nationalism and National Sentiment in Post-Socialist Romania." *Slavic Review* 52: 179–203.
Vicent, Mauricio. 1993a. "Las autoridades de Cuba recomiendan el consumo de hojas ante la escasez de alimentos." *EL PAIS* (April 14). http://www.elpais.com/articulo/internacional/CUBA/autoridades/Cuba/recomiendan/consumir/hojas/escasez/alimentos/elpepiint/19930414elpepiint_17/Tes (accessed June 7, 2007).

Vicent, Mauricio. 1993b. "La neuritis afecta ya a 45,000 personas." *EL PAIS* (June 23). http://www.elpais.com/articulo/sociedad/CUBA/neuritis/afecta/45000/personas/elpepisoc/19930623elpepisoc_4/Tes (accessed June 7, 2007).
———. 1993c. "Pablo Milanés crea en Cuba la primera fundación cultural "sin fines ideológicos.'" *EL PAIS* (June 25). http://www.elpais.com/articulo/cultura/MILANES/_PABLO_/MUSICA/CUBA/Pablo/Milanes/crea/Cuba/primera/fundacion/cultural/fines/ideologicos/elpepicul/19930625elpepicul_1/Tes (accessed June 7, 2007).
———. 1993d. "Verano Negro en La Habana." *EL PAIS* (August 27). http://www.elpais.com/articulo/internacional/CUBA/Verano/negro/Habana/elpepiint/19930827elpepiint_15/Tes (accessed June 7, 2007).
———. 1993e. "17 universidades españolas firman acuerdos para colaborar con Cuba." *EL PAIS* (July 12) http://www.elpais.com/articulo/sociedad/ESPANA/CUBA/CUBA/universidades/espanolas/firman/acuerdos/colaborar/Cuba/elpepisoc/19930712elpepisoc_2/Tes (accessed June 7, 2007)
———. 1995. "Milanés rompe con el Ministerio de Cultura de Cuba." *EL PAIS*, (June 11). http://www.elpais.com/articulo/cultura/MILANES/_PABLO_/MUSICA/CUBA/Milanes/rompe/Ministerio/Cultura/Cuba/elpepicul/19950611elpepicul_2/Tes (accessed June 7, 2007).
Weiss, Judith. 1993. *Latin American Popular Theatre: The First Five Centuries*. Santa Fe: University of New Mexico Press.
Wenders, Wim, dir. 2000 [1999]. *Buena Vista Social Club*. DVD. 101 min. U.S.A.: Lions Gate Entertainment.
West-Duran, Alan. 2004. "Rap's Diasporic Dialogues: Cuba's Redefinition of Blackness." *Journal of Popular Music Studies* 16 (1): 4–39.
Whitfield, Esther. 2001. "Buying In, Selling Out: Fiction(s) of Cuba in Post-Soviet Cultural Economies." Ph.D. Dissertation. Department of Romance Languages, Harvard University.
———. 2002. "Dirty Autobiography: The Body Impolitic of *Trilogía sucia de La Habana*." *Revista de Estudios Hispánicos* 36 (2): 329–351.
Williams, Raymond. 1973. *The Country and the City*. London: Chatto and Windus.
———. 1978. "Structures of Feeling." In *Marxism and Literature*. New York: Oxford University Press.
Wirtz, Kristina. 2004. "Santeria in Cuban National Consciousness: A Religious Case of the Doble Moral." *Journal of Latin American Anthropology* 9 (2): 409–438.
Woodmansee, Martha and Mark Osteen. 1999. *The New Economic Criticism: Studies at the Intersection of Literature and Economics*. London and New York: Routledge.
Woods, Alan. 2006 "Preface to *Rusia: del socialismo real al capitalismo real*." In *El Militante* (Mexico) (March 3). http: www.elmilitante.org/index.asp?id=muestra&id_art=2565 (accessed May 14, 2007).
Yang, Mayfair Mei-Hui. 2002. "Mass Media and Transnational Subjectivity in Shanghai: Notes on (Re)cosmopolitanism in a Chinese Metropolis." In *Media Worlds: Anthropology on New Terrain*. Faye Ginsburg, Lila Abu-Lughod, and Brian Larkin, eds. Berkeley: University of California Press.
Yáñez, Mirta, ed. 1998. *Cubana: Contemporary Fiction by Cuban Women*. Boston: Beacon Press.

Yáñez, Mirta and Marilyn Bobes, eds. 1996. *Estatuas de Sal: Cuentistas Cubanas Contemporáneas*. Havana: Eds. Unión.
Yoss. 2004. "Lo que dejaron los rusos." *Temas* (Havana) 37–38: 138–144.
Yurchak, Alexei. 2006. *Everything Was Forever, until It Was No More: The Last Soviet Generation*. Princeton: Princeton University Press.
Yuval-Davis, Nira and Floya Anthias, eds. 1989. *Woman-Nation-State*. New York: St. Martin's Press.
Zaldívar, Juan Carlos, dir. 2001. *90 Miles*. Film. 75 min. U.S.A.: LLC, USA.
Zambrano, Benito, dir. 2005. *Habana Blues*. Film. 110 min. Spain: Warner Brothers.
Zardoya Loureda, Rubén. 2002. "Ideología y revolución. Notas sobre el impacto del derrumbe soviético y el socialismo europeo en Cuba." In *Vivir y pensar en Cuba*. Enrique Ubieta, ed. Havana: Centro de Estudios Martianos.
Zhang, Xudong. 1998. "Nationalism, Mass Culture and Intellectual Strategies in Post-Tiananmen China." *Social Text 55*, 16 (2): 109–140.
Zilberg, Elana. 2002. "From Riots to Rampart: A Spatial Cultural Politics of Salvadoran Migration to and from Los Angeles." Unpublished doctoral dissertation. Department of Anthropology, University of Texas, Austin.
Zito, Miriam. 2004. *Avanzan estudios antropológicos en Cuba*. Havana: AIN.
Zizek, Slavoj. 1989. *The Sublime Object of Ideology*. London: Verso.
Zurbano, Roberto. 2006. "El triángulo invisible del siglo XX cubano: raza, literatura y nación." *Temas* (Havana) 46: 111–123.

Index

Abakuá, 66, 125, 169, 170, 186, 187
Abreu, Juan, 110
Afro-Cuban, 160–177
  art, 88
  culture, 82–83: transnational, 165, 167, 168
  drumming, 55
  economic conditions, 124
  identity, 80–81
  intellectuals, 82–84, 189
  music, 168, 177
  in New York, 160–161, 170, 175
  religion, 15, 51–66, 124–139, 148, 168, 189
  Theater, 94
  traditions, 56–57, 83
Aguastibias, 114, 121
de Aguila, Rafael, 21–22, 25–26, 33–35
Alamar, 143, 147 *see also* Havana, East
Alfonso, Gerardo, 86, 88, 156
Alicia en el pueblo de Maravillas (Alicia in the Town of Maravillas), 39, 43–44
Alom, Juan Carlos, 184, 190–191, 194
Alvarez, Enrique, 40
Alvarez, José B., 36
Alvarez, Lupe, 182
Alvarez, Pedro, 184–189

Alvarez Gil, Antonio, 113
dell'Amico, Souleen, 24, 31–33, 35
Arenas, Reinaldo, 27–28, 87
Asere Productions, 156, 158
Asociación Cultural Yoruba (ACY, or Yoruba Cultural Association), 63, 123, 125
Asociación Hermanos Saíz (AHS, or Hermanos Saíz Association), 113, 143–144

babalao, 57, 123–140
  diplo-babalao, 61, 129
Badiou, Alain, 1–2
balseros, 21, 152, 162, 172 *see also* rafters
  balsero crisis, 5, 167
  Balseros (film), 50
Barnet, Miguel, 30, 145
La Batalla de Ideas (or Ideological Battle), 49, 86, 89–91, 103
Bain, Mervyn, 109, 121
Behar, Ruth, 16, 47, 76, 78, 88
Bobes, Marilyn, 24, 32–33, 35
Borges-Triana, Joaquín, 156
Boym, Svetlana, 108, 111, 120
Brown Infante, Francisco, 112, 121
Brugal, Yana Elsa, 120
Buena Vista Social Club, 13, 47, 189

camello, 143
campesinos, 90–103

Carbonell, Walterio, 84, 151
Carpentier, Alejo, 48, 122
Casa de Africa, 130
Castañeda, Antonio, 133, 135–136
Castro, Fidel, 3, 4, 10, 17, 18, 22, 75, 80, 87, 93, 100, 107–109, 123, 129–130, 134, 151, 174, 181
  "Address to the Intellectuals," 22, 70, 93, 121
  speeches, 3, 4, 17, 86, 90, 94, 100, 183
Chijona, Gerardo, 38, 43, 82
Children of the Revolution, 15
Cine Pobre, 48
Cinema, 37–50, 184–194
  coproductions, 40–42
  digital, 44–46
Conjunto Folklórico Nacional, 54, 55, 61, 174
Constitution, 5, 18, 71, 79, 87, 106
Cortés, José Luis, 190, 191, 195
Cremata, Juan Carlos, 45, 73
La Cruzada Teatral, 95, 97, 101, 102, 104
Cuarteto de La Habana (or Havana Quartet), 43
Cubanía, 75, 90, 95, 97, 99, 102–103 see also *Cubanidad*
Cubanidad, 31, 70, 73, 74, 76, 86, 131, 165–166, 175–176 see also Identity
  and culture, 75–77
  Test, 73–75
Cubanness see *Cubanidad*
"Cuba-USSR and the Post-Soviet Experience," 121
cultural policy, 109, 180
Cumanayagua, 97–98, 104

Dacal, Ariel, 112, 121
Danza Abierta, 69, 86
De la Campa, Román, 78
décima, 92, 98
Delgado, Frank, 110, 118, 120

Días de la Música, 157
diaspora, 72–79, 86, 165, 176
  African, 44, 63, 83, 157
  Hmong, 165
  Jewish, 78
  Latino, 78
  Trope, 79
Diaspora(s), 78, 88
Díaz, Jesús, 21, 23, 33–34, 35, 113
divination, 57, 63, 65, 123–130, 132–135, 137, 139
dollarization, 5, 18, 23–27, 52–62, 65, 114–115, 137
Dollarscape series, 185–188
Domínguez, Jorge I., 7, 87, 107
Dopíco, Ana María, 13, 46
double economy see Dollarization
Dreke, Mario ("Chavalonga"), 169
Dulzaides, Felipe, 184, 190, 191–193, 194

EICTV (*Escuela Internacional de Cine y Televisión*) or International Film School, 38, 46
El Caimán Barbudo, 21, 111–112
ENA (*Escuela Nacional de Arte*) or National Art School, 97, 193
Encuentro de la Cultura Cubana, 21, 79
Espinosa, Magaly, 182
Esquivel, Alexis, 189
Esson, Tomás, 181
Estévez, Abilio, 21, 22, 33, 35
ethnicity
  in Cuba, 72–73, 76
  in the U.S., 114, 166, 176
exile, 40, 57, 70, 72–77, 79, 88, 165
  cinema, 41
  community, 134, 160, 165, 175
  -diaspora, 79, 86
  intellectuals in, 17, 23, 77, 87
  politics, 79
  post-exile, 78
  return, 168

Index

Fariñas, Pedro, 159, 160, 168, 169, 175
Febles, Miguel, 128, 133, 136
Fernández, Antonio Eligio (Tonel), 117–119, 120
Fernández Robaina, Tomás, 88, 130, 131, 146
Fernando Ortiz Foundation, 80, 83
Ferrer, Jorge, 121
Festival Internacional de Nuevo Cine Latinoamericano (Or New Latin American Cinema International Festival), 38, 39, 44, 48, 50, 145
Fowler Calzada, Víctor, 79, 108
Fresa y Chocolate (Strawberry and Chocolate), 39, 41
Fusco, Coco, 28, 30, 78

García Canclini, Néstor, 10, 71, 102
García Espinosa, Julio, 38, 39, 40, 46
Generación Y, 121
Gómez, Sara, 193–194
González, José Oriol, 97–98, 99, 102
Goodbye Lenin!, 105
Gorbachev, Mikhail, 8, 108–109
Grupo Uno, 143
Guantánamo, 92, 97, 102, 104, 152
Gutiérrez, Pedro Juan, 11, 24, 33–35, 36
Gutiérrez Alea, Tomás, 41, 87, 183–184, 194

Hart, Armando, 86, 98, 112, 113, 118, 180, 181
Havana, 3, 5–8, 13, 15, 17, 18, 32, 36, 41, 43–45, 58, 60, 61, 65, 66, 69, 73, 77, 90, 93, 94, 101, 102, 113, 115, 116, 118, 119, 121, 128, 135, 136, 138, 144, 145, 152, 155, 159, 160, 161, 163, 165, 169, 170–172, 174, 176, 182–186, 189, 191–192, 194
Central Havana, 135, 137, 144, 157
Chinatown, 80
East Havana, 15, 143, 147, 150
see also Alamar
Havana Art Biennial, 182, 184
Havana Book Fair, 23
Havana Film Festival see Festival Internacional de Nuevo Cine Latinoamericano
Havana's Carnival, 80, 146, 163
Old Havana, 105, 117, 172
University of, 74, 76, 87, 134
Hernández, Orlando, 182
Hernández, Rafael, 87, 112
Hernández Busto, Ernesto, 106–107, 113, 121
Héroes de Baikonur, 117–118
Herrera, Pablo, 144

ICAIC (*Instituto Cubano de Arte e Industria Cinematográfica*, or Cuban Film Institute), 37–50, 77
ICRT (*Instituto Cubano de Radio y Televisión*, or Cuban Institute for Radio and Television), 39
Identity, Cuban see also *Cubanidad*
and blackness, 146–157, 161, 189: debates, 15, 44, 69–87
and food, 114
generational, 181
and performance, 89
politics, 121, 165
and religion, 54, 62, 124–139
Ifá, 51, 65, 123–135, 137–140
independent film, 46
industrial cinema, 37, 38, 45

ISA (Instituto Superior de Arte, or Superior Art Institute), 146, 180, 181

Jameson, Fredric, 11
jineterismo, 28–32, 61–62, 136, 137
jinetero-a, 21, 29–35, 45, 60–61, 136, 137, 138, 189
Juntas de Patrocinio, 146
Jurel en Pesos, 114–115, 117

Konchalovsky, Andrei, 110
Koniec, 113–114
Koniek, 115
Kracauer, Sigfried, 2

La Gaceta de Cuba, 76, 87
La Madriguera, 144
La Nación y la Emigración (or Nation and Migration conference), 75
Lágrimas Negras, 47
Landaluze, Victor Patricio de, 186–187
Las Metáforas del Templo, 181–182
late socialism, 2, 10, 11, 124
Lauten, Flora, 93
Lenin Park, 111, 112
Lenin School, 116
Letter of the Year, 123–139
Lista de espera (The Waiting List), 42
Lourdes Soviet Electronic Radar Station, 108, 121

MacCannell, Dean, 29, 53, 57
Madagascar, 40
Manolín, 192
Mañach, Jorge, 72, 87
Mariel boatlift, 159, 161, 180
Marielito, 161, 163, 176
Martí, José, 71, 99, 100, 106, 153, 185, 187

Martínez Furé, Rogelio, 61–62, 66, 83–84
Martínez Shvietsova, Polina, 113–114, 120
Matanzas, 51, 52, 64, 65, 84, 136, 152, 170, 176
Mayakovsky, Vladimir, 117–118
MC Molano, 153
Mejides, Miguel, 30
Memorias de la Postguerra, 77
Memorias del Subdesarrollo (Memories of Underdevelopment), 183–184
Menéndez Plasencia, Ronaldo, 24, 25, 26–28, 32, 33, 35
Mesa Redonda, 49, 100
Miami, 45, 66, 79, 115, 133–135, 160, 161, 181, 192
Miguel Febles Padrón Commission, 123, 131
Miradas, 40
Mosquera, Gerardo, 11, 107
Movimiento, 154, 155
multiculturalism, 77
  ethnic, 71, 73
  revolutionary, 80
Muñequitos de Matanzas, 159
muñequitos rusos (Russian cartoons), 115, 121

Nada +, 45, 73
nationalism
  Cuban, 71
  cultural, 72
  ethnic, 79–86
Navarro, Desiderio, 33, 118, 120, 122
New Cuban Art, 179–182
New Cuban boom *see Nuevo Boom Cubano*
New Man (*Hombre Nuevo*), 93, 96, 102
New Theater (Teatro Nuevo), 93–94, 96, 101

novísimo writers, 24, 36
Nueva Trova, 88, 110, 118, 148, 156
Nuevo Boom Cubano, 22

Obsesión, 153
Ocha, see Santeria
Ochatur, 62
Oricha, 53–54, 57–65, 66, 126, 127, 131, 136–138
Ortiz, Fernando, 72, 78, 87, 151

Paz, Albio, 93
Peña, René, 85, 189, 190
Penúltimos Días, 121
Perdomo, Ismael, 45–46
Pérez, Fernando, 40, 195
Piña, Manuel, 184, 190, 193–194
Pinos Nuevos collection, 25
Piñera, Virgilio, 114
photography, 189–190
P.M., 121
Ponte, Antonio José, 29, 79, 120
Porno para Ricardo, 115–117, 120
Power, Kevin, 182, 183, 185
Prieto, Abel, 74, 75, 100
Prieto Samsonov, Dmitri, 113–115, 120
Proyecto mir_xxi_cu, 113, 115
pura cepa, 90–91, 95, 100–102
Putin, Vladimir, 108, 116

race relations, 81–82
Radio Progreso, 132
Radio Rebelde, 70, 73
rafters, 27, 160 *see also balseros*
rap music, 143–158
  agency, 146, 147, 154, 155, 156
  Havana rap festival, 143, 153
Rectification, 44, 88, 109
Redonet, Salvador, 36
Reggaeton, 85
Rensoli, Rodolfo, 143, 145
Rios, Orlando "Puntilla," 159, 161, 169, 176

Rojas, Fernando, 111–113, 115, 118, 144
Rojas, Rafael, 121
Romerías de Mayo, 144, 145
Rolando, Gloria, 44, 81, 83
rumba music, 15, 87, 157, 159, 161–177

Santería, 30, 51–66, 123–140, 147, 163, 166 *see also* Afro-Cuban religion
Santiago de Cuba, 42, 47, 94, 99, 152
Schnabel, Julian, 28, 47
Smith, Martin Cruz, 107
Smorkaloff, Pamela, 24
Solás, Humberto, 46, 48
Soy Cuba (I am Cuba), 122
Stalin, Joseph, 108, 112
Suárez, Karla, 24, 30–33, 35

Tabío, Juan Carlos, 41, 42
teatro comunitario, 91, 95–97, 101–104
Teatro de los Elementos, 97–99, 102
Teatro Escambray, 93, 95, 97, 102
Television, 17, 45, 49, 50, 81, 92, 100, 113, 116, 147, 157, 164, 167, 173, 183, 192
Temas, 76, 83, 87, 112, 157
Timba, 11, 62, 66, 69, 77, 85, 148, 190, 192, 195
tourism, 22, 23, 27–29, 34–35, 56, 62, 125, 129, 136, 149, 152, 157
  literary, 23
  religious, 55
  vs. research, 53
  sexual, 30
  tourist industry, 4, 28, 45, 52, 63, 168
transition, 2, 8, 10, 16, 17, 89, 106–109, 117, 119, 121, 179

Tropicola, 18, 47
Trotsky, Leon, 112, 118, 121

Un Paraíso bajo las Estrellas (A Paradise under the Stars), 43, 82
UNEAC (*Union Nacional de Escritores y Artistas de Cuba* or National Association of Writers and Artists), 25, 72, 75, 79, 87, 90, 100, 113
UPEC (*Union de Periodistas de Cuba* or Journalists' Union), 146

Valdés, Zoé, 23, 33
Vega Serova, Anna Lidia, 30
video, 38, 44, 46, 49, 159–161
-art, 45, 184, 190–195
banks, 167, 177
clubs, 49
-letters, 45, 169
Movimiento Nacional de Video (National Video Movement), 44, 45
music video, 45, 115, 116–117, 150, 155
religious video, 59, 66
remittances, 162–176
Vídeo de Familia, 45, 177
Volumen Uno, 180

Yoss, 107, 120, 121

Zardoya Loureda, Rubén, 109–110, 117

GPSR Compliance
The European Union's (EU) General Product Safety Regulation (GPSR) is a set of rules that requires consumer products to be safe and our obligations to ensure this.

If you have any concerns about our products, you can contact us on

ProductSafety@springernature.com

In case Publisher is established outside the EU, the EU authorized representative is:

Springer Nature Customer Service Center GmbH
Europaplatz 3
69115 Heidelberg, Germany

www.ingramcontent.com/pod-product-compliance
Lightning Source LLC
LaVergne TN
LVHW041629060526
838200LV00040B/1498